FOREWARD

My antecedent Thomas Clarkson the Abolitionist of slavery worked tirelessly with parliament described in Britain's national archives, a leading campaigner against the slave trade in the British empire. An historic figure he helped found the society for affecting the abolishment of the slave trade act 1807 which ended British trade in slaves, after Thomas Clarkson's thesis at Oxford university published 1786. President Lincoln presented resolution of congress United States of America 1865 to abolish slavery in the USA.

The campaign for sexual equality started with the LGBT movement CHE 1964 as a law reform act of Parliament 1964 to decriminalize homosexuality in the community. For 20 years Paul Clarkson and his partner Keith Bagnall campaigned to gain equality with the first open Gay travel company in the United-kingdom opened in 1974. Paul Clarkson's biography illustrates and measures the current status of LGBT rights, Laws, and freedom as well as public attitudes toward LGBT+ people during his 86- year life. Keith passed in 2025 leaving Paul to observe the development of equal rights inmemory of their life and work together.

ABOLISHIONIST' &
HUMAN RIGHTS LGBT+

LGBTQ EQUALITY 1967 - 2025

ABOLISHIONIST' &
HUMAN RIGHTS LGBT+

LGBTQ EQUALITY 1967 - 2025

Paul Robert Clarkson

ISBN
Paperback 979-8-89744-684-1
Hardcase 979-8-89906-635-1

AN

E S S A Y

ON THE

SLAVERY AND COMMERCE

OF THE

HUMAN SPECIES,

PARTICULARLY

THE AFRICAN;

TRANSLATED FROM A

LATIN DISSERTATION,

WHICH WAS HONOURED WITH

THE FIRST PRIZE

IN THE

UNIVERSITY OF CAMBRIDGE,

FOR THE YEAR 1785.

THE SECOND EDITION,

REVISED AND CONSIDERABLY ENLARGED.

Neque premendo alium me extulisse velim.—LIVY.

LONDON:

PRINTED AND SOLD BY J. PHILLIPS, GEORGE-YARD,
LOMBARD-STREET.

MDCCLXXXVIII.

TO

THE VICE-CHANCELLOR,

THE HEADS OF HOUSES,

BUT PARTICULARLY

THE REV. DR. PECKARD,

THE FELLOWS OF COLLEGES,

AND

THE STUDENTS,

IN THE

UNIVERSITY OF CAMBRIDGE.

GENTLEMEN,

HAVING received my education at the learned seminary, to which you have the honour to belong; having a regard for many of you perfonally, and confidering you all as ftanding in the peculiar fituation of guardians of humanity and religion, you will hardly think it ftrange, if I fhould addrefs you on this important occafion.

There is a circumftance, however, which renders the ftep I am now taking particularly proper. The fubject of this work originated with you.

a 3

If

If therefore, it has been at all inftrumental in itfelf, or has led me to fuch exertions as may have been in any degree inftrumental, in procuring that general attention to the flave trade, which prevails at prefent, and which I am confident in the courfe of time will be productive of its abolition, the merit of fo important an event will ultimately devolve upon you; and you will be found to have exhibited to other feminaries an example, and to the world at large a proof, that, while you have been endeavouring to promote the caufe of learning, you have not been inattentive to the unalienable rights of men.

If there is any other circumftance, that will additionally mark the propriety of the prefent addrefs, it is the very confpicuous part, which you have fince taken, in promoting the fame caufe, not only by public and private fubfcriptions, but by an application to the legiflature of your country.

To you then this fecond edition (the firft having difcharged a private obligation) reverts as to its own parents, and is infcribed with this publick teftimony of your conduct, by

Your obedient fervant,

THOMAS CLARKSON.

ADVER-

Thomas Clarkson (1760–1846)
by Carl Fredrik von Breda, 1788

© National Portrait Gallery, London

THOMAS CLARKSON
Abolishionist 1760 - 1846

Discovered the trade is at present confined to the English Dutch, Danes, Portuguese and French. The former in 1786 employed one hundred and thirty six ships which carried off about 40,000 slaves fitted out from the Ports of London, Bristol and Liverpool, the latter sent out ninety vessels alone. Two ports in England: from which ships were formerly fitted out for Africa having relinquished the trade, and to the honour of Ireland and Scotland their ports are presently untainted with human blood. I discovered my connection through the genealogy of our family tree to my descendant grandfather John Clarkson born 1640, and his grandson my grand uncle Thomas Clarkson the Abolishionist born 1764 Thirsk, Yorkshire. His Essay in 1785 'Is it lawful to enslave the unconsenting,' led him to expose the Atlantic slave trade. 'On the impolicy of the African slave trade' in 1788 lay behind the twelve propositions which Wilberforce MP for Hull put before British Parliament in his first speech on May 1789. Thomas's brother John Clarkson joined the great crusade in 1791, aided by Thom Peters the black loyalist leader, he did so with immense success and in January 1792 he led a fleet of fifteen vessels carrying 1196 settlers to Sierra Leone a settlement in West Africa named Freetown. Thomas Clarkson's indefatigable work with William Wilbeforce led to Parliament changing the law in 1840 against enslavement.

1830 Yorkshire Mr. Henry Lascelles was the cousin of the King a supporter of Prime Minster Pitt and a slave owner on his plantation in the West Indies.

LGBT EQUALITY

When in the course of human events, it becomes necessary for an oppressed and persecuted minority to declare for themselves the full rights and responsibilities that the laws of reason entitles them, a decent respect to the opinions of mankind requires that they should declare the cause which impel them to demand as such. We hold these truths to be self evident that all men and women and non-binary individuals of all sexual orientations and gender identities are created equal and endowed by the creator with certain inalienable rights; among these are Life and Liberty, that to secure these rights governments are instituted, deriving there just powers from the consent of the governed, that whenever any form of government becomes destructive of these ends it is the duty of the oppressed to deny allegiance to it with courage. This memoir is a personal narrative of the correlation between liberty and equality of LGBT human rights in Britain. The 'Wolfenden' report in 1967 allowed changes in the law giving the LGBT community the freedom today to live their lives, followed by ascent of a Royal pardon from Queen Elizabeth 11 with legal abolishment of criminalisation in 2010. My memories of his childhood from 1940 disabled from a bipolar mental health condition, he suffered through prejudice toward his sexuality in a dysfunctional family as he fought to remain true to himself in 1975 Hunter Davies editor of 'The Sunday Times' reported that Paul with his partner Keith pioneered 'Stay Gay Holidays,' offered gay travel plans to the LGBT community and the first in Europe. The UK 'Travel Trade News' featured this genesis in parallel to the campaign for homosexual equality, 'Reuters' news agency syndicated the story worldwide. This memoir is a personal narrative over eighty years in celebration of LGBT history, its impact and eventual inclusiveness resonates with 'Global Pride' today.

LGBTQ - is a term used for Lesbian, Gay, Bisexual and Tran sexual, the term in use since the nineties to designate a community of people whose sexuality or gender identities can create shared political and social concerns. This Queer umbrella term is a political statement as well as a reference to sexual orientation advocating binary thinking, recognizing both sexual orientation and gender identity as potentially fluid. Biphobia - is an aversion toward bisexuality and bisexual people as a social group. People of any sexual orientation can experience such feelings of aversion. As Biphobia is a form of may be based on negative bisexual stereotypes or irrational fear.

13

Chapter 01

THOMAS CLARKSON

My ancestor Thomas Clarkson was a Sizar student undergraduate at St John's Cambridge University 1785 received college assistance on the ground of poverty the son of a poor parent who entered college. He was allowed free education to earn his keep in consideration of performing menial duties with derogatory offices, acting as a servant who dined at the wealthier students table after they had retired. It implies a contradiction, to be learning the liberal arts and at the same time treated as a slave; at once studying freedom and practicing servitude. Thomas Clarkson died a hundred years before I was born, the lifelong International and commonwealth abolitionist of slavery. His work with William Wilberforce in passing the act through Parliament for the abolition of the slave trade in 1807 was with his younger brother Lieutenant John Clarkson in the Royal Navy and their cousin Granville Sharp social reformer in the eighteenth and nineteenth centuries in Sierra Leone and America.

Unlike my ancestor Thomas Clarkson, my memories of a naive childhood in the post war 1940s developed after independence of youth, before the diagnosis of my bipolar condition and coming to terms with the prognosis. Working in partnership to pioneer gay travel in support of the campaign for homosexual equality in Britain and change the law since 1967 with its impact on human rights in Britain. A triumph in the diversity of love that transformed lives was the abolition of clause 28 in education, followed by decriminalisation and progression toward same sex civil partnerships and marriage is a history of LGBT's emancipation.

I worked in Theatre 1959, acting in Television in the UK untill the 80's, later travelled in the 90's to Beverly Hills and San Fransisco California USA working as Major Domo. On retiring I decided to carry on travelling through China and India from 2000. Observing the International art market of Forbes 'Fortune 500' client's collecting art purchased with the banks foreign exchange mechanism for their corporate clients with $265 billion off shore funds transferred by 2% of the richest global clients. 2400 billionaires own eighty per cent of the global wealth. During my travels, gained insight into the demography of modern international slavery during the 21st century.

In an article published in the New York Post in November 28th, 1950

Albert Einstein wrote:

A human being is part of the whole, called by us 'Universe' a part limited in time and space. He experiences himself, his thoughts and feelings, as something separate from the rest — a kind of optical delusion of consciousness. This delusion is a kind of prison for us, restricting us to our personal desires and to affection for a few persons nearest to us. Our task must be to free ourselves from this prison by widening our circle of compassion to embrace all living creatures and the whole of nature in all its beauty.

In this biographic memoir I have come to the realisation that happiness and the solution to our human problems is not in material possessions and power over others. Happiness and suffering are states of mind, the cause is not found outside the mind. If we want to be truly happy and free from suffering we must learn to understand our own mind. Difficult situations are not problems but challenges to be overcome as the key is within our self to transform. In Thomas Clarkson's Cambridge essay published in 1785 he wrote, 'Is it lawful to enslave the unconsenting.' Today's answer acknowledges inequality by passing laws to eradicated slavery but remains ineffective in the implementation while International human trafficking still remains. In the 21st century, Governments cap millions of vulnerable immigrants entering their borders as eight million homeless men women and vulnerable child refugees roam the planet without rights, or access to education, health or basic facilities as necessities. They play lip service to human rights in principle but do not apply the law successfully while each government condones to allow corporations to manipulate cheap labour as an asset that offers an increase to their profit margin. Education enlightens the mind, but if we remain ignorant of the true facts surrounding international slavery and human trafficking, it is our undoing as a human race.

No matter in what shape it comes, weather from the mouth of a King who seeks to bestride the people of his own nation and live by the fruit of their labour, or from one race of men as an apology for enslaving another race, it is the same tyrannical principle. Let us unite as one people throughout this land, until we shall once more stand up declaring that all men are created equal. 1858 President Abraham Lincoln.

NPG 599 The Anti-Slavery Society Convention, 1840   Benjamin Robert Haydon   © All rights reserved www.npg.org.uk

ENSLAVEMENT

Slavery of the mind leads to expulsion from intellectual freedom leaving fewer conditions for growth and development. Equality in the true sense must include all the parameters of human experience, physical, sexual and spiritual in all its diversity. We cannot pass laws on how to control minds, but we do have the freedom of thought without infringement on the right of others: but unless we as individuals contribute to make this world fit for purpose for all humanity, we may live to see our own erode. We are able to challenge our own prejudice With compassion and kindness, as part of the human condition is greed, hypocrisy, war and lies. To believe we are able to look beyond our own subjective suffering by acknowledging love is the journey of humanity. Divisive elements are constructed, subject to the litany of religious and political interpretation to reject inclusiveness out of fear. To love your neighbour as you would yourself demonstrates there is only one human race that populates the earth by creating mindfulness with compassion to extinguish the heat of hate, rather than launch rockets of mass destruction in the killing fields of war. Self delusion exists only in the mind of the person conceiving of the notion in this ephemeral world. According to Buddhist principles a fault is not culpable unless the perpetrator realises they have done wrong. Many of us maintain ourselves in a state of heartless ignorance. To learn to live from the heart is a re-birth of the spiritual human being to go forward and sympathise with others through pain and suffering to reach for the truth.

Shakespeare wrote 'Wether tis nobler in the mind to suffer the slings and arrows of outrageous fortune or to stand against the enemy' is a personal choice. We can practice tolerance and understanding through diversity of culture, gender, race or sexual orientation. Bigots can drink at the fountain of ignorance, intolerant of the human condition in all its diversity. No one is immune from human frailty so could we take action against inhumanity where we see it, with courage to question everything.

I salute the media practitioners who get to the truth and take heart in the investigative journalist whistle blowers who display transparency and conviction to expose the truth. Eric Snowden informed the world of the real threat to the individual right of privacy with integrity, to expose the unsolicited invasion by governments NASA and GHQ, of personal freedom and human rights, we salute you. George Orwell wrote the book '1984,' of a society that becomes a police state run by an autocratic regime not a democracy. The narrative could become a reality if we allow the autocrats and despots to become power brokers in our time. Vigilance and transparency are operative keys words to the global future. This memoir is not intended to discredit any person, though some names have been changed to respect the privacy of those mentioned is truthful and a record of historical events are available in the public domain. Learn to live in the moment, to a future from now, and realize that we may not be here tomorrow. None of us are given a guarantee from birth of a date of our demise from this mortal coil, but we can be certain of our departure in the self realization that life is a work in progress, let's give it our best shot.

A LETTER FROM MARTHA GRAHAM

This letter from Martha Graham was written as inspiration from an artist to inspire any one to consider their own expression, was to the dancer Agnes de Mille.

Their is a vitality, a life force and energy, a quickening that is translated through you into action, and because there is only one of you in all of time this expression is unique . If you block it, it will never exist through any other medium and it will be lost. The world will not have it, it is not your business to determine how good it is or how valuable not how it compares with other expressions. It is your business to keep it, yours clearly to keep the channel open. You do not have to believe in yourself or your work.

You have to keep yourself open and aware to the urges that motivate you. Keep the channel open. No artist is only a queer divine satisfaction whatever at any time. There hing and makes us more satisfaction, a blessed unrest that keeps us marching alive than others it is the journey, not the arrival that drives us all forward to our destination.

If Rembrandt had not painted his own portrait several times through his life, we would never have know what he observed of his own physical journey from a young man to middle age in sickness and health, his self image 'warts and all.' He expressed what he knew to be the truth in what he saw without deception. Michelangelo carried his Portrait of the smiling lady' always with him to the end of his life his genius of self expression was to discover the way forward as truth. Finding your own journey does not require a map but requires courage to face the unknown that befall us through personal experience, with compassionate understanding for others on the journey of life. To discover our spirituality not of the physical world or of religious trappings in search of inner peace gives meaning to our life and learning to love others. We share this Earth from birth to death in love and war, the challenge is to leave it a better place for the whole human race.

BIRTH

I was a war baby born in Leeds west Yorkshire in the north of England 13th of December 1940 at 22.50 in the Chinese year of the Metal Dragon. As Luftwaffe pilots unleashed their bombs of destruction over head as I entered the world under the terror of war. The battle of the Luftwaffe in the sky was one of seventy two consecutive nights above Britain. My Mother spent all night crouching and frightened under the basement cellar stairs of our small terrace house in Pasture Place Chapel Allerton: she waited for the all clear siren after the Blitz bombs hit the nearby Kirkstall munitions factory in Leeds. Nazi pilots in Messerschmitt planes released their loaded bombs as they returned to Berlin before she ventured upstairs. My absent father had been out all night on home guard duty as he had not being called up for active duty due to a perforated eardrum examined by the army's medical examination board. I was expected to be born Boxing Day but arrived thirteen days earlier that night in the first floor bed room, not exactly a Christmas gift but a premature birth. During the following months the German Luftwaffe increased their successive bombing raids over Leeds as war progressed in 1941. I succored at my mother's breast but three months later was sent with her and my older brother as evacuees from the city of Leeds, to a rural farming community in the Yorkshire dales. We arrived at our adopted village of Burley Woodhead welcomed by the Greaves family at 'Cragg Cottage,' situated 350 feet above sea level on Rombalds moor in Wharfedale near Ilkley five years before the world war was to end.

In the spring of 1940 1 had been conceived in a moment of parental passion in March on the Cow and Calf rocks, five hundred feet high on the windswept moorland under low hanging clouds. When I asked my mother to confirm this, she was shocked, and asked me how I knew. I told her this image had come to me in a dream so she accepted it.

During 1940 hundreds and thousands of children were transported by train from metropolitan cities carrying small travelling cases containing our few toys and possessions on the British railways. Children were dispersed into the country side under advice from the war office of the British government to live in safe family homes within rural communities for the duration of the war. We were sent to avoid the 'Blitz' and carnage of war with Germany as evacuees during the second-world war, organised by the British Government, in their belief of the possibility of imminent invasion from the European continental mainland by Nazi oppression. The concentration camp holocaust was in full momentum of Hitler's plan to complete his 'final solution' before planning his intended invasion of Britain. We arrived by rail on a steam train in the late spring at the village of Burley-in-Wharfedale, after what seemed a long journey from Leeds City to the two platform station, hanging baskets with flowers in full bloom in a riot of colour nodded in the breeze to greet us. Flowerbeds filled with pink foxglove and yellow primrose at the side of the neatly tended station entrance. Passengers offioaded with the slamming of carriage doors behind us. The uniformed station master blew his whistle and the train moved off in a haze of steam, black smoke and clouds of soot from the funnel into the distance. Leaving us standing there in the morning sunshine surrounded by our suitcases and pram, we continued the journey to our adopted home as guests of the Greaves family at Crag Cottage. The bedroom windows looked out over Ilkley moor and the Cow and Calf rocks which lay in the horizon on the distant landscape.

As the second of four siblings with two brothers and a sister four and eight years apart my childhood was not a happy one. At the age of four I was taken away as an infant with my elder brother to a preparatory boarding school away from home in the spring of 1945.

St John's preparatory school was a day's journey by steam train on the 'Flying Scotsman' from Leeds, stopping at Crewe station to change via Uttoxeter to Alton in Staffordshire. While waiting on the platform I cried to be picked up by the fireman on to the engine footplate who allowed me to pull the cord on the steam whistle. I was fascinated by coal being thrown into the engines flaming furnace by fireman as the guard pulled me away from the hot belching conflagration before closing the iron plate door under the boiler. I hastily retreated to the arms of my mother on the platform below A few minutes later we sat back comfortably on the velvet bench seats to start our onward journey. As the train pulled out of the station past rows of derelict bombed out terrace houses, we looked out over the Suburban landscape where families had lost their homes and loved ones in night raids of the Luftwaffer bombers.

Arriving at Alton village in Staffordshire we took a taxi from the station to St John's my new boarding school, the large Victorian Gothic stone edifice designed by the 19th century architect Pugin who also designed the Houses of Parliament in Westminster, London, built on an elevation above the village. In the school brochure the monochrome aerial photograph showed impressive crenellate battlements and high stone walls framing the leaded roof with a union jack hoisted on a flagpole flying in the breeze.

I remember feeling abandoned and isolated when my parents left me at the age of four even though my brother was to stay after the long journey. They returned home to Yorkshire without us and my tears flowed. The dependency of being at school with my older brother David did nothing to alleviate the anxiety of my leaving home, in retrospect it seems a strange thing to do to an infant child. Four years later, suddenly, without warning at the age of eight as a result of my father's business failure and following financial difficulties he was declared bankrupt, this caused us both to be moved from the private preparatory boarding school in rural Staffordshire at the end of term 1948, to attend St Augustine RC Leeds city council day school in post war 1949.

The post war class of forty eight was complicated by the poor quality of teaching in noisy overcrowded chaos. I lost interest and became bored in class without mental stimulation from the curriculum and syllabus. The lack of control caused the teaching staff to become irate and adept at throwing metal rulers and chalk in the classroom with skillful aim in the direction of the protagonist or disturbance from a pupil of contestable humour or a budding comedian. This physical attempt to quell apparent anarchy failed. Such was the standard of post war education, with distinct emphasis on religious Catechism and dogma, rather than concentrating on the three R's reading writing and arithmetic. After any misdemeanor I was sent by the teacher to the convent of Catholic Carmelite nuns across the road from the School to receive corporal punishment ordered by teachers administered with enthusiasm by the mother superior. This physical abuse given to an eight year old boy was both degrading and painful.

At the convent the holy Mother nun approached her task with sadistic determination, applying several forceful blows to the palms and fingers of my small hands. The number of blows depended on the severity of my misdemeanor. I suspect she received some degree of pleasure giving abuse to a very young child of eight. I have since wondered what motivated the nun to perform this harsh ritual. No word was spoken as she applied energetic force from her cane which was carefully covered in hard brittle plaster the edge cut into the skin and bones of my hands and brought tears to my eyes. The stinging pain stayed with me even after the feeling had returned, endured as part of the school curriculum for the next seven years. Today's legislation would not allow it, as it would be considered physical abuse. I still remember the pain and emotional anguish after seven decades which served no useful purpose other than physical assault.

During my first school term-time at St Augustine's Mr Burns, a fresh faced young teacher from training college asked the class to bring their favourite piece of recorded music to be played on his gramophone.

The next day he brought his new high fidelity 'Bush' to play our forty five and thirty three rpm vinyl records. The class responded enthusiastically bringing Elvis Presley, the Everley brothers and Chuck Berry, with contemporary favourites of the late 1950's. I chose Richard Addisons 'Warsaw Concerto'. During the first movement the class shouted and jeered, blowing raspberries drowning out the first bars of the opening. Mr Burns patiently allowed the second movement to be played before the passage ended. By that time most of the class began to listen curiously, but the point was made. Mr Burns said everyone has a right to their democratic choice even if the class did not want to show their appreciation in general consensus.

Reading was a highlight, I remember waiting eagerly every Thursday of the week after my paper round when the 'Eagle' comic came out I picked it up eagerly at the news agent to read the next episode of the sheep dog and find Black-Bob's next adventure before

'Black Beauty' the wonder horse: The 'Beano' was filled with desperate Dan's escapades who lived on a diet of cow pie enjoyed with his bristly cartoon beard, he shared pages with the latest episode of the 'Bash Street Kid's and Minnie the Minx.' At weekends the prospect of a peaceful day with Dennis the Menace and borrowed books from the local public library always filled me with expectation. The discovery of learning facts from fiction it offered me a quite space not available at home. A library card allowed reading to become my passport and entry to another world of knowledge from the manifest shelf at my disposal.

Mum & Me

PROSPECTS

On leaving school at the age of fifteen without academic qualification I started work as trainee in the advertising studio of a multiple department store in Leeds. I joined the Art department, after a successful interview became studio assistant creating visual aid props for exhibition in the marketing promotional-in-store display department, as I had an ability to draw. Further academic education at College was way beyond my parents reach or pocket and no grants were available from the government in 1956 to aspiring students. At fifteen I was made to realise I had to contribute to the family budget. Previously I passed the eleven plus examination which would have allowed me to go further academically, I looked forward to the exciting prospect of starting a new term at a Grammar School, but instead of encouraging me, mother refused to discuss it and would not allow me to go to the Grammar school as it was 'non Catholic'. As no alternative place was made available I quickly lost faith in a system which completely let me down at the eleventh hour. To reflect on this bigoted religious belief serves no useful purpose.

Becoming a wage earner in 1956 with my own pocket money I could afford to take piano lessons and studied practical and theory over the next three years privately with a music teacher Miss Eileen Smith, who patiently inspired me to pass four theoretical music grades and pianoforte instrument. She was one of a few people in my young life who taught me to recognise humanity and how to focus on my own capabilities. Once a week in the evening after work I went to her music studio for tuition. Sitting outside waiting to enter for my lesson I heard a performance piece I had not recognised before, when the playing had finished I was astonished to see Ms Smith's husband leave the studio, he had just finished playing a piece on her 'Bluthner' grand piano, an 'Etude' by Chopin performed with such musicality and professional technique. I was moved to wonder why he left me with such an indelible impression to respond that music offered a range of emotional response as a new language to me.

Miss Smith had compassionate understanding of my vulnerability and the patience to persevere with my moods and often my over emotional reaction to difficult circumstance at home which interfered with the lesson. She firmly encouraged me to work hard to enter four theoretical grades of music over the next two years. I responded working at night and weekends with success, to pass four grade examination certificates from the Associated Board of the Royal School of music. It was my way of pursuing an academic choice of musical expression which gave me a sense of achievement and personal satisfaction as I had been such a poor scholar at school.

GRANDMA ROSE

My Grandmother Rose Mcmann's maiden name descended from McMann the Irish Anglo form of Gaelic claimed descent from the 11th Century high King of Irish Chieftans in county Fermanagh. Descended from Mahon Maguire a grandson of Don Carrach Maguire and related to Marshal Macmahon(Patrice de Mahon) Elysee Fr. Duke of Magenta 1808-1893 second president of the third Republic of France 1873 -1879 also a politician B Sully in the Saône-et-Loire 13July 1808. The Macmahon family originally came from Ireland. A French General and statesman served as President of France's third Republic from 1873 -1879.

A relative of Irish descent Aline Macmahon American actress 1899-1991 worked in Broadway theatre from 1920 alternatively Hollywood in film and television until her retirement in the mid 70's she

was awarded the Oscar in 1933 for 'Dragon Seed'. As a Classic Hollywood actress of 23 movies, she became president of Equity Library Theatre. She also worked with John Lithgow and Meryl Streep.

MOTTO : "Thus we defend our sacred rights"

It was my habit after leaving school each evening to walk to my grandmother's house Rose McMan who loved making me afternoon teatime of warm Irish potato cakes, fresh from the hot griddle. Warm scones were served with butter and fresh strawberry jam, accompanied by steaming hot tea in china cups served with much sweet kindness. My maternal Grandma had departed Ireland as a child, immigrating with her family to a cold water tenement in the Gorbal's of Glasgow in Scotland from her farming community of Enniskillen in county Fermanagh Ireland during the great famine of 1845-52, looking for a better life as housemaid. My daily detour to Grandma's house was arranged to avoid my returning to an empty house after school for an hour, but I did not need to look for an excuse as I loved my Grandma. My mother worked full time as civil servant for the Government Highways authority. She arriving home only after business hours to take care of the family the best way she could and ran the home with added domestic responsibility of my memory of her darning our socks and ironing the school uniforms until midnight or the early hours before she would go to sleep.

After tea at Grandma's I practiced on the upright 'Bechstein' over strung upright piano, which was installed in the front room filled with sunlight in the summer months, Geraniums planted in terra cotta pots were arranged neatly on the wide window sill, releasing their heavy intoxicating fragrance in the heat of late afternoon, from plump green leaves and red garnet flower's. I would lose myself for hours playing Beethoven's 'Fair Elise' or practice scales and arpeggios, except on Sunday afternoons when Grandpa Gaston Maximillion-Liotard banged loudly on the bedroom floor overhead, I had forgotten his afternoon nap. He had to start work at 7am six days a week as Chef de Brigade and did not appreciate me disturbing his weekend siesta.

My Paternal grandmother mother Agnes nee Stephenson, I never met or was ever shown a photograph. I was told she had died in a sanatorium before I was born from severe depression and alcohol addiction. Grandma Agnes Stephenson married my paternal grandfather William Henry Clarkson who was later diagnosed with bowel cancer. I was taken by my father to meet him only once, not understanding why he sat on a commode shouting at everyone during our rare visit. I realise now he must have been in painful physical decline. Life was difficult for the family of nine children as three siblings died within a year of their birth. The family lived together, in a small two up and two down inner city terrace house in Holbeck, with an outside privy in the yard shared between six other families in late nineteen century slums of Victorian England. Another memory of a rare visit with my father to his sister my aunt Polly occurred in a blaze of green feathers as her parrot flew around the room screeched its way round the sofa fluttering (into to a large cage) until a black velvet shroud was draped around its darkened home, as peace reigned once more. Aunty Polly made a fuss of me as an infant. I remember her as a tiny woman dressed in a brightly coloured apron which she never took off during our visit, after that visit I never saw her again.

My father told me we were descendants of Thomas Clarkson the abolishionist of slavery, and shared a direct connection to our paternal great Grandfather John Clarkson 17th century, which at the time meant little to me but I was later to discover the historical and personal significance. In 1663 King Charles II chartered a royal company with a monopoly of the African. Trade of slaves to America. ASI (Anti Slavery Internation) is world's oldest human rights founded in 1839 with Thomas Clarkson as its first president. It has consultative states at United States.

During the festive season once a year my maternal aunts, uncles and cousins gathered at Grandma Rose Mcann's and Grandpa Maximillion Liotard on Christmas day. For my party piece I played Beethoven's 'Fer Elise' on the piano and warbled Mendelson's solo 'Oh for the wings of a dove' in the small front room. Seats at this event were at a premium for the whole family as there would be more than twelve of us. Mother played 'Lieberstraum' on the piano also taking requests for carols, Aunty Marguerite did not play the viola as she had apparently lost her confidence, the house filled with excited children opening presents, chattering loudly at the table opening crackers and wearing paper hats blowing whistles before serving Christmas dinner. New Years evening was brought in by me as tradition, as the sibling with the darkest hair and colouring. I had been elected to take a piece of coal and a loaf of bread with a pack of salt into the house as the first person to walk in over the entrance at the stroke of midnight through the front door of the house to bring in good luck for the New Year as was the custom.

Then one day to my horror, the piano had gone, it had disappeared and was not at Grandma Rose's house. It had been confiscated by my aunt Margaret to her house without notice or approval. I was mortified as we did not have the means to purchase a replacement piano, I could no longer continue to practice on the keyboard. The takeover of the family heirloom had been arranged by my aunt Margaret with Grandpa. She could not play the instrument or any of her family, when questioned why? She told us 'it made her front room look more interesting'. Mother discovered the vanishing trick but the clandestine move had been completed in secrecy without any debate on the subject and our joint disappointment went unregistered and ignored causing a family rift through selfish motives.

At weekends during 1953 taking a tram car into the city centre I boarded the Sammy Ledgard 'Bone shaker,' a pre-war Leyland omnibus exhumed with creative ingenuity referred to as being road worthy, an assurance I doubted. The omnibus journey was very painful to a passenger posterior as the hard wooden bench seat provided little comfort during the journey of over an hour crawling the twelve miles slowly between stops to my final destination, the torture finally over. The objective was to get away from home. I walked up the hill to 'Crag-top Farm' from Burley-in-Wharfedale bus stop with a further two mile walk to Woodhead to the moor gate, stopping beside the iron gate entrance at the small wooden cabin where Leonard Wetzel the village cobbler mended shoes for the local village. He acted as caretaker and key holder for the primary School at the moor-side he kindly allowed me access to play the piano out of school hours, But it was no substitute as it was always out of tune but enough for me to continue to practice on the keyboard whenever I could as it provided me some consolation.

ANOTHER SURPRISE

During one of many argument between my father and mother I overheard one of significance, to discover that my father had a son from a previous relationship in the late 1920s before his marriage to mother My half brother had been referred to as born out of wedlock. I was surprised as I had never met him or allowed to see him by design or circumstance. Apart from him meeting my elder brother David, he apparently showed no interest in meeting his other sibling's as this was only by arrangement through my father who had kept in contact with him over the years. They carefully avoided any aspect of my involvement when I had eagerly suggested the possibility of my meeting him this request was met with sullen disapproval from my elder brother and ignored by my father. I was told years later that he had moved to the south of England with his wife and family and realised a whole segment of a life that I did not know had been excluded and consciously edited out of mine. To my greater surprise my mother told me in later years that she had lost a baby brother before she carried me which was still born. He would have been another sibling I never new and often wondered what might have been as I cried myself to sleep, wondering why this situation had left me confused, feeling a loss for someone I never knew. My older brother David was sent to a boarding school for the deaf at the age of ten as he was found to be falling behind in the class not hearing the lessons. When he left home my sense of increased isolation in not sharing his company was acute as I was thrown further on my own resources without an ally or emotional support. He was sent away from home to a special school as full time boarder until he was sixteen and had the good fortune to be out of the abusive domestic loop I remained in only coming home for brief holidays when permitted. I stayed in Leeds at day school and lived at home a further seven years alone from the age of eight until my sister Celeste was born four years later as I was unable to share my brothers company. At the age of four my little sister Celeste took ballet class with me every Saturday morning until she attended a convent day school at the age of sixteen until her surprise pregnancy facilitated a shotgun wedding an arrangement agreed to by my father which enabled her to leave home and country immediately as she thought it was her only means of escape. She had met her future husband stationed at Menwith-Hill United States American army base in North Yorkshire. As an American marine he planned to return with his sixteen year young English bride my sister to the USA. I realized that another relationship was now fractured as we had shared a close bond as siblings I felt abandoned. To my further surprise, my younger brother Nicholas was born later with an eight year age gap between us. As a baby he was too young to comprehend anything other than being the youngest sibling, he became the apple of father's eye, he could do no wrong without censure or chastisement from my father. By the time he reached the age of ten I had left home. From that moment I sensed a bond between them, and learnt to accept the fact that as he was the baby of the family deferred to with pride particularly as he later became a school sports swimming champion of the team much to fathers delight. At school I showed the same interest in sport's activity as a fish does out of water. My interest at that time was in theology as a philosophical discipline of religious speculation, fascinated though I was of its traditional restriction because of the origin and format of belief system to explicate faith. The Roman Catholic catechism and dogma helped me understand the scripture for choir practice as an altar boy and chorister. The code of scripture is compiled as a network of logical gates and circuits it demonstrates how the code itself can become the object of perception and savouring of the embodied code. Scripture is distinguished by its dependence on the primacy of the wording that is more important for how it says than what it says, and therefore can never be rephrased. The historical narrative of faith morphed as a matter of factual meaning, that is, what it says is more important than how it says it, and can be rephrased, multiplied. When both these wordings and meaning are subordinate the aesthetic process itself has primacy, we refer to it as art and literature. It did come to pass in time as my curiosity got the better of me. In knowing something threw up another question later, why the something was obstructing what might happen as I matured to embrace life as an independent adventure.

Chapter 02

A MUSICAL PERFORMANCE

On becoming a boy soprano and lead in the Church Choir at high mass and one of the few who could hit and hold high C and an altar boy at the age of ten: it was the only time of my childhood I felt in control in having a choice that I was involved in. When the Choir rehearsals for 'Adeste Fidelis' in Latin with other hymns at Christmas came to a climax on Christmas Eve against a backdrop of fully decorated garland's of holly and spruce the carol singers warbled 'Away in a Manger in Bethlehem' gathered around the nativity scene in front of the altar. The Church was adorned expectant of the Holy festival. The congregation expressed their interest by joining in reciting the 'Te Deum' at the midnight mass on Christmas Eve. The celebrant priest father O'Meara from the emerald isle, dressed in gold brocade over a long white surplus with sleeves edged in fine white lace, while incense smoked in a gold lantern. The priest walked down the aisle in front of the altar fanning the burning conflagration from a long chain toward the supplicant congregation. Mrs Burns the music mistress and mother of the new fresh faced teacher from classes was beside herself with joy at my solo vocal performance. She immediately arranged for me to enter future competitions for a showdown between school rehearsals. Future music competitions were to be organised strategically as an away match, but within weeks of my thirteenth birthday my voice had broken and its dulcet tone had gone.

The sport lessons at school in the form of football and cricket was a complete mystery to me and no alternative activity was offered. I could not appreciate the need to compete or actively take part in games, so my refusal to change into shorts for PT and sports lesson was consistently met with loud verbal reprimands from the sport teacher who marked me absent. I sat on the floor determinedly gazing into the middle distance as in a daydream of my missing riding the Highland pony at the Farm where my thoughts drifted, of being thrown, landing hard, bouncing into the soggy reeds of the hilly paddock, the prospect was a load more fun at Crag-Top farm.

FATHER

Father was an ex-army man who had been stationed in the hills of Khasi and Jiantia in north east India as a nineteen, traveling on horseback along the north-west border in East Bengal with his regiment on patrol duty from Shillong to Srinagar a Kashmir north east India. He signed on to join the army when he was little more than a boy soldier as he had lied about his age.

On my eleventh birthday, he gave me a pair of red leather boxing gloves which I rejected but reluctantly tried as he persisted in coaxing me to put them on with an intention to give me rules of the sport. He had been ex- middle weight boxing champion in the British Army, but I could not see the point of punching other boys and told him I much preferred to continue taking ballet lessons. As I went to a class with my younger sister it appealed to my sense of theatre in movement and drama. When he heard of my preference, my recalcitrant father got over his indignant horror by forbidding me to go to further ballet lessons after an incendiary row with my mother on the prospect of it 'not being a suitable future for a boy'. I was twelve when he told me to stop taking ballet class and my sister had to continue on her own. As an unwilling participant I could not see the logic for the choice of my father's preference for the sport of boxing it completely turned me off which further alienated the paternal relationship.

Back at school the physical education teacher way past his prime had been relegated to perform the segment referred to as PT (Physical Training). He could never persuade me to change into a short's for sport activities due to my intransigence and refusal to join in games.

As a result I remained on the fringe as none competitive passive spectator for all sports activity, looking on at my school peers in the class. Becoming a spectator left me feeling isolated and socially inept. I continued to bury my head in library books and referred to as 'Professor' by my classmates a title which was easy to understand as I did spend most of my spare time in the local Library after school hours.

TRUST

Walking home with Tony Bell a school friend we passed by his house and paused as he proudly showed me his father's car parked in the drive, a 1938 black Ford ten saloon. I looked admiringly at its shiny black paintwork and split windscreen with two wipers. On closer inspection I lifted the right wiper gently examining closely to see how it worked against the glass, It plopped back safely to its recumbent position against the windscreen. The next day Tony Bell's father came to the house to see my father loudly proclaiming that I had broken the wipers on his car. It was the left wiper that he was waving about in his hand with a rubber blade which had departed from the motor arm making it inoperative. I knew I had not done it, but my father had lost face and gave me a beating with his army belt on the end of the sofa. It was his endorsement and acceptance without investigation as he believed I was the culprit and I never forgot his lack of confidence in me.

Some weeks later a bizarre incident occurred on a weekend visit to Crag-Top farm, my father told me to get out of the car to guide him through the gated entrance to the farm between two wide stone posts either side to drive his pride and joy an Austin A40 into the home yard. The family watched me while I guided him carefully through the gateway. He accelerated the vehicle, while it crept forward the front bumper scraped past a dry stone post creating a metallic scream between the wall and the adjoining door panel. Without stopping he drove on as the dent deepened on the driver's side door. As the situation unfolded before us I looked at my father's face which began to turn crimson through the wind shield of the car, wide eyed with rage, unholy words emanated from his mouth in invective expletives. As his door opened he catapulted out like a jack-in-the box-in an apoplectic spasm from the driving seat running toward me in a fit of rage. I bolted and started to run as fast as my feet would carry me as he obviously blamed me for his accident chasing after me shouting 'you stupid little bastard.' I shot off into the long meadow until he gave up the chase. I knew in his sudden rage, he had forgotten to put the handbrake on as the car carried on its trajectory to increased momentum without him, ending in a dull thud against the stone wall. To this day the memory gives me much amusement, in the display of malicious intent he had projected toward me. It was evident he was responsible for his own driving but quick to blame others for his own action.

BROKEN FRIENDSHIP

Shortly after my fourteenth birthday, a school friend Tony Bell caused me to lose my newspaper paper round that I had kept for over two years I was told by the news agent he had decided to change to a new delivery boy. This caused me loss of my only independent means of financial support, I wanted to find out who had taken my delivery round from me and decided to wait one evening half way through the round, I stood in heavy rain within a gate between hedgerows as the bike and rider came round the corner. In the twilight I saw the bundle of papers carried by my friend Tony Bell. Shocked and humiliated, I asked him why he had taken the paper round from me he replied mockingly 'for less money than you.' Without thinking I saw red and pushed him off his bike shouting in surprise and anger, 'So it's you'. He fell off the bike landing on the ground with copies of the 'Yorkshire Post' newspaper strewn over the wet pavement in the evening twilight. I jumped on the front wheel of his bicycle, the wheel spokes bent as the tyre folded on impact under my foot I hit out at him with my hands in a rage. He ran off not waiting to face any further display of my anger at his deceit. I broke off our friendship and never heard another word from him or his parents. Sad as I was at losing a friend, realised that the lesson in loosing trust with someone I had befriended was part of growing up.

At school a month later during the usual playground morning break, a tall fat older boy I knew by sight as a school bully but did not know well approached me in the playground while I sat on the wall top, He shouted in my face with what I understood to be a threat. I looked at him walking toward me, his hands clenched at his side with one raised fist ready to strike. I did not reply but moved without thinking, I turned to grab a loose coping stone I noticed on the wall top beside me, lifting the projectile in one swift Zen movement and released it. The consequence of my action was critical, as gravitation pull guided the stone directly to his head, on its impact he dropped to the ground bleeding from his head and nose laying motionless on the ground. I looked at his inert form surprised at my own uninhibited action. The commotion and shouting brought the playground monitors and teaching staff running to the scene. I was marched off and taken to see the head master with threats of expulsion, I told him the true facts, which he accepted as he knew of the boy's history of bullying. The fat boy was taken by ambulance to hospital A&E for medication and stitches. A few days later the boy returned to school, but never approached me or attempted to bully or threaten anyone else to my knowledge after the incident. I would not recommend anyone to follow my example as the way forward, or encourage others in my behaviour. My reaction to intimidation was effective as it did provide a dramatic solution to a dangerous situation. School lessons for me were a blur of uninteresting tedious curriculum. During break times the adolescent boys beat up the small boys to impress the girls in the segregated lower while girls stared over the wall in romantic yearning of their fantasy hero. The boy's testosterone differences played out in pugilistic antisocial behaviour against smaller boys provided a suitable rehearsal for a maladjusted future.

As my two school friend's, Italian immigrant brothers Julio and Dino from Anzio had newly arrived from their southern Italian village they were unable to understand the constant rows and abuse between my parents on their rare visits to my home. When I accepted invitations to visit their home I could not understand the warmth and kindness shown to me by their family, the complete opposite of mine, taken by me as the norm. It was a new experience for me sitting at the lunchtime table waiting for their Mama to ladle pasta and hot broth into our bowls as 'laughter filled the kitchen with animated conversation I could not understand, but I could comprehend their infectious laughter. Their Italian Mama was happy to be involved in this loud exchange of a new language. In Contrast, my tense domestic trauma exhibited during their visits to my house, added a dark drama they did not eagerly wish to repeat as a result of bizarre behaviour from my Father. Our dinner often ended up on the wall as the plate Of food had been flung by him to vent his temper accompanied With expletives during shared mealtimes. I watched the contents of the plate sliding slowly down the flowered wallpaper creating its own bizarre motif left me wondering why, had he not like mum's cooking. This volatility created an environment of emotional conflict and constant animosity, no guarantee of winning friends. This was my normal domestic experience which continued until I left the bosom of the family home at the age of eighteen.

An alarming feature about my Father was that people outside home, congratulated me on having 'Such a wonderful man for a father,' I could not understand whom they referred to. Apparently he presented a charming and concerned personality to the external world with a reputation that preceded him I could not comprehend this anomaly. The duality puzzled and disturbed me as I caught glimpses of his erratic behaviour on meeting his associates in public, or on a bus or in the street engaged in conversation that focused on him. He would often go out of his way to cultivate a caring attitude in a situation that always seemed to put him in the best possible light I tried to understand the conundrum.

When he was out of reach of his public persona in the home, apart from outbursts he resumed taciturn behavior toward my mother which I found confusing. I was fascinated by his a talent for acting the chameleon he presented.

To escape the domestic torpor at weekends I would go to the Saturday matinee for two old pence at the local 'Forum' cinema. In those days during intermission the organ slowly rose from floor in the front of house pit played by a resident soloist in the glamorous beam of a spotlight to accompany the Ice cream girls at the front of house either side of the auditorium. The house lights dimmed into the magic of darkness .as the draped red velvet curtains opened wide to disappear before each film performance. After the interval a moment of sudden darkness before the house-lights returned mesmerised me, before the big screen and flickering beam of light high above the audience onto the silver screen projected magic.

As a ten year old I was- fascinated by 'Sylvester' the cat chasing 'Tweety-Pie' who sang 'l thought I saw a pussy cat a creepin-up on me,' in a vocal solo (with full orchestra) sung in a heavy lisp by Mel Blanc with an American accent. His voice over gave each character a personality to the cartoon animation. Sylvester the cat rarely got the advantage over the tiny yellow budgerigar, in the safety of his birdcage he bravely swings from his small perch in spite of the cat's protest, the little yellow bird felt threatened and ridiculed constantly, a situation I could easily identify with. In other comedies the Marx brothers in playful chaos got the better of Harpo, whose elegant antics and dexterous performance on his golden harp providing a hilarious backdrop to the more serious existence called life as I knew it in 'Duck Soup'.

In 1942 during the war we moved a short distance from my birthplace to a pretty Edwardian bungalow 'The Lodge', it had a small garden surrounding by a low sandstone wall. A young soldier had been billeted in our house directed by the war office. The public where possible during the war was asked to offer a spare room to billet soldiers, according to mother he used to take me out in my pram to the local park, he gave me a small brown teddy bear one Christmas which I do not remember. We made another domestic move in 1948 to a rambling red brick Victorian house with an open garden on three sides. I kept two rabbits in a hutch in the back garden to which I played them tunes on my 'Hohner' accordion, but to this day I cannot remember how it came into my possession so I must have borrowed it. During intervals of my serenade after cleaning out their cage the pets ran off to hide in the undergrowth of weeds to munch on cabbage leaves which had gone to seed. I took this to be a lack of appreciation of my musical talent which extended to their multiple droppings they arranged in small black semiquavers in a line, as if in graphic disapproval of my own musical notation.

My father was inclined to spend time planting and weeding in our sprawling front garden. The big lawn was given pride of place as he tended it preened to a velvet green after sprinkling moisture on it, from a watering can through the summer months. Liberal watering and cutting the lawn edge straight as a die, surrounded by banks of hollyhocks and tulips. On warm sunny day's he would get the croquet balls out with the heavy wooden mallet and erect the hoop to play on the lawn after giving out the rules of engagement. He had earlier treated the lawn surface with a heavy cylindrical roller to a smooth consistent level before knocking the ball hard with the wooden mallet which ended up in the foliage. I ignored the competition to wander off into camellia bushes to relieve myself. I was not old enough to lift weeds probably because I could not be trusted to mistake dandelions for burdock and buttercups or pansies for chickweed. Not having completed my Sunday chores or collected my father's 'News Of the World' paper, I was reprimanded and sent to bed with a supper of dry bread and plain tap water to quench my thirst until the next day.

One summer weekend afternoon when I was six, my father lifted me on his shoulders, crawling on all fours with his knees and hands the grass wearing a silly grin, played the donkey to me as his jockey. I was not amused and pulled hard at the remaining hair at the back of his balding head tugging it with all my might. He suddenly became shouting 'you don't like me do you' as he dropped me like a filled sack to the floor. I stared at the contorted rage on his face and answered him No and I never will,' prophetic words indeed. Coming to terns with his extreme behaviour it prevented me from feeling anything than dislike. I saw him as an angry wife beater with sadistic toward me and Mother, regularly taking off his brass buckle leather belt to flog me ordering me to face down over the end of the sofa for any transgression and with his fists across my face. I felt the indignity was both offensive and cruel toward mother. He did not understand his om demons, unable to control his rage. 'Instinctively I could not like or love a coward who took such aggressive action against women and children, at that age I did know the difference and began to avoid him. When I returned home for the summer holiday, I was placed in a local day school as a result of my father becoming a bankrupt. After my at a private preparatory boarding school which he could no longer afford to end us to. These circumstances allowed me to endure returning to at home and attend the overcrowded elementary day school. The physical and verbal abuse continued toward mother and I received from my father on a daily basis, he referred to mother as the mistake and reason of the loss of his business. A stream of vindictive vitriol directed towards my mother with constant expletive abuse. Like most egocentrics they blame others for their own failures, it became his 'Mantra' over the seemed to feed an inner frustration.

MY EPIPHANY

Walking eight miles to and from school twice a day, sometimes more frequent to lunch at home, after a few months, I bad saved enough to purchase a new bicycle with the money earned from my paper round as a delivery boy after school hours. On my thirteenth birth day the freedom of independent perambulation up hill and down dales on my bicycle allowed me to travel freely quite long distances solo. Thrilled at the prospect of playing truant by choice, I planned days away to travel to a far-off location. Working during school holidays and weekends in the 'Crag-top' field's of Woodhead turning new mown grass into hay. I felt free and happy to labour on the farm, feeding and watering calves with heifer store beast after mucking out the cattle sheds. Bernard's father 'Bert' cut fresh grass with a scythe in the meadow producing twice as much as a sickle could. In 1949 during hay-making we used to turn the hay with forks and rake up the rows to gather them in 'stooks' then stand them in short double rows to dry out in the sun and wind before stacking on horse cart: Later we lead them off the field to the barn in the stockyard or to be stacked in lofts above the cattle shed, fed later to the beasts below with a winter feed. From choice this labour of love was the saviour of my sanity from the kindness of the Greaves family.

On summer holidays I cycled solo through Skipton and the bustling market past the Castle up hill and over the dales. On other day's visiting the Spa Pump room of Harrogate and stopping at 'Bettys' cafe for tea. Sometimes visiting passing lime caves of Pen-y-ghent speeding past Paterdale, free-wheeling past outcrop clusters of limestone, my classroom became Haworth in the Bronte Country of 'Wuthering Height's, and discovered Nidderdale the home of James Herriot the famous veterinarian author. I revelled in discovering the acres of pasture and moorland wilderness, with perimeters of man-made dry stone walls surrounding the farmland, creating a quilted pattern of texture to the distant horizon in shades of amber to grey on the undulating hills of Blubberhouse moor. Cycling on through the valley to Timble village beyond the river Washbum, crossing Fewstone reservoir over the green fields of Norwood in Nidderdale Yorkshire as the season's timeless cycle brought early morning dew on small bud's reflecting the bright sun. I listened to the swallows building their nests in the spring after their annual migratory fight from Africa riding on their flight path to find a home in the old barn roof trusses carrying small twigs and leaves to rebuild their nests from the previous year, As we stacked bales of fresh mown hay cut in the summer months and early golden autumns to be led off to the empty barn. We hand-picked fruit from a heavy crop of ripened pears and apples from the orchard, with hedgerows full of blackberries and gooseberries in August, to be displayed 'in the autumn harvest festival at the Method' chapel up the lane. The warm summer season was followed by ice cold winters of drifting snow, filling the country lanes to the height of dry stone walls surrounding the fields and dales in a blizzard of dazzling snow as far as the distant horizon. Leafless trees covered in a mantle of frozen ice clung to bare branches, sparkling in the pale winter sun like diamonds. We were closed off from the village and the outside world for days. This childhood wandering gave me a lifelong affinity with the countryside and open space of the sky in constant flux beyond the Horizon. Vincent Van Gogh wrote, 'if you really like nature you will find beauty everywhere'.

Chapter 03

WASHBURN VALLEY

After a long courtship my childhood friend Bemard Greaves married Janet Dibb his sweetheart and moved from 'Craggtop Farmi to start married life at 'Folly Hall farm.' It was the start of a new chapter and their family life with two children Charles and Helen at Follyhall Farm in the Washburn valley of Nidderdale, North Yorkshire.

The breeding of a livestock herd at 'Folly Hall' farm started with a Limousine Charrolaise Bull of pedigree status brought for covering Friesen heifers for calving. In March and April the welsh half bred mule hogs-scattered the hillsides in drifts of spring lambs born before dipping with their woollen winter coats clipped in late summer. The sheep wandered into the shade of hedgerow bottoms with their fronds of wild flowers, honeysuckle, daises, buttercup and cowslip. At Easter time the winter store cattle kicked and skipped their way out of the sheds into the warm spring sunshine after the rain. Calves were gelded before racing off through the early sprigs of wild rye into the grassy hills. The bottom of the big meadow lined with trees at the water's edge of the Washburn River was swelled in a rushing torrent through the pack horse bridge carrying leaves and broken branches in leaf from the oak and sycamore trees. After a heavy rainstorm. The twisting angry water ebbed and flowed dashing over dark green mossy boulders in hasty retreat, as if poured from the devils cauldron through Norwood's pastoral landscape into the Lindley reservoir below. William Tumer the English painter captured this living landscape as he walked through rural country estate when he stayed at 'Farnley Hall' estate hear Otley in the 19th Century little has changed since then of the landscape.

A man who is tired of London, and several decades working in other cities, I try to avoid loud invasive noise pollution, and the ceaseless humm of city traffic. Preferring to walk in open spaces wandering at night through the perimeter streets of London's Regents Park, marveling at the crocus and first buds of daffodils in February reflected in the sodium light, giving them a nocturnal profile against the dark foliage behind the me railing and well kept lawns. This gave me thoughtful insight of the garden as a place of contemplation, a garden as a place of quietude not only the physical or metaphysical sense but as a place of public or private event. The park became the garden of Gesthemane entertaining disciples, gathered to hear the words of Christ at the speaker's corner: or the garden of Lumbini with the Buddhavista under the shade of the Bhodi tree to hear his words of wisdom. The gardens of Versailles where formality meets floral- horticulture for regal splendour laid out 'in precise logic from the untamed wilderness of the mind, or the garden of Eden and the serpent with the forbidden fruit in a mythical romantic tryst of the lover's assignation. We could all enjoy a garden of the uncorrupted mind walking on the grass and reach out to touch and smell the roses.

We can leave the wild flowers to grow and cultivate the distilled essence of joy in our own allotment of wild jasmine, picking ripened fruit from an outcrop of windblown berries from hedgerow fields Picking sweet apples and ripened pears from the orchard, their fragrance mixed with petunia, sweet pea blossom, orchid and hyacinth grown for pleasure, walking among wild hedgerows of the mind. We need nature, it does not need us, look for it where you can and treasure it.

As 'Padme' the genitive form of 'Padma,' the pure Lotus rises immaculately out of the muddy water intact, even in the midst of the mental poisons we humans fabricate.

Outside my daytime routine not realising the time, I departed Wigmor Hall; after a Debussy piano recital feeling depleted and unfocused. London offered all that one could want but knowing what to choose created yet more Possibilities than I could realise. In a diary of the 1700's was written, la man who is tired of London is tired of life.' Living in the twentieth century and not sharing the sentiment I took a bus up Regent Street to NW1 BBC Broadcasting house walking the rest of the way home. My interest was further-a-field for want of a better place to go in the evenings, I chose the 'Kalabash' coffee house in South Kensington as a meeting place. In the early 60's it became one of the night haunt's for the gay fraternity, mine host was Leon Maybank. The transient crowd was an option for those interested in making personal contact. At the time raids were conducted by the London constabulary in public parks, a venue I personally baulked at the activity of open air exhibition, preferring to learn my preference for a slower pace in a more sociable environment.

SURVIVAL

Needing to find work to support myself, pay rent, and put food on the table, I found it at the Haymarket coffee house next to the Theatre Royal in London's Haymarket in the west end. The coffee house gave me opportunity to meet my contemporaries in a social setting.

Not until the House of Lords recognised their errant hypocrisy did it become legal for the same gender to engage in acts of sexual intimacy between consenting male adults in private over the age of twenty one, the law remained unchanged until-1967. If two consenting male adults were caught by the constabulary in a public place in flagrante delicto with their pants or trousers down, criminal charges were made after arrest and taken to Court, where magistrates handed down orders to administer electric aversion treatment at a psychiatric unit, or undergo estrogen hormone therapy. Electric shock aversion therapy was alternative to a prison sentence, blackmail often succeeded.

Prompting the UK plan, an extensive government survey of 108,000 people from July to October 2017 of the respondents, 61 percent identified as lesbian and gay, 4 percent pan sexual and 2 percent asexual. Transgender respondents numbered 13 percent. The practice of aversion therapy is banned by the medical profession and denounced by psychiatric groups. 'It said it will eradicate the abhorrent practice', as they have seen what damage it does, but it is still carried out by religious groups. The UK government,plans to ban conversion therapy in sweeping reforms. The plans are part of a $5.9 million, 75 point initiative to make society more inclusive for LGBT people. Prime Minister Theresa May expressed her support of the project. 'No one should ever have to hide who they are or who they love,' she said in 2018. Forty percent of the respondent group surveyed by the government said they had experience4 hate incidents, with ninety percent of most serious offenses going unreported. As author of this book I must confirm a hate crime perpetrated against me in 1983, my office windows were smashed and home broken into and ransacked in Chapeltown, Leeds. This was done by someone I thought to be a friend who decided to break into my home and violate my privacy. I reported it to the police and was told by them that as 'the area was a no go' they decided not to investigate the crime.

In Great Britain homosexuality was a criminal offence under the law of public indecency since the reign of Queen Victoria, she was most concerned that this unruly behaviour should not frighten the horses. The last two men found having sex in a private flat in south London were reported to police and sent down at the Old Bailey in 1835 and hung to death at Newgate Hill. Not until 1860 did the death sentence cease being handed down in judgment of expressing love with a person of the same gender. Since the millennium, her great granddaughter Queen Elizabeth 2nd pardoned through act of Parliament by Royal ascent the decriminalisation of 50,000 gay men in equalisation of human rights.

In 1998 the House of Lords heard an impassioned speech given by an openly gay peer and member of the house who spoke in support of the bill to lower the age of consent to sixteen. The Lords rejected it after seven hours of debate, but the House of Commons passed the bill after intervention by the PM Tony Blair. By 2013 marriage between people of the same sex was passed into law. The LGBT community had equal rights under the law of their sexual orientation.

Civil partnership and same sex marriage became the norm, with the right to adopt children followed. I thought it a mystery, why would it matter to anyone who was not involved in what consenting adults do in the privacy Of their own homes. Queen Victoria in the 19th century had asked her Prime Minister at the time to pass the law as a criminal offence but omitted to include gay women and lesbian activity which has never been illegal in the public domain, as women are not included in the act, but they did suffer as a consequence of prejudice and bigotry. The feminist movement in the 19h century was inspired by the leadership am strategies of the abolitionist movement of the century which still resonates today in the 21st century.

GAINFUL EMPLOYMENT

My contact with the Haymarket Coffee House was through Gaby who ran the place with cool discipline, I was interviewed with amused detachment. She was an intimidating figure dressed completely in black, in a cashmere cardigan and black ankle length skirt, perched on a high stool in her office like a raven. Her glossy shoulder length black hair was cut at an expensive West end salon. Her deep set eyes in a piercing gaze under arched eyebrows, her pale skin the shade of light parchment on high cheekbones with a hint of crimson outlined her lips. 'Diorama' fragrance followed her in a cloud permeating her office creating an aura of glamour where she went. Everyone under her management that stepped out of line could and would be fired under her formidable all knowing gaze. As she laid eyes on me something clicked between us, I was unafraid. After my interview she smiled and offered me a station as barista on the 'Gaggia' machine. With a maternal interest she protected me, a shy provincial youth of nineteen inexperienced in the ways of the world of work and play in London of the post war fifties. I worked hard and enjoyed learning and listened to her words of wisdom. She persuaded me to observe and recognise regular customer's which increased my social ease. After some time she trusted me to apply what I had learnt and taught me how to make a profit from a one litre bottle of orange squash to give 22 portions she managed to stretch the extra units profit by the addition of slice of fresh orange. At the end of the week her personal incentive allowed her to order a supply of hand-made Balkan 'Sobranie' cigarettes supplied by Sullivan & Powell in Burlington arcade, and her favourite fragrance 'Miss Dior'. The cigarettes exotic aromatic smoke permeated the office while she sat at her desk in a self induced intoxicating cloud. On my Birthday, Gabby was the only person to turn up at my 21st party, driving her 1949 Rolls Royce silver wraith from her home in Fitzroy Square WI driving through south London to park outside my run down flat where my Brixton neighbours in Villa Avenue were twitching lace curtains as she glided to the kerb.

Working in London's west end with the 'Haymarket' theatre audience I mingled after the shows and during intermission with actors who were currently resting. I worked the tables mixing with customers and a variety of characters who visited the cavernous two floor Haymarket coffee house until well after midnight. In my naivety I had never seen so much exciting human detritus under one roof at the same time. In 1960 the attention from house patron's was sometimes directed towards me, a painfully shy provincial youth, in conversation, I managed to impress Disley Jones the theatre Designer sufficiently to make prop's for him. He asked me to create and make several three dimensional Swans for a theatre production design for Rekyiavic Iceland which I constructed in his Hammersmith studio.

My association in 1958 with Director Toby Robertson, who was working on 'The Ice Man Cometh' at the Oxford Prospect Theatre, had become inconsistent. Toby had assisted Peter Brook on the film 'Lord of the Flies' inviting me to dinner and sometimes other social events. My friendship with Bernard Sarron the Art Director of 'Poor Cow' developed in 1969, while he worked with Ken Loach during the same period. Bernard became a long standing friend acting as my mentor. I often stayed the weekend in his Chiltern Street fiat off Baker Street, spending time listening to Bemards friends talking shop, Silvio Narrizzano was directing 'Georgie Girl' with Lynne Redgrave at the time.

FRIENDS

During the sixties in London, the person I most related too socially was Meade Roberts the screenwriter who had collaborated with Tennessee Williams on the on the screenplay 'Fugitive Kind' in 1959. I listened to his description of the dialogue he had with Marlon Brando and Anna Magnani during the shoot and on location with reference to the film 'Summer and Smoke' in 1961, in which he wrote the shooting script with Tennessee. He shared an anecdote with me, of him being at a restaurant invitation with Ava Gardner at Puerto Vallarta Mexico, with Richard Burton and Elizabeth Taylor in flowing caftan and white turban, she wore the longest diamond earrings which dangling in her soup, Richard laughed and said 'Careful love their in your soup'. She took them off and handed them to the waiter and said, 'would you be a dear and keep these in the kitchen for me.' The waiter was floored but took the earrings. Richard said to Elizabeth 'They are worth $300,000 and you gave them to the waiter' 'only for safekeeping dear 1m'e sure he'll take care of them.' Of course she could have put them in her purse, but she had a flare for the dramatic and in giving someone else their moment. After the meal she went into the kitchen to retrieve the earrings that had been put in the freezer for safekeeping, she thought that was hysterical, 'Ice on ice' she said laughing.

During the following months I received frequent frantic phone calls to my home in Richmond from Meade in the early hours of the morning while he was working in London, usually around two a.m. as an insomniac in a hyper emotional state wanting to talk, I would listen to him for hours he engaged my curiosity about the history of moving pictures. His intense emotional response to the events of his day ranged from manic hysteria with wit and humor, to sudden tearful depths of depression according to his mood. During his visits to our flat in Richmond for afternoon tea on Sunday's he often felt the need to pour out his private hell along with the tea. I perfectly understood his condition as bipolar, referred to in those days as clinical depression. My partner Keith believed Meade was not of this earth without understanding him, he often got irritated with this saga. I empathised with Meade, probably as I too was diagnosed in 1996 with the same condition. My one year of monthly tests as out-patient at the Royal Free Hospital in London's Hampstead resulted in prescribed medication which made my condition worse, but no further actual therapy intervention was offered due to a lack of Government resource, though my thoughts of self harm in the extreme had occurred. My decision to discontinue taking the medication with the GP advice and guidance allowed me to come to terms with my particular prognosis.

AN EQUITY MEMBER
In the sixties

After working late nights in the west end, I often walked passed Notting Hill gate a few minutes distance to my room in Westbourne Park Road where I happily shared rooms in a garden apartment with actor Lloyd Reckord and Colin Garland the theatre Designer. I made detours to visit Keneth Hendel who at the time was appearing in the cast of 'Wait until dark' with Honor Blackman in the West End thriller. Keneth lived in Ladbrooke Grove with his partner John Inman, at that time a well respected Pantomime Dame in 'Mother goose' who was later to play the part of Mr Humphreys in 'Are you being Served,' a camp send- up of a long running TV series set in a menswear department store which had become a successful situation comedy for TV and film. Over the next thirty years John and I were often sentimentally disposed to memories of our northern roots and our days living in Blackpool over many a midnight coffee, and of his overnight success which had actually taken him thirty years to achieve. John was a kind and trusting friend to me and understood I was looking for work, he suggested I could find a position in wardrobe at the Scala Theatre London in the 1959 annual 'Peter Pan' season. He was already in the cast as 'Tinkerbell when I joined the Scala Theatre production to obtain my coveted equity card, after introductions I got a job as wardrobe dresser to Donald Sinden in 1959 before he became a knighted thespian who played both the roles of Mr Darling and Captain Cook in 'Peter Pan'. I remember him as a kind and generous man who always considered others. The production's Xmas party was at his family home's in the country with invitation's to the entire cast and crew, we were all made to feel part of the family at Christmas .dinner. Julia Lockwood was cast as 'Peter' and Juliet Mills played Wendy. The Christmas eve party at her Dolphin Square flat and later New Years Eve party at John and Keneth's Ladbroke Grove flat. Julia arrived with her surprise guest Sarah Churchill the daughter of Winston Churchill, Sarah had played the lost boy 'Peter' in the previous year's production and accompanied Julia as her guest to the party. A week later with friends we all toasted in the New Year at Dolphin Square.

After working for the WAAF until 1945, Churchill's
daughter Sarah returned to her first great love: the
theatre. In 1958, she played Peter Pan in London.

Churchill and family after watching Sarah in *Peter Pan*,
Scala Theatre, London, 30 December 1958
In 1949, Sarah Churchill made her first appearance on the
American stage as Tracy Lord in *The Philadelphia Story*. That
year she married the photographer Anthony Beauchamp.
She also appeared in *Gramercy Ghost* on Broadway and toured
Britain as Eliza in *Pygmalion*.

The London newspaper *Star-News* wrote in 1958,
'[Sarah] announced she will play the part in the annual
Christmas production at the Scala Theatre, not one of
London's plushiest but the traditional place for *Peter Pan*.
Miss Churchill has been appearing sporadically on the stage
and in television in America for the past nine years... Peter
Pan at her age is not unusual. Mary Martin first played the
part at 41 in the United States and was a big hit. Like Miss
Martin and all other Peters, Miss Churchill will wear
tights and fly about the stage suspended from a wire.'

249

GRAPHIC PHOTOGRAPH OF WINSTON AND SARAH CHURCHILL 1958/59

TRANSGENDER

I cannot remember the exact circumstance or day when I met April Ashley in 1959/60 who at the time had undergone successful surgery for gender reassignment in Morocco, a rare occurrence in those days, before she went on to a successful career in modeling for 'Vogue magazine': well before any headlines in the press. We went out on the town as she took me under her wing as an inexperienced naive nineteen year old youth I was surprised to be invited by her as guest to the 'Fiesta Club' in Notting Hill and 'The Gateway' in Kensington used as location for a Robert Aldrich film 'The killing of sister George'. Closed in 1985, at that time it was a revelation to me as no men were allowed to enter the famous strictly gay women private membership Club. These beautiful women were recognisable from the fashion houses and cosmetic commercials of the day and in 'Vogue' and 'Harpers Bazaar' magazines. The members impressed me with their candour and choice of gender preference, it was their private world. The frisson of being in April's company at that time allowed me into their inner sanctum. It was an exclusive and memorable experience of my youth and early social constraint in a secret setting only by her private invitation. April Ashley was one of the first Britons to undergo sex-change surgery received an MBE in the Queen's Birthday Honours list for her services to transgender equality. In 2004 the Gender Recognition Act allowed people to legally change gender. Achieving real transgender equality is a big issue for many people in modern Britain, but all too often it either fails to gain any real publicity or is misunderstood. The term 'sex-change' has segued into the politically correct term 'gender reassignment'. Public attitudes in the western world have become less judgmental and tolerant of sexual differences. Most importantly, the legal systems of many countries have recognised the rights of transsexuals to appropriate social documenti0n and to marry and lead socially LGBT lives. A few years before, Jan Morris CBE, fellow of the Royal Society of Literature with Honorary degrees to Universities of Wales and Oxford was born. James H. Morris 2nd October 1926, known for the trilogy Pax Britannicas (1968-78) as a trans-woman she published under her birth name until 1972 when she transitioned from living as a male to living as a female. She accepted a CBE in the Queens honour's list out of respect for a lifetime of distinguished service to literature with 'Conundrum' 1974, with a personal narrative of her transexualism. In 1953 James Morris completed the first climb 20,000 feet up Mount Everest in the Himalaya, Nepal.

Attitudes began to change as 65,000 LGBT gay and bisexual men were pardoned of the 15,000 who were still alive in 2010 in the UK as a result of criminalization abolished later by the change in law. In 1967 Sir John Wolfenden the author of a report published in 1957 recommended the decriminalisation of homosexuality which became law in 1967. At the time LGBT communities suffered loss of their jobs and were victimised and blackmailed for their sexual orientation. Original records were expunged as a Royal pardon was given posthumously by the Queen to Alan Suring the scientist who broke the Enigma code during the second-world-war. The court gave him a judgement of guilt and he was ordered to be sent for hormone injection aversion therapy as an alternative to a prison sentence. He eventually committed suicide in 1952. The harm to the LGBT community was later acknowledged and the draconian law was repealed in 1967. Until then the ignominy remained, finally in 1992 the World Health Organization WHO confirmed homosexuality was not a disease or illness as previously been listed. He now appears on the new €50 notes.

TRANSGENDER

At this time there are 14 gender identity clinics run by the NHS in the UK, each has a high demand and a long waiting list for treatment. A private MD practitioner is offering on line treatment at a private clinic which started 18 months ago where the 2,000 patients have been advised of suitable medical treatment in each individual case. BBC radio 4 listeners in first April 2016 listened to the programme 'identity enquiry transgender.' Great Ormond Street Hospital pediatric surgeon consultant Dr Mashtar neurologist confirmed 1,500 births are not born as gender specific. In other words biological gender is none binary or fluid sex between the legs, gender is between the ears and one birth in a hundred are indeterminate. The hospital consultant thought parents need not be uncomfortable with indeterminate sexual identity before the individual child has grown to accept their own sexual identity, which could be a personal choice of the individual.

Professor Julie Bakker lead researcher at the University of Liege in Belgium confirmed: 'Although more research is needed, we now have evidence that sexual differentiation of the brain differs in young people with GD Gender Dysphoria, as they show functional brain characteristics that are typical of their desired gender'. The study included biological males and females with GD and male and females without GD as controls, with ages ranging across childhood to adolescence. The team used MRI (magnetic resonance imaging) tests to examine brain activation upon exposure to a steroid, as well as measuring gray matter and white matter microstructure using a technique called diffusion tensor imaging. The male foetus for example has genes that trigger the mother's body to produce the hormones testosterone during development. This physically alters the male foetus brain, priming it to produce male sexual behaviour.

If the male does not receive the hormone treatment, his brain is likely remains typically female: if a female foetus is exposed to a male hormone sequence, she is likely to be more masculine.

Gender Dysphoria affects an estimated one percent of the population, according to the Gender Identity Development Service, rates of diagnosis are increasing due to public awareness. Scientists believe GD may be caused by the exposure of foetuses to additional hormones as a result of medication taken by the mother, as well as foetal insensitivity to certain hormones while in the womb.

Analysis of around 160 participants showed that biological males with GD — the experience of discomfort or distress due to their biological sex- had a brain structure and neurological patterns similar to biological females, and vice versa. The analysis revealed that the distinct neurological differences are detectable during childhood. This breakthrough research revealed for the first time evidence that the brain activity of people who feel they inhabit the wrong body closely resembles that of the gender they want to embrace, and revealed that the distinct neurological differences are detectable during childhood. Scientists behind the new research say their discovery promises doctors a potent new tool with which to offer better advice at an earlier stage. People questioning their gender identity could be offered brain scans to determine whether they are transgender, we will then be better equipped to support these young people instead of just sending them to a psychiatrist and hoping there distress will disappear spontaneously. Currently, children complaining of GD typically Undergo psychotherapy. They can also be given hormones to delay puberty, so that decisions on further transgender therapy can be made at an older age.

IS THEIR A GAY BRAIN?

In 1991 the prestigious 'Science' Journal published a study showing that the brains of homosexual men who had died from Aids were structurally different from the brains of heterosexual men. The nucleus in the hypothalamus that triggers male-typical sexual behaviour was much smaller in gay men and looked more like that in the brains of women. The author Simon LeVay, then associate Professor at the Salk Institute for Biological Studies and Adjunct Professor of biology at the University of California, was immediately attacked by gay activists who feared that the recognition of homosexuality as a physical based condition might lead to it being stigmatized. LeVay is himself gay then went on to discover that the brains corpus callosum differs between straight men too - in gays it was found to be bigger. Three years later a study led by molecular biologist Dean Hammer of the National Institute of Health in Washington, DC, evidence suggested that a specific gene-carried on the maternal line-influenced sexual orientation in men.

In 2008 Swedish scientists studied brain scans of 90 gay and straight men and women, found that the size of the two hemispheres of gay men's brains more closely resembled those of straight women than they did of straight men. In heterosexual women, the two halves of the brain are more or less the same size. In heterosexual men, the right hemisphere is slightly larger. Scans of the brains of gay men in the study, however showed their hemispheres were relatively symmetrical, like those of straight women, while the brains of homosexual women were asymmetrical like those of straight med Put together, these studies provide strong evidence that homosexuality is rooted in Biology — and hostility to the idea has largely disappeared.

Being transsexual is not an illness and should not be treated as such. Last year UK Prime Minister Theresa May pledged to amend the Gender Recognition Act to allow people to legally change gender without medical authorisation. The findings, presented at the European Society of Endocrinology annual meeting in Barcelona, are likely to provoke controversy among groups who argue gender identity should be a matter of personal choice.

Source : The Telegraph (22-6-18)

INDIA

In India, 'Hidra' is a third gender accepted under legislation (2015) under Supreme Court ruling. Other examples exist, in Mexico, Phillippenes, other areas of human development, hormonal variance development suggest that effeminate boy's and masculine girls grow up as a normal human experience

India's LGBT people on prime time television discovered a new found openness, which rested with the Supreme Court's decision in September 2018 which struck down a British Colonial law since 1880's as Victorian era India had kept on its statute since 1947 criminalizing gay sex, though this law was changed in Britain in 1967.

According to 800 million viewers across India the Audience Broadcasting research council, campaigners are now hoping that television can now smash stereotypes about the LGBT+ community. We finally have legal recognition, but the fight for equality starts now, we need societal acceptance said Sushant Divgikar a performer on the singing realty show SA RE GA MA PA on TV.' With my drag persona I am challenging gender stereotype characters that served to mock members of the lesbian, gay, bisexual and transgender community in a negative light, not just on Indian television but in cinema'.

Aparna Bhosle business head of 2 TV said on a special episode of MTV 's reality dating show 'Elovator Pitch,' a gay man was wood by 10 contestants including one who had not previously been open about his sexuality. Rahul Bharti said he chose the opportunity to come out on television as a way to tell his parents. 'I felt I could not tell them personally as I was scared how they would react', I took part in the show only because I wanted to tell my parents. Bharti's parents did not speak to him for days 'But they are now dealing with it'. He said he hopes for wider acceptance of LGBT+ people now as many in the entertainment industry are breaking down harmful perceptions they helped to create.

While MTV had LGBT+ characters on many shows in the past, this was its first attempt in unscripted content to include the LGBT+ community said Ferzad Palia head of youth division at Viacom 18 which operates MTV in India. The Supreme Court's decision has widened the scope for such conversations, so it was a natural progression for us in story telling Palia said.

In India February 2019, Bollywood lead actor and his daughter played their filmic roles in the recognition of Lesbian love, revaluating the parent relationship in a family paradigm wanting their child's happiness. The premier of the movie was in London and Directed by Ms.Dupredar presented from a women's perspective.

The gender of the individual does not necessarily conform to societal acceptance. In the 21 st century the acceptance is sometimes forced on the baby at birth by the child's parents depending on a particular religious, political or societal bias or social acceptability, the individual is compelled to be binary. Dr Mashtar Great Ormond Street hospital say's 'gender need not be a component of a legal requirement, but should be accepted as a myriad identity "choice of an individual of a biological spectrum'

HOMOPHOBIA

In Dhaka Bangladesh, gay activist in the Islamic State were hacked to death with a machete in 2015. Organised (Zulatha) was Bangladesh protesting against violent secular killings, the information Minister confirmed this under the radical Sharia law and denied there was a problem.

RUSSIA

In 2018 Gay activist in Russia are rounded up in public by police then placed in custody later, given a prison term by the court. President Putin ratified illegal any homosexual reference in education to minors as unlawful. This has created conditions of terror as male gangs now roam the streets of Moscow and other metropolitan cities organising gay bashing, with official acceptance, thus violating human rights. In Russia LGBT activists claim at least two people have died by torture in a purge of Gay people in Chechnya. The Russian LGBT network alleges about 40 men and women have been detained following the arrest of the administrator of the online group for LGBT people at the end of 2018, in 2017 reports of more than 100 gay men being held and tortured mainly in the Muslim region. The authorities denied there had been any persecution. Chechen president Ramzan Kadyrov has been accused personally of organizing the repression. Igor Kochetkov of the Russian LGBT network said 'Persecution of men and women suspected of being Gay never stopped' it's only that the scale of the operation has changed.

BRAZIL

Brazil 2018, President Balsanaro's hostility say's' he would attack Gays if they display affection to each other in public' as 300 LGBT's were murdered in Brazil. FIFA fined championship league games for homophobic chanting during soccer matches Tournament's. The National Gay tournament soccer team played on the pitch during 2018, out members as professional players faced prejudice while their team 'Bees Cats trained in San Paulo, were exposed to placards displaying 'Footballs a man's game' but their team mascot Drag Queen opened the game.

In 1979 Brazil's woman team was also banned for playing as they faced prejudice against their women playing football, LGBT confirmed women were facing inverse prejudice as a case of hostile identity politics. In January 2019 'Crossing continents' BBC Radio four reported Jim Slim the first openly gay LGBT Congressman as being subjected to serious abuse and threats of death having faced physical intimidation in public, he has now decided to leave the country as he considers he and his family are no longer safe. Brazil's President Balsanaro has made repeated homophobic comments in public and in the public domain.

KENYA

As reported in 'The Times' in 2016 the High Court held the use of anal examinations to determine a suspect's sexual orientation, dismissing the argument that the procedure amounts to torture and a degrading treatment. There was no violation of rights or the law, a high court judge Mathew Emukule said. 'l find no violation of human dignity, or right to privacy and right to freedom of the petitioner' he said. Two men had sought a court ruling to stop enforced anal examination and HIV tests of the men accused of being gay after they were subjected to the procedures. The two men were arrested in a bar near Ukunda a town on Kenya's Indian Ocean coast, in February 2015 on suspicion of being engaged in a sexual act with another man which is a criminal offence in Kenya. They still face the charges, and if convicted, could be jailed for 14 years. In their petition, said examination's amounted torture and degrading treatment. The judge said they should have used their lawyers to seek injunction orders to avoid undergoing the tests. I sat in court holding my chin in disbelief said Eric Gitari, the executive director of the Kenyan Gay and Lesbian rights Commission, which has supported the commission. He said the men would appeal. This level of discrimination and insular homophobic attitude toward a minority is further evidence of the lack of progress in human rights' it is not unfortunately rare in the case of Kenya's judiciary.

INDONESIA

18 May 2017 in Indonesia, for the first time two gay men were sentenced to public flogging, further undermining the country's moderate image. The Sharia Court in Aceh province said the men

twenty and thirty year old would be lashed eighty five times. The
lead judge Khairil Jamal said 'As Muslims, the defendants should
uphold the prevailing Sharia law. They were sentenced yesterday, the
International Day against Homophobia and Trans-phobia.
Human rights groups called for their release. Human Rights Watch
says public flogging constitutes torture under International Law. Aceh
is the only province in Muslim-majority Indonesia that practices
Sharia law. Other punishable offences include men skipping at Friday
prayers. Homosexuality is legal elsewhere in Indonesia, but a case in
the country's top Court seeks to criminalise gay sex. Reuters.

MALAYSIA

A gay Teen died after being beating, burned, and raped for hours
by eight men. It happened outside a burger shop the evening of Friday
16 June 2017 near a Mosque in Gelugor a southern suburb of George
Town in Penang, Malaysia. The teenager Nhaveen Shanmugan had
decided to get together with a friend to celebrate quitting his job and
going to College in Kuala Lumpur on Saturday reported 'Free
Malaysia, but he never made it. Police say Nhaveen and a friend
were just outside Taman Sardon Mosque when they ran into two
former classmates Who had bullied Nhaveen for being effeminate.
Reports say as many as six more young people then rode up on
motorcycles. All eight men then started beating Nhaveen and his
friend Prevlin using their helmets. Prevlin managed to escape and
ran away, and headed to Penang Hospital where he was treated for
crushed cheekbones. Hours later, a brother of one of the attackers
brought an unconscious Nahveen to the ER of that same hospital at
2 am Saturday. There he was treated for severe head injuries and a
wound on his groin that was oozing blood. Gay Star News reported

his family was informed he had been sodomised; there was evidence of forced penetration to Nhaveen's anus, he also suffered severe burns on his back. Doctors declared the student brain dead. At least four of his alleged attackers were college students police confirm. The fifth under arrest is unemployed the three others have not been apprehended. Nhaveen had hoped to study music composition. 'He loves music' said his aunt, Nahveen is so friendly and jovial I spoke to him last week and he wanted to come over to my place for chicken curry but looking at the way he is now, I do not know if he will come back at all.' This story filed under: Hate crime, Homophobia, Bullying.

1931 GERMANY

Ernst Rohm leader of the brown shirt Nazi movement in 1931 exposed as Gay was murdered when the Nazi's came to full power and Hitler became Chancellor January 1933. A 'Pink List' drawn up by Himmler to expose and eliminate publications in print and to raid gay bars, bathhouses, and meeting places of the Gay community where arrests were made and human rights violated. In 1934 interagation and torture were made to 56,000 convicted homosexuals who were sent to concentration camps as prosecutions were brought under enforcement of section 175 of the German criminal law. In Dachau camp interragation and torture was rife use as a tool of oppression. Prisoners were made to sew a pink triangle on their uniforms for easy identity and raped by guards and other inmates. After the Second World War post Nuremberg trails persecution under section 175 was overturned and decriminalized in 1968 in West Germany.

Chapter 04

GREAT BRITAIN

In 1974 before the law had changed, my partner Keith and I were actively involved with CHE as members of the British CHE campaign for homosexual equality and supported the annual national conference and other regional meetings. The CHE was one of the earliest gay rights organizations in the 70s, with GLF gay liberation front in the 80s, 'stonewall' and 'Outrage' had become more influential. By 1972 CHE had 2,800 members in the UK it grew out of the Law reform society. Leading members included the broadcaster Ray Gosling, and the academic Michael Steed. Dereck Oyston presented film awards in conjunction with the London Lesbian and Gay film festival. Lord Smith of Finsbury (A former cabinet Minister) was vice president of CHE. Author and playwright Peter- Scott-Presland wrote three volumes 'Amiable Warriors' Volume and published 'A space to breath'

LONDON
A night bar

KAY MALON HITCHED HER short stubby body on her high bar stool with legs encased in forty denier stockings into shiny black patent leather boots in the public bar. She was a proud product of London, and a street wise cockney from the East end wanted to be noticed. 'Hello dear what's your tipple tonight' the barman wheezed, 'usual darlin' Kay slurred her speech in a whispered baritone. Her plastic surgery had been completed twelve weeks before, with cheek implants that had healed, and the prescribed hormone oestrogen therapy reduced her surface body hair after cosmetics had been massaged on to the bruised skin's surface. The dark roots under the highlight accented her coiffed blond wig, but something was not quite right, as her large masculine hands were carefully manicured with painted extensions. She fondled the whisky tumbler that Leo the barman placed before her lighting up a cigarette swiveling it around in her fingers before raising the glass to her lips, sipping the contents left smudged red lipstick on the rim. Kay's trans-sexual metamorphose three years earlier toward the operating table, had been a long personal journey. Giving it much thought and with an eye to the future his boxing career had come to end. He decided on greater stardom with the glittering prize of successful boxing promotion. It was not just the bright lights and the late night with the boy's splitting deals that he made, but the legitimate move was final.

He had always wanted to be one of the girl's. His ex partner Casey and he had produced two wonderful baby girls together and she was old enough to understand his new found happiness in the public eye. He had always looked after his girls and provided well for them, now approaching the stage when he wanted to be a she, and take care of herself. The statistical possibility of the population believing they were born in the wrong body as a gender is 0.01 %. The belief that denying it to themselves affects their lifestyle which can result in cases of attempted suicide or critical depression as it was a direct negation of their sexuality not as a result of it. Their sexuality was nothing to do with self acceptance of gender but the understanding of their self identity acceptance was. Kay may not have kept her gonads, but she did have the courage of her conviction. The macho world of boxing sport either accepted or rejected it through ignorance and misunderstanding of his new identity as a woman. Could the question of his self image and acceptance of the notoriety Of coming out in public with a new identity be a statement of intent; or of others questioning her individuality, a new self assurance gave credibility to Kay Mallon being interviewed on British television on BBC 'Hard

Talk' providing a degree of celebrity after the journalist Steven Sakur had eschewed a sensitive approach to the subject let the viewer decide. The cell phone rang in her patent handbag piercing the clubs silence. Grabbing it she punched the key pad, 'Hello Dad its Noreen when you cumin ome for dinner' her daughter demanded. 'Soon Reeny won't be long just got a bit of business dear' the cell screen flickered in the club's low lighting and died away. 'What business you got doll' turning on her swivel bar stool to face her old adversary in the ring and sparring partner Robbie, 'still ducking and diving' he snorted, 'what you doin in this neck of the woods. Kay sneered, 'well I'me not ere pimpin for the duchess like some' 'Ooh' you can be an evil cow'. In the darkness Kay could make out the late and loud Daniel Farson perched on a banquette with his young protégé sitting beside him at the far end of the room. Kay fixed a glare at the table across the room 'Look's a bit of a lad,' well dear they do say its love at first sight.' Robbie answered in a low voice 'more like lust at first sight if you ask me, but im'e sure he has a more spiritual side.' Kay made eye contact with Robbie under hooded lids gave nothing away. "Well her grace should have, he drinks the distillery with no short measure and more than makes up for it with his new love interest'. Suited and booted, the sullen youth offered them a smirk over the top of his lager glass. I watched Daniel drained his pink gin before the youth walked to the bar for fresh orders. 'He looks well hard 'muttered Robby who stared at him as a cat looking at a canary, 'didn't know you'd been looking dear'. Kay's laugh hissed like a deflated tyre stepped on after a puncture. 'Anyway I had better go its way past my bedtime Robbie, I promised her indoors I'd be home for dinner an hour ago.' 'Never mind I'll give you a weather report dear, Kay turned and said 'as long as it's not wet and windy' as she dipped off the stool with a flourish of her hips. She walked on high tilettos toward the exit pulling at the strap of her bra with a theatrical gesture. With the other hand waved as the skin flapped hanging loose from her arm, she gave a lewd wink to the barman, threw a cupid bow smile as she giggled and wiggled through the door marked EXIT......

FRANCE 1934

Simone de Beavoir noted in her memoire that she placed some importance of agreement with the existentialist Satre that she viewed Olga through his eyes. Olga Xavier was nine years younger unusual and unconventional. Simone incorporated her into their relationship. Beavoir formed a deep attachment to Olga for ten years to the point they became lovers. Olga was one of many lovers she would have through her life. She became involved sexually, as Beavoir played the role of mentor with whom she was unlikely to experience equal reciprocity, she placed great value on these intimate relationships with younger women. The challenge of becoming a desired object she argues was one of which all women face in a patriarchal society, regardless of their sexual orientation. Although heterosexual conditioning within a patriarchal society predisposes women to pursue erotic relationships with men, the polarization of gender roles signifies personal independence.

Her first volume in 1949 'Les Deuxieme Sexe' sold 22,000 copies in the first week of publication, the publication by 1969 had sold 750,000 copies.

OUT OF THE CLOSET

Louis B. Mayer Hollywood MGM studio boss gave an ultimatum to his biggest box office star William Haynes, 'either get rid of your partner Jimmy Shields or get out of the studio contract' he was a major star from the 1920s to the 1930s, and lived openly with his marriage to Jimmy. At the time history showed little tolerance to any suggestion of homosexuality, particularly toward contract stars not conforming to the studio heads predilection for the status quo, 'Billy' to his friends, decided to give up his career to stay with his life partner as his preferred choice and became Hollywood's most successful Interior designer to the stars. The Hayes' production code gave restricted sexuality and good taste which enforced the standards and status quo to film production in the 30's. The standard contract was a one way bet for the studio. The small print was full of surprises for the unwary. A morals clause demanded that the artist would 'conduct themselves with due regard to public conventions and morals' and they would not commit any act or thing that will degrade them in society, or bring them into public hatred or contempt scorn or ridicule, that will tend to shock, insult, or offend the community or ridicule public morals or decency, or prejudice the producer or the motion picture industry in general.

UNDER WRAPS

In 1924 at the age of sixteen Archie Leach arrived in New York USA from Bristol England with the Pendle group of performers as an acrobatic juggler. He decided to stay in America, when they returned to London, his aim was to get to Hollywood. He walked stilts as an acrobat on the boardwalk of Coney Island, and sold ties on Broadway NY to eventually arrive in Los Angeles. On his first screen test he was rejected as 'having bow legs and a funny walk.' This did not deter him from getting signed with Paramount Studio on contract and working with Mae West, his name was changed by the Studio to Cary Grant and he became a leading man. In 1932 at the age of twenty four Cary Grant met Randolph Scott both worked at Paramount, they lived in a shared apartment and later moved to a beach house together on Malibu beach referred to as 'Bachelor Hall' until 1944. At the time both stars were on contract signed with Paramount Studio. Cary advised by the studio, married Virginia Cheril divorcing her after 13 months, he returned to live with Randolph for twelve more years. Both stars were given an ultimatum by the studio heads between them they went through seven divorces. Cary married actress Betsy Drake, he divorced her in 1936 though they remained friends for life. After four more marriages later, he had numerous therapy sessions with over 100 session of LSD and tried to commit suicide twice during a nervous breakdown. Being gay was the last taboo in Hollywood tinsel town as image was everything and remained a burden for a performer and financial liability and investment for the industry if the code was broken. In 1941 Cary Grant became an American citizen. In 1999 the American Film Institute named Cary Grant the second greatest male star of Hollywood's Golden age Cinema, an image he carefully Preserved as a top box office draw.

HEDY LAMAR
Hollywood film actress 1914 - 2000

Often proclaimed the most beautiful woman in the world said, she sexually preferred women to men, although she was married six times. Quote: I am not ashamed to say that no man I ever met was my father's equal, and I never loved any other man as much. As well as being a top box office star she became a pioneer in the field of wireless communications following her emigration to the United States, assisted by George Anthiel, she received a patent for spread spectrum technology that helped galvanize the digital communications boom. It formed the technical backbone that makes Bluetooth, GPS, cellular phones and fax wireless operations possible. This ground breaking invention of Wi-Fi. In 1977 she with George Athiel were honoured with the EFF pioneer award. Hedy Lamar became the first female recipient the GNASS spirit of achievement prize for inventors, the 'Oscar of inventing.' She was a 20th Century visionary whose technical acumen was ahead of its time, she entered the National Inventors hall of fame in 2014.

Over a hundred years of Cinema history, Hollywood was a haven for marginal people working in the film industry, in 1920 morals were more liberal and ambivalent sexuality was accepted. Rudolph Valentino gave a bisexual effeminate aura on screen, and on his death 80,000 mourners attended his funeral. In 1938 the film 'Draculas Daughter' exhibited a display of Lesbian sexuality. The Studios encouraged lavender marriages as a cover, Marlene Dietrich's affair with Claudette Colbert and her intimate association with Mercedes De Costa. Barbara Stanwyk's marriage to Robert Taylor was arranged, suitably for both parties. In the 50s Rock Hudson, Tab Hunter, James Dean and Sal Mineo of 'Rebel without a cause' were tolerated. Macarthyism created an environment of fear after the 'Hayes' directive. Marlon Brando confirmed his enjoying sexual relations with guys in the 50s.

In 1991 pee wee Herman Paul Rubens was busted during a police raid by the police in a gay theatre found watching a pornographic movie and he was dropped from further studio work. Conversely, it appears the public tolerates straight actors playing gay screen roles as good for their careers. Hugh Grant was caught with his trousers down literally receiving oral sex in a car from a prostitute in West Hollywood which has been good for his career. 'Playing Gay' is now cool in Hollywood 'The talented Mr Ripley' presented gay roles, as did 'Philadelphia' with Tom Hanks both played by straight actors.

These roles were at odds with gay actor Rupert Everett opposite Julie Roberts as her best pal in 'My best friend's wedding' and later in 2018 as Oscar Wilde. Ellen Degeneres actress, writer, producer came out in a gay relationship with her spouse Portia de Rossi, but she has never been given a lead role in sitcom, though 'Ellen' is the number one talk show in America. 'Will and Grace' plays it straight as does 'Queer as folk' on TV. The Hollywood establishment never allows homosexuals to be seen as gay, but the great American public will one day accept alternative lifestyles. Anderson Cooper who announced he is gay and married to his husband and long time partner on the 'David Packman show. He interviewed Clint McCance an Educational School board Vice president after his anti-gay rant on the suicide of teenagers harassment and bullying, who had said he' liked it when gay people got to die'. A few individuals might have something to say in response to this. Elton John and his husband David Furnish, Thom Daley and Dustin Black are in committed relationships with their partner's. Gloria Vanderbilt advised that she had enjoyed same sex relationships in her life, as did Alan Cumming and Grant Shafner. Bella Thorne, Charlie Carver, Colton Hayes, Elena deli Don, Elizabeth Gilbert, Holland Taylor, Justin Greening,

Kristin Stewart, Reid Ewing, Rubin Lord Taylor, Sara Ramirez, Trey Peason, Aubrey Plaza, Colton Hayes, Shane Dawson, Ryan Beaty, Rayvon Owen and many others in the gay community.

OFFICIALLY OUT

The gay community does have a private life, but being in the public eye more often than most outside the entertainment industry, some have chosen to introduce themselves to the public. A few who came out of their own volition in the new millennium, and with the date of announcement of which have spouses are the same gender.

Chely Write	2007
Victor Garber	2007
David Hyde Pierce	2009
Zachary Quinto	2015
Cynthia Nixon	2015
Robin Roberts	2013
Simon Haus	2012
Symone Raven	2014
Frank Ocean	2012
Ricky Martin	2010
Ellen Page	2015
Kelly McGullis	2009
Jason Collins	2014
Mat Dallas	2015

There are many more in the LGBT community, but out of respect for their wish to be private will remain so. A few individuals choose to believe that sex is between the ears, and express that trust With their partner of choice, as does Ellen Page and Samantha Thomas. There are many other dimensions to personal relationships, as there are those who wish to create their own family. In 2017 'Stonewall' charity data confirmed that 20,000 children grew up in same sex relationships in the UK as reported on BBC radio four news.

'Speak your mind even if your voice shakes.' Maggie Smith

Extra sensory perception defined.

ESP refers to the ability to obtain information about the world around you without using the normal five senses. The term ESP was popularised by Joseph Banks Rhine a Professor at Duke University in 1934. He conducted several experiments that he believed proved the existence of ESP. There are many theories as to what causes ESP. Some individuals believe that all humans have some degree of ESP and that we involuntary experience ESP on several occasions. Others believe that a selected few individuals have special extra sensitivity sensory perception that allows them to access ESP, but only when they are in a special mental state. Most individuals who believe in ESP maintain that all humans have the potential for ESP, but some are more aware of their ability than others; telepathy, clairvoyance, precognition, retro-cognition as a medium and psychotherapy. The evening lecture at the British Museum fascinated me, in the postulation of the theory of time as a measured abstraction for practical use, which enables the human race to resonate in sympathy with others in their understanding of the Universe yet remain in synchronicity with others. Descartes the French philosopher wrote, 'If God did not exist man would have to invent him'. Procreation of the human species is a force of nature which evolves in religious or atheist belief with political fervour, usually burdened by cultural interpretation. Human life is 3.7 billion years old, as fossil and sedimentary indicate, and rock fossil chemical tracer's carbon dating of the minerals confirm. This is only part of the historical reference of our evolving planet, which existed long before the gaseous cosmos formed in the universe. 'Lucy' the Homo sapien skeletal fossil was scanned as identified from 80,000 years: University of Texas & Austin

INFINITE

I wonder at the notion of infinity which is impossible for the human mind to comprehend, as there is no beginning and no end only continuum. The agnostic and the atheist are polarised, without faith or scripture have no meeting of minds. Imagination gives birth to invention as mankind discovers through technology and science. Etymology, word formation in oral communication is subject to understanding a vocabulary enabling thoughts to be to be understood in speech and the written word. The individual instructed in academic discipline adept in a field of specialisation is subject to this process. Intelligence quotient (IQ), a number expressing the intelligence of a person's mental age by his or her chronological age multiplied by one hundred.

My own clinical analysis by three independent medical psychologists was scored at 170, which is two percent of the population. At school I studied theology and catechism and understood the dogma of the Jesuit who advocates 'Give me a child until the age of seven and I will give you the man. A prognosis that suggests theological dogma negates the individual intellectual curiosity for personal development and growth. I now understand that inculcation of a religious doctrine with the filter of dogma and cant for me is inconsistent with experiential observation and learning.

AN ARROW NEVER MOVES IN FLIGHT

Reflect on the fact that the arrow never moves in flight as the instant is held in space, released to a target of speed divided by distance as motion at a point in time. The assumed movement is crossing a distance (now) as movement in a point in time.

Zeno of Elea a 5th century philosopher held that problems generally thought to have been devised to support Parmenides doctrine that, contrary to the evidence of one's senses, the belief in plurality and change is mistaken and in particular, motion is nothing but an illusion. He offered arguments that lead to conclusions contradicting what we all know from our physical experience as a paradox against common expectations.

The potential of infinite as an abstract concept would be inadequate and unquantifiable as incalculable, the potential of infinity and the perception of its feasibility as a premise is a dichotomy of two paradox. A sensory illusion as an example: a camera shutter speed is open for a continuous time determined by shutter speed, captures the picture at 24 frames per second (1/48th of a second). This interval captures and blends all motion happening to converge on real time biological motion which is an apparent illusion of the brain. The shutter, like the eye, is always open at a frequency of 6HZ things that cycle faster, appear constant as the image is faster than our brain perceives. Or, the misnomer of the bald man having no hair is identified by the apparent lack of follicles on his scalp, not the complete absence of hair. The infinite is a concept understood by few but in faith is a belief understood by many. The Illusion of the smallest things is to wonder at the universe's miniature black holes smaller than an atom in Nano technology. Since 2006 the electron microscope PICO sees individual atoms in the structure of a nano magnified a billion times'

Quantum mechanics is provable on paper. In practical terms optical mirrors compute experimental analysis of Spenon, Holon, and the Orbiton, illustrate the fundamental particles split into three. It takes light photons 7.5 billion years to reach Earth from the universe. Theoretical physics calculate gravity as a fourth dimension string theory, suggesting a multi dimensional parallel universe.

OUR DELUSION

The elements have no distinction Buddhist verse. Finding questions to extend my boundary of understanding, I chose meditation as a practical technique, re-discovered by the Gautama Buddha taught as a universal remedy which flourished in India, lost its efficacy virtually disappearing from its land of origin. Burma preserved the original form of Vipassana through the millennia since 1969 re-introduced into India when its roots grew stronger. Compassion' yields a release of the mind,' a phrase used in Pali text is enlightenment itself. The habit of self scrutiny helped Buddhist practitioners to monitor the distractions that deprive us of peace. Through meditation we become aware of the ephemeral nature of invasive thoughts and cravings that poison our lives. In this method of training, self discipline and practice take effect slowly with no immediate perception of the ultimate truth. Gotama said it could take at least seven years imperceptibly over a long period. His teachings were handed down orally in the Pali cannon, and not written down until the first century BC. Writing was uncommon in north India until the time of the Emperor Ashoka, between 269 to 232 BC Ashoka lived two hundred years after the Buddha. He became a Buddhist follower and made inscriptions to preserve the teachings life and memory leaving ancient writings and scriptures.

Before this, myth and anecdotal legend grew in humankind from oral tradition to eventual historical fact. The Buddha is a challenge to modern society, the new orthodoxy of 'positive thinking' and habitual optimism allows us to bury our heads in the sand, denying the pain and suffering of others and to isolate ourselves in a state of deliberate heartlessness to ensure our own emotional survival. I understood the Buddha would have no time for this as he believed spiritual life cannot begin unless we allow ourselves to be invaded by the reality Of suffering and realize how it permeates our whole experience, and feel the pain of other sentient beings, even those we may not feel in accord with. We may not practice the method he prescribed in its entirety, but his teachings illuminates the ways we can reach a truly compassionate journey With intellectual and personal independence, toward expressing human kindness.

Ipassana, a Pali word meaning insight or entering into the self, seeing things as they really are not in blind faith or philosophy, it has little to do with sectarian religion. The goal is to purify the mind and eliminate the tension and negatives that make us miserable, leading to infinite happiness, to work with human nature not to fight it being mindful of self deception.

'Sati' in which he scrutinised his behaviour at every moment of the day, everything being impermanent:

'Anicca,' nothing lasts long, not even the bliss of meditation. The transitory nature of life is one of the chief causes of suffering. The Ego is voracious and consistently wants to consume other things and other people distorted by greed as we pursue an object of desire, even when we know in our heart it will make us unhappy in the long run.

Such states of mind make us 'unskilful' because they make us more selfish than ever. The purpose of mindfulness is to neutralize the power of egotism that limits the human potential, a compassionate understanding Of benevolence and goodwill can become habitual as the mind breaks free of its constriction and embraces all beings. Its expansion without limits results in the consciousness feeling as infinite as the sound of an expert conch blower, thought to pervade all space, or as a prayer Wheel follows around the axis of the globe. Without meditation prescribed by the Buddha, the truth remains as abstract as a musical score which for most of us reveals its true beauty not on the page, but orchestrated and interpreted by the skilled performer which does not preclude our self in practice. Ontology leads us down the path to self discovery through the philosophy of the nature of being. When you kill, you steal a life, when you lie you steal some ones right to the truth.

BUDDHA

'An enlightened or awakened person'

By giving in to anger, we are not necessarily harming our enemy but we are definitely harming ourselves. We lose our sense of inner peace, we do everything wrong, our digestion is bad, we cannot sleep well we put off our guests or we cast furious glances at those who have the impudence to be in our way. If we have a pet we forget to feed it. We make life impossible for those who live with us, and even our dearest friends are kept at a distance. Since there are fewer people who sympathise with us we feel alone to what end? Even if we allow our rage to go all the way, we will never eliminate our enemies. As long as we harbour that inner enemy of anger or hatred, however successful we are at destroying our outer enemies today, others will emerge tomorrow: Journal of the National Cancer Institute 92, no. 12 (2000).

On the influence of meditation: L.E. Carlson et al., 'Mindfulness-Based stress reduction in relation to quality of life, Mood, Symptoms of stress and levels of Cortisol, (DHEAS) and Melatonin in Breast and prostate Cancer Outpatients', Psychoneuroendocrinology 29, no.4 (2004) M Speca et al., A randomised controlled clinical trial: The effect of a mindfulness meditation-based stress reduction programme on mood symptoms of stress in Cancer patients.

MBSR — Mindfulness-based stress reduction- is a non religious form of training based on Buddhist mindfulness meditation which was developed in the United States hospital system more than twenty years ago by Jon Kabat-Zin. It is now used in more than two hundred Us hospitals for the palliation of post-operative pain associated with cancer and other serious diseases as a gateway to stress release.

Tenzin Gyatso — 14th Dalai Lama, means Ocean of Wisdom told the story of a monk who keeps promising his pupil that he will take him on a picnic but is always too busy to do so. One day they see a procession carrying a corpse 'Where is he going,' the monk asked his pupil who replied 'going on a picnic'

At the beginning, nothing comes.

In the middle, nothing remains.

In the end, nothing goes away.

Thinking of the emotional state of happiness brings me to illustrate there is no better way of putting it as written by His Holiness The Dalai Lama, in his book 'The Art of Happiness' when he writes. You can have two different types of individuals. On the one hand, you have a wealthy successful person surrounded by relatives and so on. If that person's source of dignity and sense of worth is only material, then as long as his fortune remains, maybe that person can sustain a sense Of security. But the moment the fortune goes the person will suffer because there is no other refuge. On the other hand, you can have another person enjoying similar economic status and financial success. But at the same time that person is warm and affectionate and has a feeling of compassion, because that person has another sense of worth, another source that gives him or her, a sense of dignity, another anchor. There is less chance of that person becoming depressed if his fortune happens to disappear. Through this type of reasoning you can see the very practical value of human warmth and affection in developing an inner state of worth. The Dalai Lama clearly sees modern materialism as a source of destruction he sees real happiness coming from within.

Knowing, is what blocks creative energy. Knowing what will happen, why it won't work, you will have experienced this process. Life is in truth a mystery in which we don't know what happens next. Approach it from a different perspective and by becoming friends with mystery, you will unlock creativity in every aspect of your life. Curiosity is the fuel of creativity. In Zen the phrase 'Don't know go straight' means in any given moment to look with fresh eyes and hear with fresh ears and stay free of thinking. This is the Zen practice of the beginners mind as the way to live is now in, and of the moment, let sparks fly to a final conflagration of creative energy. Stress ends when you step out of judgment because when you know, you stop looking. Letting the world be, invite it and embrace it to allow you to be calm and effective.

OUT OF THE BOX

Picking up a book after breakfast during school holidays at the local library, historical subjects interested me. I turned the faded pages and found Copernicus who understood the world to be flat in 15th century Europe as the Pope dictated and the Vatican decreed. Galileo had observed the world as a round spherical planet with two poles axis. He discovered through his telescope new stars and continued his Observation and discovery under the threat of excommunication by the Roman Catholic Church for his scientific work. He was imprisoned and kept under house arrest for fourteen years by a Vatican decree unless he recanted his work which did not receive the Imprimatur. In spite of this apparent form of spiritual blackmail (at a time when the Vatican sold Novena's for financial gain) he pursued the truth, discovering the Earth's trajectory round the Sun. His scientific contribution achieved worldwide recognition on his death in 1642, and Rome decreed it to be so as an infallible fact. The search for truth in discovery leads to better understanding than oppression.

In 1737 John Harrison a Yorkshire man from England presented the Royal Society his longtitude marine time keeping clock. The very Reverend Maskelyne published his Nautical Almanac and Astronomical Ephemeris twenty nine years later in 1766. Both inventions gave mariners the ability to navigate the seas for new lands to discover, pushing forward the boundaries of travel and securing shipping lanes to trading posts in distant continental harbours.

In the 20th century the British inventor John Logi Baird discovered the cathode ray tube, this enabled BBC to broadcast the first live television from Alexandra Palace London, with entertainment' information and education to the people. Sir Tim Berners-Lee introduced access to information and the World-wide web to the public domain for all, creating social networking and commercial application to the Media. Science in the 21st century discovered Quantum mechanics, nuclear fusion, Bio chemistry and Nano technology.

Percy Shaw OBE, of Halifax in west Yorkshire invented the cat's eye which reflects light enabled aviation and shipping safer landing in harbour ports, roads and runways to a become a safer world. Government authorities do not necessarily comprehend or take into account the individual need to experiment in discovery and invention. Percy found his way home from the village Public House one foggy night in winter he managed to see his cat waiting outside his garden gate in the fog, as the light of a passing car reflected in the eye of his feline friend he set about reproducing what inspiration nature had to offer in his hut at the bottom of his garden. Adversity brings enlightenment to the human race as in the challenge of space travel to the planets of our galaxy and beyond into the Universe.

FILTRATION

The single atom thick two dimensional nature of grapheme is particularly useful in the application of filtration of pore size of 5nm. The smallest membranes today are much coarser at 30-40nm. This material has the potential to revolutionize water filtration and desalinization as we know it. A more cost effective way has been found, to use molybdenum disulfide (Mos2) thin-film membranes designed to let high volumes of sea water through but keep the contaminants out. A next generation material filtering up to 70 percent more water: University of Illinois 2015. This could lead us to adequate clean water from desalinization to supply to over a billion people in need, and the irrigation of crops in traditionally dry zones. We have two thirds of the world's surface as Oceans to take from. Water, water everywhere, but not a drop to drink, this is a reality in the 21st century unless the prospect of drought is eradicated now in the developing countries. When the G20 industrialised population turn on their garden sprinklers for their acres of lawns and irrigation systems to green-up the landscape. Cast a thought to 350 million people on the planet without irrigation for crop, or a tap to wash and drink from or flush effiuent. This should be a basic right in this technological age, but it still remains a problem that water is not freely available to all. It is apparent that a global priority of caring for human kind is way down on the list of developing nations. [World Bank and IMF please take note]

Chapter 05

FOR ARTS SAKE
Kerela 2015

Yoko Ono wrote her book on conceptual art in 1964 called 'Grapefruit', in which she encouraged the audience to watch the sun until it became square. At the Kochi Muziris Bienalle a three month art festival in Kerala, India. The Japanese artist urged the audience to listen to the sound of the earth turning on its axis. Ono the wife of John Lennon sent postcards from the US that contains instructions on how to do it. Starting on December 12 in Kochi it will feature reproductions from limited edition postcards printed in 1999 featuring the relevant piece from the book. Her art work will be part of the works of 93 prominent artists from 30 countries displayed in various venues in Kochi- from a historic waterfront warehouse and a 17th century Dutch bungalow. The sea facing Aspinwall House, displayed an installation to be unveiled by Indian origin-British artist Anish Kapoor. The winner of the prestigious Artes Mundi Prize Chinese artist Xu Bing's work is inspired by a landscape painting by Xu Ben who lived during the rule of the Ming Dynasty. Artist NS Harsha who won the Arte Mundi from India presented an installation of an enigmatic sage-like monkey pointing toward the mysteries of the Universe as a challenge for the art lover. Who knows what the cognoscenti will make of it all. The visitor could leave inspired and return to their sunshine beach parties fulfilled. It's not all smooth sailing though, with an estimated budget of Rs 26 Crore there were concerns if it be possible to sustain the Biennale over 108 days. A crowd funding platform was launched on-line to garner Rs 15 crore in 90 days. It was hoped that the participation would allow people to take ownership of it and feel pride in it. Perhaps that will be 'The road of hope' from the title of Yoko Ono's acclaimed 2011 installation.

My own ray of hope dictates that the round sun will rise at dawn. I have lived 27,375 days to the time of writing, I can confirm I have never observed a square sun, but there is always a first time for everything, I will keep an open mind.

CLIMATE OF FEAR

We live in a time when Government and corporations in the 21st century spend vast amounts of public money and private funds on a 'red flag theory' to pacify corporate economic interest against Global equality. Creation of millions of security personnel contracted to CIA and M15 monitor individual Citizens emails. BBC world news on 20th February 2015 gave details that the world's biggest producer of smart cards in Holland was hacked by NASA and GHQ Government intelligent agencies to enable them to listen to millions of phone calls of private citizens and access electronic mail world-wide. This gets round privacy laws as application of warrants from a court are mandatory, but it does circumvent the legal privacy of individual citizens. Profiled listed extremists phone calls, their emails are under surveillance monitored rightly so, but to extend powers through Parliament to pass new laws allowing government to include the general public at random is an erosion of individual privacy, free expression and indiscriminate. Maintaining observation of suspects profiled by the authorities as a potential public enemy by surveillance of suspects, to monitor them and stop the suspected culprit creating anarchy and murder in the public domain is currently on government database. It needs political will to implement the efficacy, not a blanket cover of intrusion on a whole population with the assault and violation of individual human rights. Democracy flourishes in an environment of freedom of expression for mankind to thrive through a vote, not by invoking draconia laws to impinge on the human right of freedom of thought and speec The opposition of minority views expressed in a vote is a corner stone democracy vox- populi. Political expediency and self interested group manipulate statistics to further their agenda, the means justifies thei ende Governance by oligarchy produces a climate Of controlled intelligence which can dictate the conditions leading to a public siege mentality, by producing a political climate of fear. The global order is in disarray of geopolitical direction. Russia is trying to redraw borders in Europe. The middle-east is in conflagration, European unity is fractured. Jihadi terrorism is spreading pluralism challenged by authoritarian regimes. China is contesting the status quo in the south China seas. President Donald Trump wants to build walls in the USA and stop all immigration from the Islamic countries to keep out illegal immigration as part of his message to the American nation. With divisionism as a strategy for the future of his Presidency including his objection to 'transgendeds serving in the armed forces' who wish to protect their country, we should all fight against exclusiveness and be aware of inclusiveness as the antidote to isolationism.

CRONYISM

Multinational corporate security companies make their shareholders a safe investment for future dividends from a multi-million dollar business for the few super rich investors. They receive high dividends via the stock exchange from security companies run by ex-army personnel who operate in all areas on continents in every area of government intelligence in collusion under the guise of national security. Royal protocol elevated Timothy Laurence the husband of the Princess Royal to the title of a knighthood, which provides kudos and a highly decorative feature on a letterhead for prestige in the city role of non executive Director on the board of the Dorchester property group. His previous position until he retired from the MOD was chief executive officer at the Ministry of defence land office, when he represented the MOD sale of the Prince Phillip barracks site for development. It was later discovered that Sir Timothy Lawrence had a role in the sale of this large site which was investigated as a conflict of interest, reported in the TV 'Dispatch' August 1b 2016. This detail was gained through the freedom of information act.

CREATIVE ACCOUNTING

Ernst & Young have the distinction of having been auditor to the two biggest banking blow-up's ever. The firm did the accounts for Lehman Brothers who collapsed in September 2008 caused a near Armageddon on Financial markets. Lehman Bank had used some pretty fancy techniques to make its balance sheet look better than it was. 'Including Repo 105' that classified debts as sales. In December 2010, New York State attorney general, filed a civil fraud case the lawsuit sought the return of $ 150 million in fees plus other damages. E & Y is also being sued by Alameda County Employees retirement

Pension Association alleging they made misleading statements about Lehman's finances before it went belly-up. Chief Executive and later Chairman Sean Fitzpatrick of Irish Life & Permanent was involved in a scheme to conceal over $100 million in personal loans advanced to him by the Bank long before the Dirt scandal and tax inquiry was exposed. Paul Smith a qualified Barrister and tax expert, became managing Partner of Ernst & Young in 2000 and was elected three times.

The appointment of John Murray as Chief Justice of Ireland in 2011 retained his position on the Supreme Court until 2015 was described in the Examiner as the highest paid judge in the world, based on a 2008 study by the Council of Europe in forty-five developed countries. His annual salary of 295,000 Irish pounds as Chief Justice picking up pensions on the way, as two-time Attorney General he simultaneously drew a pension of 67,686 Irish pounds. As a judge at the European Court of Justice from 1991-1999 his annual retirement package was estimated at 70,000 Irish pounds. At one point in 2011 the rewards from all his judicial posts came to a staggering 440,000 Irish pounds a year. The establishment certainly knows how to take good care of its own. His take home pay was more than the president of USA and considerably more than the UK prime Minister.

Chapter 06

MODERN CORPORATIONS

Create strategies of investment through foreign exchange mechanism as inward capitol for start-up factories in the developing world, to produce cheap garments using cheaper local labour as the main objective without minimum wage to generate maximum profit for the overseas retail fashion company without actually improving the conditions of those workers. Bangladesh has 200,000 textile workers mostly women, who were killed working in dangerous buildings that collapsed due to building codes being ignored by corrupt officials who supply permits to developers in collusion who ignore the official regulations and safety rules. Human resource is squandered by employers as a quantitative competitive cost factor as collateral to be offered for a profit on a global scale.

MODERN SLAVERY

In India the NDA started schemes to provide social services to unorganised workers including landless agricultural labourers. The problem remains this and other health schemes are not being implemented to alleviate the conditions of the worker. Working conditions offer little safety regulation, polluted environments and undernourishment result in exposure to hazardous work. Inability to continue such work, such as old age and disability, insecurity of a major illness or being laid off at the will of the employer for which they have no legal remedy. It is common among poorer parents to let their minor children work to supplement the family income this also benefits the indentured workers employer. This is a major reason for the widespread prevalence of child labour in the unorganised sector and related illiteracy in not attending school due to economic necessity.

Women are given low and unequal wages to men and sexual harassment is common but not discussed for fear of losing employment. This is a major source of profit for employers and contractors who exploit the workers lack of bargaining power and state legislation. Studies have found that on average they earn no more than Rs 300-500 around five dollars per day. The work is seasonal. In order to earn more they work longer hours and harder in inhospitable working conditions, in buildings that sometimes collapse from building regulations being ignored by officials who accept bribes to pass phony building certificates in Bangladesh.

In India Rajendra is a self employed Chai vendor his wife is a rag picker and his oldest son works at home assembling micro-electronic piece work for a local industrial manufacturer of parts. Between them on a seasonal average a joint income of Rs.3500- 400 per week, their disposable income is less than $5 a day. Multiply this over a 1.3 billion population and 70 per cent are agro-centric workers with no rights. In 2018/19 the new generation of over six million university educated post graduates looking for work in the next year five years with higher expectations suggests a sociological future miasma of civil unrest and high illiteracy.

All I ask is a chance to prove that money can't buy happiness.

Spike Milligan

CAPITOL WITHOUT BORDERS

Seven million documents leaked by 'Zudeche Zietung' were published, exposing the UK as the tax haven of the world, with London's network as its hub. Offshore British protectorates Bermuda, British Virgin and Cayman Islands offered tax avoidance schemes arranged through financial services of such companies as Appleby, they also have offices in Crown Dependant Jersey, Guernsey and the Isle of Man offering their rich clients and corporations the opportunity to take advantage of tax exemption advice. With the blessing of the UK financial services authority FCA European savings Directive, a $252 billion offshore client fund exists without borders.

Paradise papers BBC Panorama

Meg Hillier-UK Public accounts when interviewed spring 2018 expressed surprise and concerned that tax lawyers assist their clients to circumvent tax in the UK by opening offshore accounts approved under the new rules of 4% tax on capitol tax evasion is a serious offence, but the Isle of Man customs gave approval to Formula One racer Lewis Hamilton to land his private aircraft once on the Island to avoid 20% VAT by allowing the leased jet, business use only: thus avoiding a tax bill of $4 million in 2012. Lewis bought the jet transferring ownership to be leased by him from his offshore company. The Isle of Man customs office refunded $2 billion VAT to other aircraft under similar scheme to dozens of companies. Funds are set off shore by clients to overseas registered company accounts to substantiate loans to their personal bank account in the UK, $3 to $4 hundred billion fund of capitol exists outside the UK in tax havens offshore facilitated by tax lawyers to the wealthy which are exempt from full UK tax. Many British schools and hospital closures and the overburdened NHS budgets would not be cut annually illustrates the rich getting richer and the poor getting poorer.

GREED AND AVARICE

My fascination with the hypocrisy of red-tape vigorously invoked through endemic corruption enables the abuse of power. It made me aware of the International scale and depth of collusion. The world's G20 Banks fixed interest rates between the global banking fraternity and were left by the UK Government to self regulate. After the 1985 big bank debacle, fines of $35 billion were imposed after being exposed. A clear case of the patients running the hospital, as the global pandemic of economic decline provided no efficacy to treat the symptoms which still exist. During the non regulated period 2007 through 2008, no less a person than Mark Dearlove at the Bank of England was told by the Government to lower the international bank rate of interest LIBOR, the cost of borrowing between banks, an illegal gesture. A recording obtained by the BBC provided their radio four audience, with audible proof of the conversation on the news bulletin 16 of April 2017.

On the same day the News bulletin, Jez Stalley CEO Of Barclays Bank had his bonus cut because of similar reported irregularities. Further to this broadcast, the report of Shell in 2011 who took over the Nigerian oilfields, when a $1 Billion payment disbursement led to Tete and payments to Good Luck Johnson who was Prime Minister at the time. Corruption takes place at the highest levels of Government and social class.

Hong Kong Savings Bank HSBC CEO Mr S. Guthrie faces criminal charges at the time of writing for putting $7 million into his own Swiss bank account covertly through an offshore Panama company to evade tax liability to the UK Inland tax revenue department. While watching the BBC 'Panorama' and Guardian Newspaper investigation, it showed substantive proof that HSBC allowed their clients to draw large cash amounts from their account to move to their Swiss operation evading tax. HSBC assisted seven thousand of their rich clients to move $118 billion into their Swiss operating bank account to avoid tax liability beyond the UK authorities. The HSBC bank offered a wide range of services to shelter funds by client personally collecting cash not declared. Their Bank customer Mr Herman, an up market London furnishing company was assisted by HSBC to transfer his $1.8 million cash to a HSBC Swiss account. Another client Stoke football club Chairman Mr Humphries was assisted by HSBC to move over $4 million of his undeclared cash through a similar route with the banks advice and full cooperation. The abuse of the European savings directive of client funds in another country came to light from the 'Falcciani' files as a result of an investigative Internet Technology employee of the banks services, who presented them to the relevant UK tax authority, who ordered criminal investigation to hold the bank and their clients to account for a tax liability.

UNDER THE INFLUENCE

The Global $270 Billion business turn over in illegal drugs and arms deals requires the transit of FOREX funds referred to as black money, can be laundered into white money in the blink of a cursor by electronic means. Other methods involve cash on a massive scale. Drug cartel boss of bosses Guzman escaped from prison in 2006, one of the 50 most wanted people in the world. During his reign 60,000 people were killed in turf wars and gang to maintain his supremacy through corruption. Tunnels built under the Mexican border to the Southern State of America designed by architects to be distributed from Chicago. Cheating, steals the right to the fairness of collecting tax for public investment to spend on improving the infrastructure and future life of National interest. Tourism is another high return investment for a low risk assessment. Hotel conversion of the infrastructure offers high yield through low occupancy rates, the manipulation of low bookings reflected high occupancy on the final audit referred to as money laundering. Catering offers multiple opportunities to investors who literally pay their staff to eat at empty tables in restaurants with ambiguous guest who don't turn up for fictional reservations processed on a chart flow as fully booked. Rental accommodation channel funds through the books. Business proliferates and is multiplied to launder black money into white, an alchemy which persists today. According to the United Nations UN, the largest recipient of foreign direct investment FDI in 2013 was the British Virgin Islands an Archapeligo with 23,000 residents: $92 million dollars in foreign cash funds was deposited in this tax haven receiving massive investments include the Cayman Islands, Lichenstein, Monaco, Andora and Vanuata In 2014 the Chinese overtook the Russians as the largest buyers Of condos in New York. Other laundered money is used to purchase London Mansions, Yachts, securities and Art. Switzerland's $3 trillion dollars secret banking Jurisdiction for corporations.

Source; 'The Laundryman and the sink' Author Geoffrey Robinson

I lent a friend of mine ten thousand dollars for plastic surgery, and now I don't know what he looks like.

Emo Philips

DISPROPORTIONATE CONCENTRATION OF WEALTH

The richest 10 percent of the population own 85% of the global wealth. In 2017 the richest 2% in the world own half of the world's wealth as the world's 2,043 billionaires. Less than 0.000015 percent of the world's population own equal to twice that owned by the poorest to date. The world's 250 biggest companies account for more than $14 trillion dollars in annual sales, or about one third of all global GDPs. The top two thousand employ over seventy million people around the globe. The Sunday Times 'Rich List' 2017 named 134 Billionaires resident in the UK, among the list is the Duke of Westminster of the Grosvenor Estate who own large portions of London's west end including Mayfair. Additionally, over a million acres of land are held in private hands by aristocratic families in Britain. The Lascelles family wealth came from slavery in the Caribean originally their vast wealth was generated from the slave trade in the seventeenth century, this allowed owners to buy and develop these vast estates. Tinsley Castle estate in Herefordshire England, owned by the Parkinson family, who in the 1800's held 33,000 acres in Trinidad according to the National archives at Kew. Records in the register show as slave owners they were compensated in 1834 with 46,000 Other slave owners in the UK who jointly owned 84,000 slaves. The British owners were paid compensation totaling seventeen billion pounds sterling equivalent of today's value, the 40% of total expenditure in 1834, these funds were transmitted into property, infrastructure and land. The land act in the 18th century property was the key, and rights to the property. The abolishionist's denounced the concept Of slavery as property Emancipation Of the slaves only occurred because the UK Commissioners valued slaves as assets to appease the slave owners. This State sponsored financial compensation was the largest payout in British history, paid to British resident slave owners of the British Empire as the price of slave freedom. These wealthy owners kept their slaves a further six years without wage as part of the settlement of release. Thus investment of this inherited wealth was transferred as property of those families such as Lascelles at Harewood Estate in Yorkshire who owned five plantations in Jamaica and Barbados, the Duchesse of Chalders who owned 300 slaves was an absentee owner 1770-1780. Thirty seven Peerages of the House of Lords owned slaves in the West Indies and London the global financial centre.

According to Forbes, in 2012 there were 421 Billionaires in the USA, 96 in Russia, 95 in China, 48 in India. The richest 0.01 % control global wealth, these super rich 660 individuals own 90% of the world's personal assets, and the list grows annually.

Of the seven billion population of the human race 600 million defecate in public, 2.5 million have no toilet access. 1 billion people have no sanitation facilities this cause's a health pandemic with open sewers exposing toxin and cholera, diseases responsible for children's deaths. One in ten deaths are due to poor sanitation, The World

Health Authority confirms $53 million dollars are lost annually due
to lost productivity through illness and death.

Every gun that is made, every warship launched,

Every rocket fired signifies in the final sense a theft

From those who are hungry and are not fed,

Those who are cold and are not clothed.

Dwight Eisenhower

CIVILISATION UNDER ATTACK
2002 to 2016

The so called Islamic state ISIS without a country destroyed priceless art antiquities of world heritage sites of priceless and irreplaceable historic value, to further their religious and political objectives. The terrorist organisation obtains funds through sales of crude Oil of $365 million annually. In March 2002, the so called ISIS blew up and destroyed the Buddha heritage site a direct attack on cultural identity. ISIS is intent on destroying world heritage and any cultural art and history of the human race other than Islam. They declare their authority as caliphate, their religious fanaticism and military expertise provide currency 0 fuel violence against any historical reference to the humanities. rh0usands of years of human expression and thought in historical terms being eliminated in irreplaceable works of art, the Nimrod frieze lacked to fragments. Their narrow and distorted vision of hate is in violation of the Koran interpreted by ISIS is a portent of what is to come.

Art and architecture from over 5,000 years ago of Babylon, Samarian Mesopotamia and Roman Islamic art Co-existed for Millennia have beer broken and bashed to wanton destruction by the fanatic sledge hammers of the Islamic state in their interpretation of the Quran Iraq museum curators record relics as an irreplaceable expression of human history now under intentional attack. The Buddha sculpture, a venerated world heritage site in Bhatra blown up with dynamite in 2002 symbolically reflected human suffering in civil war. On BBC World News Usama Assam a senior researcher of Islamic studies and a Muslim Iman stated. 'A fanatic ISIS mindless approach to their interpretation of the Koran is extreme, the words of the prophet Mohammad was ambivalent with idolatry from other religions strictly forbidden in the Koran by the faithful Muslim. The unbeliever in words of the prophet is not subject to Koranic law.

This history of where we come from as a human race is subjected to actual deliberate destruction in second's, the testimony of common human heritage that has remained with us through the ravages of time has now gone. While I was an infant in 1940 the Nazis in world war two marched into Europe destroying Jewish history before getting to the people who were then targeted for elimination. The Kameer Rouge destroyed all reference to history and culture before they came to power in Cambodia before getting to the people to destroy them. The so called ISIS is using the same technique in violence and destruction with success across borders which they ignore as sovereign states but as a necessary means to an end. The kidnapping of hostages raise further millions, in January 2013 Al Khaida hostages taken in North Africa, associated press reported that Nazar al Khaidi raise 50% of their budget from kidnap and ransom from taking hostages. Four hostages from Finland had their $20 million dollar ransom paid through Oman indirectly. Lela Kaleva and the other three were released. American and British governments together with other governments officially refuse to pay or negotiate with terrorist organisations, James Foley, Kosloff, Kaila Muller killed after their capture.

Negotiation between France and other European countries by sale of illegal drugs and armaments provides further funds. King Abdulla 2nd of Jordan confirmed 'this method of raising funds furthers the aims of the ISIS reign of terror and violence in Arab communities'. The so called Islamic state murder the messenger, journalist reporting facts on the ground at the battle front become targets for ransom, a price is on the head of a third of all foreign correspondents, three hundred journalist are murdered annually abroad attempting to bring true facts into the public domain confirmed by Cardiff

University Head of journalism. In October 2015 the IS murdered 272 passengers aboard a commercial jet in Shar-el Sheik resort in Egypt, a devastating and cowardly act of annihilation of human life to further their cause. In Paris France during November 128 innocent people were murdered by suicide terrorists to give their message of destruction, as in London, Brussels and Copenhagen.

Foul-cank'ering rust the hidden treasure frets, but gold that's put to use more gold begets. Venus and Adonis.

BANKING PROBITY

MONEY BLACK OR WHITE, legal and illegal, is moved internationally as of necessity to its final destination. Banks are part Of this process, at the time Mr Steven Green at HSBC ran the banks department offering covert devices through the banks Swiss operation, at an annual salary of $4.5 million, was responsible and prepared to break the law in 2013. Mr Green was later made a Peer of the Realm he joined the House of Lords as an ex member of the cabinet and Tory Minister for Trade and Investment in the period referred too. Now Lord Green with the authority invested in him as Peer of the realm declined an interview as did the UK Government on this matter. Lord Green put over $4 million of his own funds into his Swiss account via the Panamanian registered company route which is an illegal act. A Queen's council gave legal advice to BBC 'Panorama' producers that: notes of meetings between the bank and their client clearly showed secret tax evasion cheating the United Kingdom Inland Revenue to the amount of $118 Billion of the eleven thousand clients that the HSBC bank assisted.

Out of 11,000 people who evaded tax in 2010 only one person has been prosecuted under the criminal law, justice was clearly not done, nor seen to be done. In 2015 Chairperson of the UK public accounts committee MP Mrs Hodge made placatory noises verbally admonishing the errant system, but did not clarify what action should or would be taken. In 2013 Ms Sue Shelley working at the HSBC employed as tax compliance Officer was fired by HSBC bank when she upheld the UK law bringing the facts before them. Later she was judged as wrongful dismissal later recompensed by tribunal accordingly. HSBC was responsible in helping client's access methods of wide spread tax evasion estimated at over $100 billion. The bank advised clients how to avoid tax by offering to facilitate this action through a Swiss account to avoid a UK tax liability to Her Majesty's Inland Revenue in the Criminal High Court'.

Future proceedings against the Bank will now cost the UK taxpayers millions for legal costs for the banks wrong doing. Heads will fall to be buried under the carpet until next time without independent regulation, is corrupt practice indeed.

Barclays Bank has had to set aside over a billion dollars for fixing exchange rates in April 2015 pending investigation but announced a 25% increase in profits in July of that year. In June 2015 HDFC Bank's international operation 4,000 jobs were downsized to coin a phrase, with the object of saving funds, not jobs. In June 2017 CEO Mr Varley and four other Directors are facing criminal charges from the serious fraud office in conspiracy to commit an unlawful loan to Qatar and other Middle East clients of $7 Billion dollars in share conversion to prop up investments in Barclays shares after the 2008 crisis.

Commerzbank:

In March 2014 were found guilty of collusion in money laundering on a huge scale and fined $1.5 Billion as they had turned a blind eye to this criminal activity over years of operation on a grand scale.

Deutcherbank:

Was made to pay a penalty of $2.9 Billion for manipulating interest rates and penalized further for misleading regulators and corrupting evidence, and a further $5.4 billion in the USA for selling toxic mortgage products. Banks in countries of the G7 lead global corruption get away with a derisory fine which they pay without appeal as guilty as a method of deferred prosecution by arrangement with government to avoid impacting on fiscal policy.

The French government initiated Court proceedings against HSBC as a result of the heiress granddaughter of Nina Ricci Fashion house fortune being convicted of tax evasion and money laundering operation through HSBC's Swiss operation. In November 2016 RBS Bank put aside over four hundred million pounds sterling in the event of customers claims, as a result of their admitted inferior customer service. The UK tax payer has to pay the legal costs of prosecution for the Banks mistakes in the final account.

American and European Banks bought bad debt in 2007 and continue to do so while the traders retain their bonus payout annually. We are informed that this specialist banking fraternity are available to the highest bidder, and we are told for economic reasons it is necessary to keep paying them over and above the average to keep them. This same fraternity contributed to the cause of the world recession in the seventies and nineties which continues to jump start, nothing has changed to prevent it recurring in future. The bankers, hedge fund manager's and private equity bosses, the pantomime characters accused of causing the financial crash of 2007-08 are still raking in the bonuses. A pattern emerges nothing is unique to its time as history has a habit of repeating. In an attempt to balance the nation's books in 2015, UK tax authorities received a sixty billion pounds contribution to the exchequer, forty billion pounds directly from the city of London banks and a further twenty billion pounds from their employees. The banks arrogance and greed led to the financial crash was replaced by self pity. Some were forced to retire, but the blow was softened by extraordinary and overly generous pensions they had been provided with on exit. Few seemed able to explain their actions. A number of practitioners are back in the banking world at prime ministerial and presidential top tables. It would seem historical amnesia will assist in softening attitudes in public opinion as economies recover and memories fade. The rich can usually secure rehabilitation no matter what their wrong doing. Borrowing, like scratching, is only good for a while.

WHAT THE PEOPLE WHO HAVE EVERYTHING REALLY WANT.

Discovering Israel's Prime Minister Binyamin Netanyahu and his wife Sara cost their countries taxpayer's $542,000 over five days according to a detailed breakdown published 16th June in the 'Financial Times' 18 June 2016. The cost of his five day trip last year includes hairdressing and make up for Netanyahu was released as a freedom of information request exposes the overt and luxurious lifestyle enjoyed by the prime Minister and his wife. His visit to the UN's general assembly last autumn were the cost of maintaining his at $1,600, his make-up artist billed for $1 , 750.The state comptroller considered excessive expenditures on take away meals, cleaning, and hairstyling. Expenses incurred by Sara who could face charges of expenditure at the couple's official residence not included. The list includes minor items such as chocolates costing $4 and matches charged at $8.69. The Israel government's official auditor alleges, holidays paid for by wealthy friends of the PM includes Arnaud Mimran a French businessman currently on trial for fraud. Three years ago the Israel government paid for a specially commissioned $127,000 'resting chamber' on a plane taken by Prime Minister Netanyahu for a five hour flight to London three years ago. A year earlier it was revealed Netanyahu had an annual contract of more than $2,000 with a Jerusalem ice cream parlour to supply his residence with his favourite pistachio. Other items listed during their New York visit were the removal of furnishing's from the hotel rooms to meet needs of the guests cost Israel almost $20,000 - $30,500 for their removal and $16,000 for 'storage of the removed furniture. The couple's meals cost $1,860 while, 'special cleaning' was listed at $6,900 though it was unclear weather the item was charged or recouped. A total cost to the taxpayer's of Israel $542,000 for the five day trip to New York. Details of the five day trip were revealed after Shahar Ben-Meir an Israeli lawyer had pursued the FIO through the court and won. In December 2018 Police had sufficient evidence to indite the P.M. for multi corruption criminality.

If you have to ask the price you can't afford it — J.P. Morgan

EVASION AND CORRUPTION

600,000 employees of Mitsubishi woke up 20th July 2015 to find their CEO had fraudulently inflated $1.22 billion dollars false profits in the company tax returns. Political appointments protected self interest through corrupt practice against the interest of the shareholder and ordinary citizen were ignorant of the facts now exposed in the public domain. Extremist holding power and autocracy over others not subject to checks and balances could result in anarchy augmented by ignorance and motivated by political or commercial belief acting in the name of the State. In Britain the Magna Carta written 800 years ago frames a fair system of justice that 'All free men shall be allowed to be judged by his equals in a court of law ,the information was announce over the speaker. let us see the Judicial wheels turning imperceptively.

Make crime pay become a lawyer.

Will Rogers

TURMOIL

I could not concentrate, polarised by a feeling of sadness which did not abate. No joy, an emptiness followed by frustration at my inability to share intimacy. My personal relationships punctuated with irregular activity gave little gratification, feeling disconnected in deep loneliness. It was as if the act of intimacy had no relevance in achieving a peace of mind which remained in turmoil. Passion rarely transported me to a level of emotional tenderness to last longer than the act of physical intimacy. My diary was filled with appointments indicating time and place but did not translate into building a shared future with another human being. I experienced a state of Isolation and dislocation of non commitment, while employing methods of social intercourse which added to the confusion. The opposite applied to my work and business plans which I approached with care, skillful as the surgeon's knife in operating. Like a moth I had been near the flame of love but my compulsion had been thwarted by inexperience and naive trust.

Ducking for apples change one letter and it's the story of my life.

Dorothy Parker

SUSPIRO DE LEMONA

(Sigh of a woman)

One Sunny summer day in 1960 walking along a Liverpool Street browsing in a shop window I had noticed her reflection following me as an androgynous shadow. I turned and stopped, we acknowledged each other and contrived to talk. She introduced herself as Jeanette and we walked together to a city coffee shop with our cappuccino's to enjoy a common conspiracy, where we sat for two hours. The next day after work we met as arranged, taking a bus together to the suburbs to baby mind a friend's sleeping infant upstairs. While watching TV on the first night of baby-sitting she promptly seduced me downstairs on the ubiquitous sofa This new development became a fiction of fantasy, as she offered me a leading part into accepting her androgynous habit of occasional dressing as a boy. As a piece of theatricality this added an experimental dimension, far more interesting than the traditional one I had perceived This new world opened up during my twenty second year in which we shared in monogamous relationship, we both enjoyed the commitment. Losing my virginity to a more experienced female predator became a consensual reality. During the second year we decided to be engaged as she turned twenty, we planned a future marriage. After inviting our two families to celebrate the engagement, the ring was presented sealing the union at a joint family celebration at Jeanette's parent's home in Liverpool. I loved her, and wanted to spend my life with this woman who touched me body and soul, enveloped in the intensity of sentiment and emotion. Children and a family was a dimension we looked forward to as partners of mutual choice. I did not see a cloud in the sky, until one autumn weekend during her a stay over in my flat after what had been a mutual idyll she left, suddenly announced without warning ' I will not be seeing you anymore'. I laughed thinking it was a joke, but she left closing the door without laughing.

I sat in quite disbelief for a very long time in shock. It took hours before I could accept the realisation that I had been dumped unceremoniously. Jeanette explained later to a mutual friend she had met an American Airline pilot while on a flight to Speke airport Liverpool on duty as she was air steward in the cabin crew and that it was final. The way I was told and the manner was with cruel disregard for our engagement commitment and gave me cause to doubt the veracity of her empty words. There was no argument or raised voices, she just calmly informed with a cool callousness. I realised love is an inexplicable irrational phenomenon having a dependency component and took the situation badly. In a condition of traumatic distress I fled to London which led me into a deeper depression leaving me feeling vulnerable, isolated and emotionally inept in a City of strangers. The emotional pain was excruciating, but I lived with it and was in a deep depression and emotionally unstable for three years after until my decision to consciously change direction which I eventually did.

That's the trouble with life — crap dialogue and bad lighting.

Elizabeth Taylor

A PARTNER

In 1964 at Easter weekend I took the train from Kings Cross returning to Yorkshire to close up my flat in Leeds after making a decision to move back to London at the age of twenty four. The Bank holiday steam train was packed full of standing passengers, but in the carriage I found a last remaining carriage seat in an overcrowded carriage. 'Is this seat taken?' without waiting for a reply I sat next to the smiling youth full face. In the sixties it was a four hour journey which turned into a flirtatious conversation between us with thigh and knee contact under the table. I understood this as a signal to either enjoy or endure. His pale blond hair bleached by the sun fell straight over a smooth forehead. His fine cheekbones and strong jaw line framed his dimpled chin with a flawless porcelain skin. His eyes defined his face, they were cornflower blue which overpowered his other features. With a captivating youthfulness he was hard to resist, Keith was eighteen years of age living and working in west Yorkshire our mutual destination. After what was then a four hour journey we enjoyed a mutual attraction. We met later as arranged that night and consummated our attraction in loving tenderness until first light, which was transformed over time into a strong bond we shared over the next twenty three years. A lifelong friendship not always understanding our differences but accepting each other with a deep affection and trust over the next half a century. During our two decades together we worked with a middle aged irascible Austrian woman in the travel industry, whose worldly stories were told with gratuitous detail as she unfolded her life story. She was born the daughter of Loti Lehman on the Covent Garden Opera house stage in London between the first and second act of 'Jenny Lind'. Her mother Loti Lehman the Metzo Soprano and international star gave birth to her during the interval, singing the title role of 'Jennie Lind' A plaque is placed on stage in memory of the historic occasion of

Jenny's birthplace. Jenny grew up to be one of only six woman marine engineers educated in and qualified to be part of the navy fleet in the second-world war, a remarkable achievement in itself indicating her firm grasp on reality. This certain waywardness brought her to settle for a while in Malta where she entertained the war troops with a unique ability to negotiate and pick up cash from the bar with her genitalia needless to say without underwear, she was allowed to keep all the cash coins left on the table.

After the war Jenny became an air steward with British airways based at Northolt Middlesex. In the cabin crew the Captain was Hughie Green later to become show host of TV 'Opportunity knocks'. She remembered that after each flight arrival on the apron of the runway he would relieve himself by urinating on the fuselage of the aircraft in the parking zone not wishing to walk to the passenger terminal facilities. A man distinctly inclined to a future in television history and the father of a child who then denied it publicly 'He vos an arrogant bastard darling' was her final comment. She married a De Kuyper salesman but was a teetotal, but she never remained completely sober, he died early, but for her, life without him was like a broken pencil, pointless.

THE TRAVEL BUG

In response to the LGBT community, Keith I decided to start up a niche travel market under the name 'Stay Gay holidays' as a marketing concept in 1975. My ingenious idea initially did meet with some resistance from Keith who was not to be ignored, but after listening to my business plan came he on board. We became the first original 'out' gay travel company and the genesis to make an impact in the mainstream travel industry. To reach a wider audience we were hungry for publicity and I phoned the features editor at the Sunday Times news desk and put through to the Editor Hunter Davies in Fleet Street working at the 'Sunday Times' as correspondent, he listened to my story and grasped the genesis proposing we meet and suggested an interview. We met over a pint of best bitter at lunch time in 'The Old Bell' public house. Hunter was intrigued as I presented him with a thousand words of copy text from our printed brochure. Hunter read it and intended to edit and place it in the 'Compass' Travel section. We reminisced about our northern origins for an hour before departing. Six weeks later the four column quarter page article appeared with our naked torso's photograph on the bonnet of our 'Bentley as the headline 'Happy gays are her again' The Sunday Times published March 1975. 'The Travel news' published a follow up as we became bona fide ABTA members.

All hell broke loose as the news story was picked up by Reuter's news syndicate. It was only seven years after the homosexuality white paper had been passed into law through parliament. Reuter's news agency syndicated the story world-wide we became front page news on the 'San Fransisco Chronicle' and 'USA today'. 'South China Daily' in Hong Kong, 'The Irish Times' followed by 'The Observer'. Over the next few weeks numerous publications picked up the story globally. A four page spread appeared in the Belgium Sunday tabloid: graphically illustrated after a visit from their news editor to our London office, he stayed with us for a weekend to get more background detail of our operation with a full pictorial double page spread. On my visit to New York USA, interviewed on coast to coast public radio in New York to Los Angeles it was the beginning of a Gay odyssey and a dramatic impact on a future LGBT community.

SUNDAY TIMES EDITORIAL

9th March 1975.

'HAPPY GAYS ARE HERE AGAIN'

Paul Clarkson has known for years there was a need for organised gay holidays. When he was 18 and went into travel agents and tried to describe the sort of holiday he fancied, the girls behind the counter giggled. 'They could not relate to my requests'. When he went into the travel trade himself he realised even more that the demand was there. Last year he and his partner Keith Bagnall began 'Stay gay holidays' limited -the first tour operators in Europe catering for homosexuals. Last summer at their first gay attempt they sent 150 gay people to Europe. This year they have had 700 bookings so far. We advertised in the Sunday times travel section last autumn and received 1,800 replies- 20 percent of those who answered made booking's. 'We've stopped advertising we don't need to.' This caused the travel trade to copy our programme during the following three years and amused sensationalism enabled expansion at no Ad-cost. Their brochure is highly suggestive. Apart from very arty photographs of Paul and Keith both naked, the copy is full of jokey remarks, "let us help you reach your holiday climax. at night a mixture of the outrageous prevails....nudist beaches famed for their permissiveness ....enjoy the bazooka in gay abandon...small boy souvenir sellers whose innocent smiles hide a remarkable talent for bargaining   muscular attendants compete to massage customers Clients go on normal scheduled flights- it's only when they get to their hotels or villas all personally vetted by Paul and Keith that the gay times begin. In Amsterdam where a two night all in holiday costs 39 Pounds many of the hotels they use are either gay owned or exclusively gay friendly. They even have a gay courier to show customers the gay beaches bars and clubs. Their two most popular tours are to Amsterdam and Athens to Mykonos but they also have gay holidays in Paris, Malta Tunisia, and Turkey, in October they start in Bangkok. One in six of the British Population is gay so we are obviously on to a winner. We did offer to do a similar service for gay women to arrange tours to the isle of Lesbos in Greece but they were not amused. They said they did not want to get mixed up with a male oriented organisation. I said 'listen sweety, we would not be asking you if you were male oriented'. I think really they were a bit put off by us being an organised commercial company, they thought we should be completely philanthropic. 'Almost 40 per cent of our clients are married men, blokes who have realised over the years they are bi-sexual and want to let their hair down once in a year. Then they go back to being respectable married Solicitors or whatever' On April 2 Paul is beginning his first series of gay tours of Britain, 'Stay gay round Britain' is aimed at foreign visitors especially Americans and Japanese, the price is 80 pounds for three days and two nights. During the day the tour is historical, at night it's hysterical. Paul is personally taking the first party round in his Rolls Royce.

Hunter Davies. *Sunday Times article, 9th March 1975*

In 1975, We had published the first open and out Gay brand travel brochure in Europe offering the travel trade and public a genesis gay travel package programme selling direct to the LGBT community. Reaction to the story syndicated by 'Reuters' news agency was read in over 130 countries. The 'Travel News' the trade paper made impact in the travel industry on publication, which caused 8,000 readers to request our brochure directly from multiple International editorials. Over the next few weeks our post was delivered daily in the little red vans of the Royal Mail to our Wimbledon office by the sack full. It took the two of us, and four full time women including my mother, to answer the post over a period of six weeks of constant deliveries by the red Royal Mail van's daily postal service. We had as they say 'arrived'.

At this time the seven day Yom Kipor war in 1974 between Israel and Palestine pushed the OPEC countries to hike the oil price from $40 to over $100 a barrel, this immediately caused fuel surcharges too be levied by the air transport carrier direct to travellers on arrival at the airport in 1975. This shot a hole in the traveller's budget and caused cancellations of advance bookings following media reports. The deleterious effect on our travel programme was factored negatively beyond our control. In addition, petrol ration cards were issued nationally in the UK. The following year OPEC decided to ration further supplies to the west in retaliation of them losing the Yom Kippur seven day war against Israel. The next season looked unstable for the travel industry so we reluctantly decided to stop operating it had become unfeasible to continue our packaged programme with government petrol ration cards and airline fuel surcharges, escalated costs beyond our control. Since the 70s the vacuity we created in the LGBT community has now been fulfilled the demand by gay travel specialists globally into the new millennium. Our presence made an important contribution toward the equality of LGBT and we are justly proud to be the first gay travel company to present an 'out' gay programme to the LGBT community in 1975 to have broken the mould in Europe and the UK, opening the way forward for 'Gay travel pride' and the International travelling community

NORTH AFRICA -1967

Keith and I travelled to Morocco North Africa after our first summer together. We encountered a chance meeting in the Tangier Kasbah, namely Esta Ackerman Who befriended us one morning over mint tea. Esta was dressed in a multi coloured curtain swathed about her ample portions, her face was weathered and wreathed in smiles no longer youthful. She wore distinctive heavy horn rimmed glasses perched on a large proboscis, shaded by a wide brim straw hat which had seen better days. She informed us she took a month off every year to visit each country. As a single middle aged Jewish lady of virtue and probity unencumbered by family, travelling alone she referred to joining us in a trio as 'the three musketeers' her choice of Nom de plume in our enjoyable and warm friendship. The first week after breakfast we fell into a daily routine of wandering down the souk to the promenade followed by an entourage of youths offering us personal guidance to locations unknown and of ulterior intent while we sunbathed on the beach. Later we three musketeers each purchased a Djelaba each in the Kasbah and walked through the souk in them, these garments were woven from the finest ivory linen edged with silk and gold brocade worn with dramatic flair• As characters in a pantomime, we had turned into over the next few days not agreeing who was to play Cinderella or the ugly sister.

Esta dancing the Hora under a murillo sky each afternoon in the midday heat snuggling between hotel sheets in her siesta, dreamt of a tryst of passion with Hassan, while we flirted with Mustapha the room boy from Cairo during Ramadan until the first light of dawn.

Happy gays here again

SCENE ONE

PAUL CLARKSON has known for years there was a need for organised gay holidays. When he was 18 and went into travel agents and tried to describe the sort of holiday he fancied, the girls behind the counter giggled. "They couldn't relate to my requests." When he went into the travel trade himself, he realised even more that the demand was there. Last year, he and a partner Keith Bagnall, began Stay Gay Holidays Limited, the first tour operators in Europe to cater for homosexuals.

Last summer, at their first attempt, they sent 150 gay people to Europe. This year, they have had 700 bookings so far. "We advertised in The Sunday Times last autumn and received 1,800 replies—20 per cent of those who answered made bookings. We've stopped advertising. We don't need to."

Their brochure is highly suggestive. Apart from very arty photographs of Paul and Keith, both naked, the copy is full of jokey remarks. "Let us help you reach your holiday climax . . . at night a mixture of the outrageous prevails . . . nudist beaches famed for their permissiveness . . . enjoy the Bazooki in gay abandon . . . small boy souvenir sellers whose innocent smiles hide a remarkable talent for bargaining . . . muscular attendants compete to massage customers."

Clients go on normal scheduled flights—it's only when they get to their hotels or villas, all personally vetted by Paul and Keith, that the gay times begin. In Amsterdam, where a two night all-in holiday costs £39, many of the hotels they use are either gay-owned or almost exclusively gay. They even have a gay courier to show customers the gay clubs, beaches and bars. Their two most popular tours are to Amsterdam and to Athens and Mykonos but they also have gay holidays in Paris, Malta, Tunisia and Turkey. In October they start in Bangkok.

"One in six of the British population is gay so we are obviously on to a winner. We did offer to do a similar service for gay girls, arranging tours to Lesbos in Greece, but they were not amused. They said they didn't want to get mixed up with a male-orientated organisation. I said, 'Listen sweety, we wouldn't be *asking* you if we were male-orientated.' I think really, they were a bit put off by us being a highly organised commercial firm. They thought we should be philanthropic.

"Almost 40 per cent of our customers are married men, blokes who have realised over the years that they are bi-sexual and want to let their h once in the year. T go back to being r married solicitors or w

On April 2, Paul is his first series of gay Britain, Stay Gay Roun Ltd. This, is aimed a visitors, especially Amer Japanese. The price is three days and two "During the day, the historical. At night, it' cal." Paul is personal the first party round in His ambition is to be gay millionaire.

Brochures and further tion: Stay Gay Holida 112 Bolingbroke Grov London S.W. 11. Send. S

Hunter

Bring back sex and

Opinion

▶ Did you notice the article few weeks ago in the Scen pages about Stay Gay Holiday the homosexual travel agency Disgusting. I expected million of letters from Yours disgustec Tunbridge Wells. Instead, we gc two people cancelling their sul scription while 7,500 (repea seven thousand five hundred readers wrote to Stay Gay Hol days for further information. I just goes to show that as a con troversialist I'm a dead loss. If keep on at this rate, I'll end u on Any Questions.

Paul (top), Keith (bottom), directors—and models—of Stay Gay Holidays Ltd:

LGBT
GLOBAL PRIDE

Six years before Keith and I travelled to Morocco in North Africa, the global Gay Pride 'Stonewall' movement had started June 26 1969 in New York, when NYPD police raided the Stonewall Inn, a gay bar on Christopher Street in West Village, Manhattan New York. This had Provoked a riot among the patron's that lasted for two days. Poet Allen Ginsberg living nearby hearing the commotion remarked, 'Gay Power! Isn't that great 'It's about time we did something to assert ourselves'. This reverberated around the globe and now celebrated in the enlightened countries of the world, ten years later I visited Manhattan New York as guest of a Radio station being interviewed as representing the first out Gay Travel Company in Europe.

Every gay person in some way is defined by how their sexuality affects their life. Weather it be that they felt the need to hide it for part of their life, or how they came out early and dealt with it, or how they dealt with finding a significant 'other'. Sex may not define you, but in a greater sense your sexuality does help define a part Of your identity Learning about intimacy and interpersonal relationships or not getting a chance to learn those things early on that defines one as in the British film 'My beautiful Laundrette' in 1967.

Over three decades later 'Broken Back Mountain' remains the most commercially successful LGBT themed film ever produced. The Academy award winning epic American love story is set against the sweeping vistas of Wyoming and Texas. The film tells the story of two young men a ranch hand and a rodeo cowboy, who met in the summer of 1963 as they unexpectedly forge a lifelong connection, one whose complications, joy and tragedies provide a testament to the endurance and power of love between two men. In contrast Dirk Bogarde as the 'Victim' in the British cinema of the nineteen sixties showed a different side of sexual inequality as unsettling in the pre-Wolfenden report era. Gender identities are disposed to suffer, when such evils are sufferable, than to right themselves by abolishing the forms to which they are accustomed: Example the celluloid closet and reinforcing the British stereotype 'Carry on camping'.

The history of humanity is a history of continued persecution on the part of the heterosexual majority over those with differing sexual orientation or gender identities, having the direct consequences of leading to a complete tyranny over LGBT people. They required LGBT people to hide their true sexual orientations and gender identities in order to be accepted and validated by society, family and government. They contributed to the psychological abuse of LGBT people by continually informing them of their differences, yet instead of validating these differences they used them as subjects of derision and ridicule; leading many LGBT people to suicide, depression and despair. British law forced LGBT people to undergo psychological treatments like reparative therapy in order to change what they believed to be a deviant nature, a process which causes irreparable psychological and emotional harm to LGBT people. Parent's using religious text use it to validate hatred against LGBT people and instil in their children the notion that this hatred is legitimate as the will of God, and choosing to the above despotism through the force of law. It is demanded that the walls of hatred and condemnation be torn down, to be replaced with the bonds of equal rights, respect, and affirmation.

OUT OF THE CLOSET

Times have changed in the USA, LGBT and the New York Police vehicle's now paint rainbow stripes of the International gay flag bearing the sign reading 'NYPD out and Proud' as part of the parade. The appeal of the gay community to brand's combined global spending power is estimated at $3.7tn a year according to LGBT capitol a corporate advisory investment management company. Two Million spectators watched the diversity and inclusion reflected in the Pride march in the US. In 2016 the Gay pride march attracted sixteen Global fortune 500 companies including Wall mart, Delta, AXA, Netflix, Bud light, Unilever, BNP Paribas, Nissan, and the Disney Corporation. In January 2015 the jeweller Tiffany's featured a gay couple in an ad for engagement rings for the first time in its 178 year history. Elsewhere in the world, the oppression of transgender and same sex relationships is often a punishable offence. 2015 Credit Suisse employ none binary gender 'Pipa' or Phillip as lead executive at the banks headquarters at Canary Wharf London, gender assumption is incorporated by supporting identity of gender of the individual, as gay, lesbian, and transsexual employees. LGBT say's this reflects on employer recognition of minority rights.

2016 In Uganda, Kampal, homophobic rhetoric from government officials over the last 10 years arrested 16 pride demonstrators. Ugandans would look at this as a human rights struggle as would Rwanda and Jamaica.

2 June 2016, Omar Mateen shot and killed 49 people in Pulse a gay night club in Orlando Florida. The President of Interpride organisations so far identified 944 'Pride Event's in the world. Gay

people still suffer in the US which still goes unreported. Drive by shootings is a form of terrorism when you are perceived as a gay, or subject to violent attack. It's something we have been conditioned to deal with it on a daily basis. Bruce Springsteen cancelled his concert 2016 in North Carolina USA because the State government passed a law banning gay or transsexual people from using public toilets by people whose birth certificate does not match their sexuality or chosen gender. Bryan Adams did likewise in support of gay rights as the same includes trans-genders as discrimination under the law passed by the State.

Legislation in Belize disproportionately affected homosexual men it was ruled unconstitutional by their Supreme Court in a challenge led by the UK former attorney general. Belize criminal code section 53 banned 'carnal intercourse against the order of nature' and made consensual sex between adult men in private illegal. Chief Justice Kenneth Benjamin said the legislation violated the constitutional rights to dignity, privacy, equality and non discrimination on grounds of sex The London office of Debevoise & Plimpton a US based law firm led by Lord Goldsmith QC the former UK Attorney General, advised the human dignity trust which intervened to support the challenge led by a coalition of caribean lesbian, gay, bisexual and transsexual (LGBT) activist's academics and legal experts. The individual claimant is Caleb Orozco a Belizean gay man and prominent LGBT human rights advocate.

On the 14th September 2016 the BBC one Television programme 'Unreported' confirmed that the Gay refugee population in cologne and German camps were subject to abuse and violence, from their fellow Iraq and Syrian immigrants. Fear of repeated threats of male to male rape and homophobic attack from their own countrymen with further beatings, drove the ninety LGBT men interviewed out into the general population of the city. This has created homelessness and further distress, causing many of the mainly younger men to be exposed to working as male prostitutes for less than one hundred German marks per client at half the local rate. They expressed their fear at returning to the refugee camp. As one million refugees are to be assimilated into the German Democratic Republic in the future things do not auger well. The Cologne 'Pride' parade gave a feeling of inclusiveness and freedom to the oppressed minority.

THE KILLING TRAIL

1991 Texas Dallas USA Hate crimes of homicide, torture and several beatings by young adolescent's blood lust against gay people in Houston, these predators savagely beat and later 'shot gays' after 30 minutes in a park a 19 year old, the three youths received life sentence. Thirty gay men in Texas were killed in the same fashion, Police and the media linked this by hatred of a teenager 15 year old. This action tolerated by the Church and Police and a Donald Aldridge on Citizen Band radio justified this murderous attack on Gay victims.

In 1993 in Tyler, Texas, Nicholas West a 23 year old man was taken by Donald Aldrich and his gang, driven to a local reservation spot, who terrorized the victim by beating him before pulling a gun on and riddling his body with 25 gunshot wounds before he died.

FILE PHOBIC CONTENT REVIEW

HATE CRIME AND MURDER

At the ' London Pub' in Oslo a gay venue in Norway, a crowd was filling the bar celebrating the end of LGBTQ Pride week, terror reigned as Lars Arleson a 42 year old man used his two guns to shoot into the crowded pub killing two people and injuring twenty one the night of 16 July 2022.

Source : BBC

CIVIL RIGHTS CAMBODIA

South East Asia's connection to modern slavery and civil rights: The BBC report women being held against their will in a scam operation from China transporting them to Cambodia via the global internet associated with the Prince Property group. Hun Sen Prime minister of Cambodia is aware of Senator Ankors connection to this slavery in Cambodia, with sales of eighteen to twenty thousand per person. Local Police are working with the Property Company,

Source: BBC July 16

Chapter 08

GLADRAGS THEATRE CLUB

With some initial misgivings after 'Gay Travel', Keith and I decided to open 'Gladrags Theatre club' in 1979, in what had been a silent cinema theatre in 1905 in Kirkgate, Leeds city centre. It had originally opened with the movie 'Gay Times,' a portent of the future.

In 1979 before the club opened, our Barrister made two separate application's to present arguments to the Court for a private members gay club license, the first application had been refused as the Lords day observance society objected. It took us a further year of objections before we were granted a full license to eventually open in the summer of 1980, with a restaurant and bar, centre stage with two dressing rooms, tiled from floor to ceiling with hand painted ceramic tiles in panel's scenes from the 20s. The dance floor for 450 guest's opened for private membership and became established quickly as the first 'out' gay club in Leeds. On our opening night we exceeded the fire regulation numbers and had to close the line which had formed several hundred two deep round the block, indicating a successful opening. Helping us in the restaurant was our heterosexual friend Dominic Hoffman our visiting seasonal American actor friend from the TV series 'A different World' who elected to run the tables and became a 'Lothario' with the ladies his seasoned hamburgers in hand.

The opening stand up comic act entered stage left, announced to the Club audience it was 'The biggest urinal he had the pleasure Of working in' pointing to the ceramic tile wall's floor to ceiling, I paid him off after his first set. Following live acts included 'The Rocky Horror Show' kindly staged by the cast who were appearing at the Grand Theatre on a UK tour, with established regular live gigs Gino Washington and the 'Ram Jam Band'. In direct contrast author of 'The naked civil servant' Quentin Crisp graced our club with an invitation to his 'question and answer' evening personal interview, much to the consternation of the 450 audience who did not quite know what to make of his distinguished appearance. Pianist Mike Terry of 'Wheel tappers and Shunters' ITV series was fully supported by the cast and crew from the Leeds Grand Theatre. The lighting was designed by Geoff Riley who later joined Northern Contemporary Dance as their lighting resident designer, posthumously named their Theatre after him in 1980. He had become a frequent visitor and a valued intimate friend and member of 'Gladrags' The 'Kenny Everett's dancers' adapted their TV routine and later Helen Shapiro the 60s pop star did a one night gig. Other guest artists appearing at the Leeds BBC Television Studio at the time were Yorkshire Television's 'Emmerdale' cast and crew supported the opening weeks, as I was in the cast of the series at the time, Keith and I had just finished a few days shooting on the set of the 'Chariots of Fire' in York on location.

We arranged an interviewed for opening night in the club with Radio Leeds for their 'What's on' programme and the live entertainment was reviewed in 'The Stage' news paper. For two years it was a roller coaster of highs and lows. The novelty wore off as the second winter approached the second year of the lease. Quentin Crisp appeared as himself at 'An evening with' before he left to live in America. Running the club together seven days and half the night was exhausting, Keith and I decided to sell the business after the second year as our commitment to it and each other had gone. The fact that our relationship had also suffered, partly due to my bipolar condition, and Keith's heavy drinking became a cocktail for disaster. Exhausted in the second year we lost interest and sold the Club before the end of the lease. It was the beginning of the end of the change in our relationship after twenty three years.

I will be so brief I have already finished -Salvador Dali

LONDON
FLIGHT OF FANCY - 1984

I WALKED FOR three hours before getting a cab to Regents Park, my intention of providing funds to charity evaporated into the cold night. Arriving at the reception of my apartment building, nodded to the uniformed doorman who touched his peaked cap in deference as the dawn chorus was breaking, and took the lift to the penthouse for a welcome hot shower followed by a strong black coffee. Sleep was out of the question as I had decided to take a flight to Los Angeles to the auction house of Sotheby's. After an hour checking my email and packing a small valise,

I ordered a cab on-line and minutes later checked in at the Heathrow terminal. My habit of grabbing sleep at thirty five thousand feet gave me the option of mobility with an element of rest as part of multiple tasking I found it attractive. During the eight hour flight I was seduced by the dream of acquiring the painting legally or otherwise. I set the wheels in motion putting a call through on Skype to Claudette who answered a little wearily as she had just completed fifteen lengths of backstroke in her pool before breakfast. Grabbing a towel and her cell phone she breathed 'Hi Paulie where are you now'? Hesitating a moment before replying 'on the way to the airport Claudette I shall be with you in a few hours' 'Ok sweetie I can't wait to see you after so long,' and cut the call short. He understood her abbreviated reply to speak volumes; smiled and completed packing to leave London on the LAX flight from Heathrow.

In my fifth decade having enjoyed peripatetic years on the sunshine- coast of California between LA and San Francisco I decided to return to Europe as mother needed help at the age of 85, so four five years I nursed her at my home for the last five years. On my return to the UK I decided after the death of mother at the age of 91 in the new millennium to travel to Goa the sunshine state in India which had by then become 'Little Moscow 'with Russian tourists. The sybaritic location offered multiple personal contacts but I was none the wiser as to the machination and complexities of human behaviour, but did learn you can't take the bias out of bigotry.

Before leaving San Fransisco my old friend Billy Holdroyd a British ex-pat asked me to deliver a car he had sold to a client in Los Angeles an Oldsmobile 1969 V8 Classic from Monterey and he needed it to be delivered to his customer in East Los Angeles. Due to his commitments he was not able to drive it down the Pacific coast highway so he asked me, as I was going to LA I agreed. I enjoyed the eleven hour drive down the Big Sur coast from Northern California Monterey past 'Hearst Castle' through south LA to Watts in south central south Los Angeles, some seven hundred odd miles journey. The Corvette car was sleek black and powerful, an exotic combination of a design statement of American Classic automobiles. At my journeys end I delivered the car to his Purchaser, it gave me the added bonus of seeing 'Watts Tower' an architectural Ikon created by Architect Simon Rodia at the front of the house in the south central neighbourhood known as the hood in Watts and Compton home of the 'Bloods' gang.

Gladrags Theatre Club

Chapter 09

MY HYPOMANIA

In the summer of 1995 my GP diagnosed my clinical depression referred me to a year's specialist clinical observation as out patient at The Royal Free Hospital London for twelve months for tests as a suitable candidate for therapy. I was diagnosed suffering from a Bi-polar condition as a disability. The doctor prescribed medication which made my invisible condition worse in my considering suicidal thoughts. After months of delusional self harm, I decided to stop taking the prescribed pills. The discovery of recognising and knowing the symptoms added to learning to control the hypo-ups with manic-downs after realising I was on a Bi-polar roller coaster. The diagnosed condition indicated a direct physiological hormonal imbalance affecting the forty billion cell syntax neuron contacts. The symptoms manifest in sudden and extreme neurological mood changes, an illustration in point was as if by touching a white hot poker or deep frozen metal it creates a similar reaction of a burning sensation. The brain reacts without the sense of touch before the actual event. This condition can provide the occasional bizarre reaction, not exactly an attractive feature while engaged in social interaction or understanding intimate relationships. My episodic depression and irritability created an emotional liability over the years, especially tears and anger with rapid changes in cyclical bipolar disorder, hard to endure in relationships.

Hypomania Bipolar episodes, is a mood state characterised by a persistent disinhibited pervasive elevated or euphoric mood, with a rapid irritation mood less severe than full mania. Characteristic behaviour is extremely energetic talkative and confidence commonly exhibited with a flight of creative ideas. While hypomania behaviour often generates productivity and excitement it can become troublesome if the subject engages in risky behaviour, according to symptomatic severity, associated hypomania constitutes the first stage or stage one of the syndrome wherein the cardinal features, euphoria or heightened irritability, pressure of speech and activity increased energy decreases the need for sleep, the flight of ideas are most plainly evident.

Source: christopher M Doran (2008) 'The hypomania Handbook 'The challenge of elevated mood'

CLINICAL DEPRESSION

People with manic-depressive illness and those who are creative share certain features: the ability to function well on a few hours sleep, the focus to work intensively and an ability to experience depth and variety of emotion. Where depression questions, ruminates and hesitates, mania answers with vigour and certainty. As against five percent of the general population who met the diagnostic criteria for a mood disorder, thirty per cent artists and writers needed treatment, and fifty per cent of the poets — the largest fraction from any one group had needed much extensive care. : Source. Kay Redfield Jamison, Professor of Psychiatry, John Hopkins University School of Medicine

BIPOLAR

THE PHYSIOLOGICAL CAUSE

I thought it necessary to understand my mental condition fully, with the aspect of its existence that involves the consciousness in critical Physiological causation. In basic brain activity, neurons communicate in the production of thought to process emotional memories and sensations. The cells send and receive messages through Axon or trunks branching out to gaps called Synaps. The actual messages flow across these gaps carried in the form of chemical molecules called neuro-transmitters to create electrical signals that can be measured by EEG. Some of these neuro-transmitters are known, for example as the hypothalamus Which process serotonin, a chemical substance which is influential in depression and a bipolar condition. The scientific term for the transmission Of electrochemical signal from one neuron to another is connected when the production of serotonin is evident biologically in the brain, as insufficient serotonin in the brain affects the Synaps connectivity.

Biological psychology(BBC Radio 4) announced 19 June 2018 that new studies show conditions in the womb of a pregnant mother communicates to the child connected through the placenta during pregnancy, stressed emotional trauma experienced by the mother directly exposes the unborn child to stress hormones across the Placenta biologically. This addresses an unborn susceptibility to depression and a predisposition as infant to inherited DNA intergenerational genetic brain function. These complex points of disorder impacts on future organic brain function in the diagnosis of clinical depression as a bipolar condition of behaviour and anxiety in mental illness. The emotional interconnectivity affects connection of the mother and child, influencing the relevant stressful response.

In the Journal of psychopharmacology, BAP, Guidelines confirming the known aetiology of bipolar disorder as primarily genetic, with heritability as high as 0.93 in 2004. This means it is one of the most heritable disorders in medicine. Genome- wide association studies have now been conducted on sufficiently large samples to give complete confidence in a growing number of specific genes. Bipolar disorder is highly polygenic so leaving little room for causation, by rare genes Of large effect. These positive findings confirm that DSM diagnosis has some biological validity. Current strategies emphasis the treatment and prevention of syndromal relapse, disabling aspects of long term outcome such as chronic depressive symptoms, mood instability, co-morbid anxiety, it is usual to think of bipolar disorder as a sequence of acute illness episodes (mania, depression, or mixed states interspersed with relative euthymia.

The delivery of effective treatment within BAP guidelines illustrates a need for a service model. The neglect of bipolar patients in UK government policy 2002 justifies our restating the obvious. The term bipolar disorder or manic depression was given no special consideration and entirely omitted from the glossary of key terms in the national service framework for mental illness, which is inappropriate to bipolar disorder in the United Kingdom (Department of Health 1999). It remains a monolithic social model of acute mental illness 2007. Bipolar disorder has been a relatively neglected condition. Their is a lack of understanding among policy makers of the need for high quality specialised services for bipolar patients, either in relation to early intervention or to provision of adult services in the Department of Health's national service framework in the UK.

Mental Health Provision : January 2018

Prime Minister May promised extra funds of over six billion pounds for NHS mental health made in the budget and confirmed by the Secretary of State for Health Lucciana Burgess MP on 22-01-2018, the funds were not ring fenced and had been drawn on for other health procurement.

The Royal College Society of Psychiatry spokesperson Dr Sandy Laroo said on BBC 'Today' programme though training had started, it was a long way off being able to deliver a mental health pathway service commensurate with the expertise required as a shortfall of 40,000 nurses nationwide 5,000 trained nurses in mental health had not yet reached the frontline patient: therefore 22-01-2018 BBC radio reported access to a full NHS mental health service was lacking. It will take a three year effective training period before a comprehensive mental health provision could be provided until 2020/21. Mental health is accepted as a personal priority by the Prime Minister supported by law passed in Parliament 2014 for parity of treatment in the NHS.

• In June 2018 Minister for the Disabled Sara Newton MP confirmed that the government appointed agencies paper based claimant patient review had received 26,000 appeals, which would now be based on face to face interview system for the physically disabled for those whose benefit had been reduced or stopped due to the adopted new point system.

To explore the boundaries of 'Three brains in one', the brain is not a single object additional levels of complexity are grouped by function. First the brain stem at the top of the spinal cord. Second the limbic region, which includes the Hippocampus located in the temporal lobe. Another significant part of the limbic system is the amygdala which plays a critical role in emotional memory. Linked to significant biological reactions, events that generate strong biological response such as release of hormones occur. These message patterns can be stored or triggered in more personal experiences of a highly charged nature. Activities of the limbic system or 'Emotional brain' balanced by the third and most recently developed layer of the brain, the Neocortex. This layer provides capacity for reasoning and imagination. The human Neocortex develope into a larger more complex structure over hundreds and thousands years, providing Homo erectus with the capacity for language, Writing music, art, and empathising with others. The production of a single thought requires a series of complex interactions among all three layers of the 100 billion brain cells. This bio-physical support system offers the concept of the mind as a perpetually unfolding experience of the self which is actually an illusion generated by the unceasing flow of thoughts emotions, sensations and perceptions. Experience changes the neuronal structure of the brain that perpetuates the experience of self. In the natural mind there is no rejection or acceptance, no loss or gain.

In mindfulness, the Buddhist tradition and practice of 'how,' lies in learning to rest in the awareness of thought, feelings and perceptions or sensations. Becoming mindful is a gradual process of establishing new neuronal connections, neither rejection or of acceptance, but acknowledge the experience and to let it pass.

MY SUBJECTIVE DESCRIPTION
Of the disorder

This description is anecdotal, someone asked me to describe what it is like to suffer Bipolar disorder. To relate the question to a relevant scenario is like arriving at Disney world with friends. They want me to join them on the big dipper. To share in the roller coaster ride in an attempt to share the journey and experience the ride. When we get on board to be connected into the seat with the safety belt strapped firmly with a safety bar secured in-situ. We start the journey in a rapid climb which develops immediately into an episode of despicable manic horror for me as in an out of body experience. From a complete high to enter into sudden and abrupt traumatic physical lows, the turbulence is followed by agonizing physical response as the anxious emotional revulsion intensifies. Disconnected, I see my friends are exhilarated, clearly enjoying their experience of the ride which I am not. During the repeated experience, absolute panic sets in with the realisation that I can't get off this trajectory. My repulsion is not over as the ride continues onward accelerating upward, toward an immediate non-gravitational descent. My feeling of desperate panic intensifies in complete helplessness feeling out of control, this offers a physical analogy. My perception and subjective emotional response continues from a physiological chemical imbalance of the brain, as this contributes to my mood disorder. This out of control feeling of helplessness continues on the big dipper called Life. Depression is a dryness of the heart that sometimes made the Mahatma Gandhi 'want to run away from the world'. The Dalai Lama referred to it as thoughts and emotions that undermine the experience of inner peace.

John Keats the writer told 'If I were under water, I would scarcely kick to come to the top'

'No great mind has ever existed without a touch of madness'
Aristotle

Suicide is taking one's life to get rid of feelings of emptiness hopelessness, guilt or shame. Mental disorders including depression, bipolar disorder, schizophrenia, personality disorders, overly anxious, agitated substance abuse and alcohol are all reasons leading to suicide. Learn to be sensitive to those you care for and their needs and be an empathetic listener and develop a strong communication bond. No person who ends their life wants to die but just end the pain, hurt hopelessness and loneliness. We need to realise that the one who takes his or her life does not see an alternative other than death as their only escape.

A support system and talking about suicide is more that helpful for the one whose thinking or attempting it, as it allows them to express their plan and allows you to connect and understand the world the suicidal person is trapped in. This could enable you to guide or nudge him/her to seek medical help as needed depending on the severity, as the true meaning of hope is living. I suppose it was inevitable there was no moonlight only the reflection of a bright string of lights on the water outside the beach bars on Calangute beach as I walked past the edge of the lapping waves. It was nearly midnight and tourists were leaving their last drink at their watering hole. Suddenly a figure of a man with purpose walked diagonally in front of me a few feet away toward the sea. Not stopping or deviating he just carried on walking into the waves ignoring me. I wondered if a midnight swim to cool off was his intention but he carried on into the waves without hesitation. By now he was shoulder deep into the heaving current, not stopping his trajectory as the water closed in around him and his head completely enveloped by the tidal wave he was gone. I sat on the sandy beach waiting full ten minutes for him to reappear on the surface of the water but he did not. The breeze gently touched

the waves which once closed in on him. He had gone for good, or
bad. Within minutes another man appeared running from the bar
stopping beside me visibly shaken and asked if I had seen a friend of
his as they were returning to go to the hotel to collect their cases for
the airport taxi after one last drink. I described what I had seen and
the man who had gone into the sea. Horror spread across his face as
had spent the night at the bar listening to his friend say he did not
want to return to his job, home or way of life. I said I did not think
his friend would return and advised him to accept the inevitability of
life or in this case his death.

THE PROGNOSIS

My mercurial response was put to good use, with a natural creative talent I actively processed ideas like blowing up helium balloons releasing them into the sky one after another. Equally, success followed failure while accumulating experience and acumen over the years. I savoured every experience as a duck to water sometimes sinking sometimes swimming. My hyperactivity challenged an instinct to survive and prosper, with care not to explore the depth of intimacy in finite relationships. I took commercial risks anxiously endured nights of insomnia with days of endless hyper manic activity as my medical condition enabled me not being able to turn off an energy tap.

In the early 80's Prime Minister Margaret Thatcher was at political war with the coal miners union and President Arthur Scargill was the protagonist. This strike virtually closed all coal production down, and in autumn the British public had no access to this thermal source of energy in the winters of 1984/85. The strike was a major national industrial action and shut down the British coal production, enforcing divisive confrontation. Mrs Thatcher called the miners 'The enemy within'.

At this time I developed an idea to go to Lanarkshire on the Scottish border to visit local farmers to locate the availability of Peat. I drove up to the border and talked to the farming community, deciding to follow the source for the demand for energy to heat the home fires in whose English hearth had been extinguished as no coal was available. I bought an Old ten ton truck driving through the night. I gave cash to Farmer's, filled the truck to the roof with the crop, with peat logs and returned to Leeds within two days to bag it into bright yellow PVC sacks. I printed the message 'Peat Heat' on a large red flame, distributed the 20kg bags to garage forecourt retailers to be picked up by their domestic customers for their homes in Bradford and Leeds area as an alternative solid fuel. This profitable journey was repeated by me regularly during the one year strike as I had satisfied a definite need to hundreds of customers to keep their home fires burning successfully.

HIDE AND SEEK

After the private members club was sold, Keith and I moved to an old brewery with an attached house where we started producing handmade leather hide stuff-over furniture and started to export into Europe. My blind friend Michael and I would go by the ferry to Hoeke of Holland fully loaded with our furniture delivery driving through Brussels in Belgium down the Autobahn to Bavaria south Germany in Michael's company in shared humour and companionship throughout the trip to arrive in Munich to the final destination the English Strasser furniture showroom. During a previous meeting I had received an order in a chance meeting with Herr Menchen who was desperate to fulfil the waiting list of his rich client's orders. On our first visit after walking passed the extensive windows of the opulent display frontage we decided to walk in and became engaged in conversation with the owner of the showroom. During our meeting the offer of his challenge was 'If we could supply he would buy, we negotiated a cost priced to close the order. After high tailing it back to the UK to our Leeds workshop I realising a meeting with the Bank would be necessary to make an appointment. Our bank manager wanted to see the order on official letterheads for verification and decided to visit us at our place of production during which to our surprise he extended a loan against the production cost, we were in business. This impressed our new customer and allowed us to confirm delivery on time as he repeated customer orders monthly with further increased deliveries. Until one fateful day, the second year, a new retail customer had provided a deposit, but did not pay the balance of their order after its delivery to the detached mansion the balance was not forthcoming we decided to take it back without Unloading the completed order and returned it to our works. The negative impact on cash flow prompted the bank to warn us of possible foreclosure. Three months later sales of all our assets cleared the account to zero, and we had to walk away and start over. To realize risk is always balanced by mixed good fortune and the vagaries of economy. It was becoming too much for Keith and we decided to finally go our separate ways. The pressure triggered my depression when I realized the futility Of losing the material world, something we had built up over the years With property as Keith had vanished overnight. For the next six weeks the banks official ultimatum was to advise us to sell all our assets, with the workshop site calling in on the business loan, a sudden and dramatic reality. A goal to the future became a vehicle which had crashed in a write off.

CHINA
CHANGING TIMES

My sabbatical and peripatetic bus journeys in the Himalayas in Nepal and train journeys to Hyderabad became a pilgrimage. Watching Sunrise on Dahl Lake in Kashmir or travelling by car through Manipor. Bus journey's through Assam to Sikkim, flights to Chennai, Pondicherry and Bengal. These retreats became an Oasis and sanctuary for me over the many years travelling, always the journey not the arrival.

In the year 2000 I travelled to China with my friend Eric Rao to his home town of Guangzhou in Guangdong Province. Our first stop was a flight to Hong Kong for a week, taking the ferry to the lift built by the engineer from Scotland up onto the mountain top overlooking Kowloon Island and the panorama beyond. We took the fast train from Hong Kong traveled through small family communities, this offered fascinating glimpses Of medieval villages. Farming communities tended their crop in the fields to market, in direct contrast to the cityscape of high rise development and modern commercial zones supported by migrant workers leaving the countryside for the factories to produce goods for export. During the few hours journey this prospect offered an endless stream of human activity during our following thirty days in China mainland in Guangdong Province. Guang Zhou had been chosen by central government in Bejing as one of the five zones for modernisation and Industrial development by Chairman Xiou Pin to bring it into the 21st century. Eric's family apartment home was next to an office complex a hive of activity with three shifts of workers 24 hours seven days a week. As a result of this herculean effort, building one floor a week was completed without disruption. The hard hat workers scrambled all over the site working by spotlight through the busy night and through the daytime by three shifts of workers as thirty floors had been completed during my month stay. Eric's father was Professor of Hydrology at Ghuanghou University. He worked for the regional government and his brief was to search for water required in the development of the new city in his region and its growing population. His mother taught at a city elementary school, she showed me round the family's expansive veranda surrounded their second floor apartment. Later, dinner was served with hot steaming rice and noodle soup with beef garlic, peppers, peanuts and radishes. After a week in the busy heaving metropolis we all decided to go to Gueylin a few hour's drive to the countryside in the company limousine, this was organised by Eric's sister who was married to a property developers lawyer. We stopped on the way at a midday rural restaurant where our party all sat round a table where lunch in multiple servings of food was cooked from the menu and served. Delicious duck in an unguent Plum sauce, with bright coloured vegetables in large steaming bowls carried through from the kitchen. More food kept on arriving attended by smiling waiters. After an hour as soon as my plate was empty I could eat no more, and asked Eric why the food still kept on arriving in such vast quantities when other guests at our table had finished their meal. I was politely informed by Eric who whispered in my ear that if I did not want more food I should leave a small amount on my plate to signify that I had eaten enough as this was the custom in China. As a foreigner not knowing this cultural nicety I tried to hide my embarrassment by excusing myself and left the room to relieve my aching stomach in the courtyard outside, before returning to hot towels brought in to end the feast. Our journey continued on through beautiful landscape along the west bank of the Li River on the border of Hunan, arriving at the twin Pagodas where we walked along the two lakes. The following night we took a night cruise along the Pearl River with the lights of the city reflected on the surface dancing and bobbing in the breeze. The all too short happy month came to an end, the last few days was spent with Eric's family I was effected by their warmth and genuine hospitality. It gave me insight in the need to accept that we are all same human race. Our return to London was tinged with sadness. This had been an epic journey as I had retained a childhood dream to go to this land of mystery since my school days, and was impressed by the changes in the contrast of modernist material ambition required to rush into the millennium, versus ancient communal traditions.

You go Uruguay, and I'll go mine.

Groucho Marx

I met Bala Jeda on the Candolim beach in Goa as I was sunbathing one morning in March with the sun rising over the Arabian Sea. I heard him say 'Would you like my strawberries' I sat up opening my eyes. He stood close beside me holding a tray, each carton filled with luscious red strawberries glistening in the intense sun like jewels. He sat down on the sand in front of me with a fixed gaze put the tray before me temptingly 'Best price for you my friend.' Staring into my eyes he was assured of holding my interest. We shook hands exchanging names while smiling at each other. I was the first to say 'If you don't sell them now to tourists I will take what is left at the end of the day'. Bala rose to his feet, 'how long will you stay here '? Oh 'All day,' and 'will you be here when I come back? Yes' and he walked off down the beach. I woke up in a torpor from dozing in the midday heat as Bala had returned with the tray still nearly full of unsold fruit 'he sat offering them 'take them please,' oh 'I can't carry them home on my two wheeler you will have to bring them to the house on the pillion seat' he looked at me with his bright intelligent eyes and a spark of recognition crossed his face. We drove slowly in the cool sea breeze past swaying coconut palms over the paddy field lanes toward Saligao village. After entering the garden gate of my bungalow compound, Bala 'carried the tray into the house leaving it on the kitchen table smiling turned toward me and asked, 'Can I have 'Pani' water and sat down at the table. I poured him a glass of iced water from the fridge which he drank in great gulps, spilling the water which ran down the skin of his slender dark fingers, coating them in a translucent film to the colour Of ripened tobacco in contrast of the dried dust. His red cotton tee shirt stretched across his smooth olive chest as he threw his head back laughing, he noticed me staring at him. He folded his arms behind his head, sitting back in the chair exposing his swimmers flat waist and toned bronze torso. His sensuous lips moved in animated curves on white teeth as he spoke, attractive dimples danced on his cheeks with a warm smile. Expressive eyes set beneath heavy eyebrows under a clusters of black shiny curls framed his fresh youthful face. He drank in great gulps as his skin glowed with beads of perspiration in the heat of day.

Bala got up slowly to wash the glass at the sink he turned to place it on the table and followed me into the house. No word was exchanged between us, an expectant glance held promise. We arrived at the foot of the day bed in the lounge on which we sat eagerly leaning forward in embrace following the ebb and tide of energy between us. As if dreaming of a far-off sound, our mutual passion turned into a tidal wave crashing with strong currents onto a hot beach. When the pounding of the waves ceased we lay in tender embrace in each other's arms. talking of future dreams until sunset with the night closing in. More days and months of hedonistic paradise followed in coexistence. Balla's sweet nature and simplicity gave him a keen perception, understanding without judgement or prejudice in joyful expectation of trust. Bala loved his family and on his twentieth birthday his parents picked him a suitable bride from his village in Andra Pradesh as the tradition and custom in India. His family decreed it and the deed was done. His new wife, a sixteen year Old second cousin chosen by his parents to fulfil the role they had chosen for him. Three aborted pregnancies later a baby girl was born, two years later Bala was happy to play with his baby daughter, but became bored by his wives ignorance and illiteracy. Their future union appealed to him less as time went by, and he hoped a second child would fill the void of loveless copulation. The plurality of purpose and the continued relationship remained constant. His marriage was a surprise to me but an acceptance of fact to him as his family expectation was as fixed as the moon in trajectory of the night sky. As if in a dream his wife screamed aloud and woke the baby to see its little face suckling on her breast. The baby lost its grip with its tiny teeth on her nipple before it tippled down her chest, landing on her lap which did not please her much, bounced off landing near mummy's feet. The babies howling brought comments from her husband, Balla cried out 'Oh what a noise it makes'. Mummy cried if you fell 'wouldn't you', within seconds, she was about the baby rubbing its little head with her gentle hand to make it better. Husband Balla moaned, well it's better than me at landing, 'when she bounced off your teat' he said looking at his wife. She turned and glared at him directly in his face to shut him up.' What do you mean you didn't say that when you fell upon me the first time.' His face reddened as he reckoned she was right: 'But you held tight before I let you go' he chuckled. Hearing him say that she slapped him hard 'what did you do that for?' he frowned, rubbing his cheek. His wife sighed, well it happened so infrequently' I did not think to hang your coat on it before you landed on my bed', with that she hurried off wrapping her Sari over her head to leave the room. A minute later the little baby meanwhile had been pacified by Daddiji Balla who returned to the scene. On hearing his baby cry, picking up the infant as it lay at mummy's feet. 'Thank God your here' said mum returning hearing him whisper sweet nothings, she thought he would not neglect the child. 'Never fear while Daddy's here' he said breathing over the little mite as he'd just returned from drinking a libation. In vexation his wife rose up from her chair and stared at him,' the baby's fine' she hollered. In your absence' I got to thinking, well, if he is out drinking, baby can drink as well.' 'Oh Nagama' he hugged his young wife in sad regret. She struggled from his embrace and said 'the babies got to feed' as her little mouth was chomping hard upon my breast',' and we will have none of that.

GRAVITATION

I gravitated toward beauty developed in the eye of the beholder, fixing my focus on art as predator to its prey to fulfil my gratification. The symbiosis, between passive and active participation merged into a subjective reality and became my modus operandi of choice. I understood love to be a force of energy embracing the predator and its prey in the ecstasy of gratification. The gravitational pull drove me to ignore boundaries and borders while migrating in seasonal flight. I believe animism to be the immortality of spirituality of the soul, and recognised that the human desire of beauty was a universal corruption of the mind. The thirteenth moon in a year is referred to as Blue moon, extra days in a year occur in a leap year. Electromagnetic pathways occur on the surface of the Earth, scientific knowledge discovers energy is matter relative to the Earth trajectory. Our physical body radiates electromagnetic energy in voltaic measurement resonating in synchronicity being existential to our existence. Our understanding of the oceans currents and tides, the electro-chemical balance of tidal waves originates from the moon. We gravitate to certain people inexplicably, and react negatively to others subjectively without warning. The dismal leaden sky, an easterly wind blows through the leafless branches fallen dry and brittle. A grey winter's day fades into black soon against dusk of sunset to moon light The shadow of the elliptic moon creeping over the oblique face forward in motion on a trajectory round the earth in gravitational pull lights the continuity of human life through millenia.

We held each other in an embrace before Bala stepped into to the back seat of the Tuk-tuk taxi. It set off lurching down the long drive over deep potholes like a noisy perambulator through swaying palm fronds into the distance. t waved farewell as he reached the busy main road. Bala turned to look through the rear window as he blew a kiss which landed at my feet like a silent bomb igniting the pain of parting. I Stood still a few moments before turning away under dark clouds moving across the grey sky before the falling rain mixed with fresh tears running down my cheeks. For the next five months we endured another long wait until our meeting in Nepal.

Behind me, the sea beat against rocks on the beach where we had walked together in the early morning mist. We had shared an understanding that our two halfs were greater than a whole throughout the ten years but our loss was not forgotten. We would survive time and tide of sorrow that swept into waves of the monsoon sea behind us.

I stood alone with my thoughts before walking back on the path to the cabin we had shared for a month then closed the door behind me to brew green tea. We had often made tea with lemon in the afternoon, his with sugar, mine fresh coffee with powdered cream as fresh milk was scarce and often unavailable in the island's local shops. The rest of the day I busied myself filling in time with small things wondering if I should pack to leave the following morning for my return to London not India. Bala had returned to Andrah Pradesh to his family. His father had sadly passed away suddenly a few weeks ago before his wife's father who had been in a coma passed away the night before. We had shared a transient month together as a gift that was suddenly over. Like life, nothing lasts forever, but next time we would be together in Kathmandu before Christmas.

INDIA
CORRUPTION

I was approached out of monsoon season one day by Franco, a partner and brother in the 'Hotel Roya'l on Calangute beach in Goa. Striking up a conversation while walking the beach in the last of the monsoon rain, he proposed his interest of leasing me a temporary shack he owned on the Calangute beach, the property was used during the tourist season as a beach restaurant 'would I be interested', after negotiating the details and signing the contract as part of the deal the following month I gave him twenty five thousand rupee (two hundred and fifty pounds sterling) deposit toward the agreed fee, on his written assurance that all permissions and licenses would be performed by him as a notarised agreement which he did. I looked forward with pleasure to summer on the beach. After refurbishing what was a timber frame to transform it to a workable enterprise took the labour of my team from Nepal headed by 'Zero' to give an attractive refurbished addition to the tourist beach. I was pleased after several weeks it was ready to open.

The other two Franco brothers decided that they would turn off the water supply and the electricity cable supply was cut with a knife and several verbal threats made to my staff that they would meet with dire consequence should they assist the foreigner to open for business, I was dismayed but ignored it. The week before the planned opening a team of local youth's directly outside the entrance played basket ball, they kicking the ball repeatedly through the access door intentionally. The ball rolled repeatedly several times inside the entrance for over an hour in apparent Provocation, they just walked in casually to collect the ball without acknowledgment. I asked them to stop. My request caused both sides to kick the ball toward me screaming expletives. After an hour of this I decided to call the Police, the control room sent a plain clothes officer to investigate the scene after the volley ball team vanished and had left the beach. The officer said I should go with him to Calangute Police station assist them 'to sort things out'. An hour later I drove my car with the legal registered contract of agreement and necessary documents. On arrival at the Saligao police station shown to into a back office and surprised to see the Volley ball team from the beach assembled in the room, As I entered the Sub-inspector shouted at me to sit, feeling threatened and sensing an impending confrontation I decided to leave and avoid any further exchange. I turned to the door an said 'I would return later.' At my response he called out in Konkani, local Goan language a command, I was forcibly stopped by fourteen uniformed officers who assaulted me physically by knocking me to the ground. They punched me on the face, kicked me in the ribs, head and ears. I became dazed and literarily thrown into a cell and left for seventy two hours without food or my prescribed medication until the following Monday 72 hours custody.

At the age of 69 I was taken in a police jeep with four officers to the Mapusa civil magistrate court without legal representation or my prescribed medication. I must have looked the part of a miscreant without being allowed to bath or a change of fresh clothes, After a perfunctory look at me and the police order form, the duty Magistrate stamped the paper and continued on with her busy case load on the bench without further enquiry. Directly driven by the police from the court to the Bambolim General Medical Collage emergency ward where first aid was administered in the emergency department. The emergency Doctor asked the two police escort's to wait outside the cubicle while she attended to me. She wanted to know how I received the wounds and contusions I told her the details as she attended to my wounds. She said 'this was not the first time this had happened to foreigners at the hands of the Police' and signed my medical report accordingly. Under the Indian constitutional law persons over 60 must not be assaulted physically as it is a criminal offence to do so. The Police ignored this, in my case their attack on me was unprovoked, the incident took place on record 2010. I was moved by police vehicle directly from the A & R General Medical Hospital to the behavioural psychiatric department at Bambolim. The police reported my court order to the Doctor who took me to the Hospital lock-up ward where I was incarcerated for two weeks under custodial observation and given multiple test assessment. After the third week a panel of three Doctors gave me a clean bill of mental health. The three independent psychiatrist's in agreement signed my release form, as 'they found no reason for me to be there' apart from a hypo episode. They also 'confirmed my IQ of 170' a great surprise to me, stated on my green legal release form. I took no civil action against the police authority, as my Advocate Anthony thought it better to 'let sleeping dogs lie'. My neighbour Kate had contacted the British Consul in Panaji who had intervened and visited me twice in the lock-up ward. I gave them my thousand word statement detailed report of the incident and of the assault. The British foreign office in London accepted this with the UK Consul file duly noted with the Indian authorities through the UK foreign office. Before the incident I had visited Inspector Wilson the Chief Inspector of Calangute Police station at the time in 2008. I reported to him personally that his duty officers had allowed a brothel to remain open on the public beach, and his officers were taking commission in cash or kind (so to speak) for all to see and this should not be treated with covert acquiescence. As a consequence his response was to orchestrate the physical assault on my person in the station. The mental trauma was intended to inhibit further action being taken by me as the official complainant.

Inspector Wilson and his sub-inspector the protagonist were fully aware of the situation by allowing it to continue. I phoned Goa's Chief Constable Braar on his Personal cell phone and home phone after I came out of hospital. This surprise approach elicited his response 'how did you get my phone number. I responded, Chief Constable 'it is irrelevant,' what is relevant is that you should be aware of what is happening in your constabulary then gave him details. A week after my leaving Hospital Inspector Wilson was immediately transferred from Calangute police station to Canacona in south Goa to take care of the flora and fauna constituents. I cannot believe that it was only as a result of my contact with his boss, I am grateful however to the Police authority to respond in such a responsible manner after the event. I could have been killed or maimed at their hands as so many other foreigners have been violated as reported in the media outside the mandate of the Indian Constitution.

The official post mortem of a 15 year old girl raped and murdered on the beach at Anjuna by two youths some months later came to International media attention. The miscreants were on bail in police custody, with no further action taken against them. Five years later September 2016 they were released with no case to answer. It was fully detailed as reported in the International syndicated media. The UK Government sent a team from Scotland Yard CID to Goa, India, were met with a degree of uncooperative silence in assistance for a positive result to be allowed to come to light. They returned to the UK with no police cooperation offered, such are the methods employed by Goa's Police Authorities from their Indian counterpart. Many other incidences are reported in the public domain and U-tube social network, subsequently met with similar lack of action due to political pressure and opposition to bad publicity which does not ingratiate the travelling international tourist to the bosom of Goa when planning a travel itinerary in India as a safe place for family and friends.

Single foreign women on their own have been assaulted by the Goan male taxi driver fraternity severally, arrested for rape on many occasions over the years. Another miscreant allegedly charged for assault and rape of a twelve year old Russian girl on Bambolim Beach, the son of cabinet Minister Monseratte was out on bail, It will take years for the case to get to a court by which time the victim would not probably be in the country or wish to be reminded of her ordeal after decades of trying to come to terms with the criminal assault physically to her and the more permanent psychological damage. In 2015 women drivers were employed for taxi's driving female passengers in the state as antidote alternative to the problem.

CORRUPTION

The sad saga of two former chief Ministers

Are they guilty as charged?, when the names Chief Minister Digambar Kamat and Churchill Alemao Minister for public works at the time who were arrested 15 August 2015 are mentioned to a Goan. An image of unbridled corruption appears of unfulfilled dreams, and the negligent and dysfunctional governance who squandered the public's patrimony in the interest of personal gain. Somehow the sight of these two former Chief Ministers fighting to stay out of jail put smiles on their faces proclaiming innocence in the face of one of the high profile corruption scandals. The Lewis Berger scandal opened the floodgates of unchecked corruption. Unites States federal bureau of investigation looked into the alleged payment of $3.9 million dollars in bribes paid by Lewis Berger International to foreign officials in several countries. Churchill Alemao was Minister for public works when the project was awarded in 2009-10 and Digambar Kamat was Chief Minister. Among the projects now under investigation is the multi-crore Japanese funded Goa water supply and sewerage project that prosecutors say involved pay-offs to the highest ranking officials in Goa. Because of the slow Indian judicial system and culture of impunity, it is unlikely the Lewis Berger scandal, will in the end claim the freedom of the former ministers. The best they can hope for is to be given bail by the court.

HERALDO NEWS Panaji, Goa

A kingfisher flies

As a bird of prey dips a long beak into the water to catch the biggest fish it can find. Its focus of attention is disturbed only by the intensity of light to follow its prey. The chairman of the board Mr Vijay Malia Chairman and CEO of United Breweries used the same technique when he avoided paying his pilots and the ground crew of his Kingfisher Airline in India for six months. The ground staff waited patiently some months to receive payment of their salaries to no avail. The Government cancelled his operating license due to unpaid taxes to fly, the Indian Airport Authority still waits for payment of landing fees, servicing and fuel bills to be settled. At the annual general meeting, The Chairman claimed insufficient funds were available to pay outstanding fees and employee wages. His employees became creditors and remained hungry. Shareholders can wait, but if whole families cannot pay their rent and mortgages, their table is bare of food for families and children's education and expectant aspirations ground to a stop. A shareholder stood up and was allowed a question, 'why does the Chairman who is a majority shareholder in Kingfisher Airlines still has 480 Crore in an account in a Mauritius bank in his name. 'He replied 'It's mine and nothing to do with company funds. It will not be used to pay any account outstanding' and he brought the general meeting to a close. Mr Malia advertised he was 'the King of good times,' his not yours. It would be easy to say that he is guilty of dereliction of duty or that he misled the very people who supported him with credit loans and labour services, this man performed a miracle. Christ changed water into wine for wedding guests Mr V J. Mailia changed beer into gold at his own parties. That said the small guy always looses out against the big guy without the financial clout to take him to Court. Twenty years is not uncommon for the imperceptible wheels of Indian justice to grind along, who is able to bear the cost. The Indian Government however is able, but unwilling to do so. It seems no one in Government wants to stand up and be counted to take up the challenge on behalf of the citizen's of India who lost their livelihood, could there be a separate agenda. In June 2016 the story of the Supreme Court order, as the media reported his assets, the amount of $240 Crore to be taken by the Court toward his creditors. Mr Malia's reply to the press was that 'he thought his case was motivated politically'. In 2016 he flew as domicile to the UK as fugitive from India Supreme Court's ruling. In 2017 UK Prime Minister Teresa May was given a request from Prime Minister Narendra Modi for his extradition. V J Malia's bill for 260 Crore is still unpaid to India, and he remains on UK soil with an appeal for his extradition to India in June 2017. In 2018 the Indian Supreme court ordered that he was an economic fugative and would be stripped of all his assets. This does not include his offshore assets.

Look around the poker table. If you don't see a sucker, get up because it must be you. - Amarillo Slim

CLAUDETTE
USA 1987

Hi Paulie, you should have phoned from the Airport and would have picked you up', Claudette stood smiling in the doorway of her Santa Monica Apartment. 'Buster' the faithful mutt at her feet wagged his tail side to side in enthusiastic adulation of my arrival. After many years 'Buster's' muzzle had turned grey, he had lost his sight and hardly had the breath left to bark. I remembered when I had taken the mutt for long walks as Claudette's room-mate down onto Santa Monica Boulevard running on the boardwalk crossing the Beach and into the Pacific Ocean to swim in the surf. As we followed each other in to the dining room Claudette said 'I'll make some coffee and a club sandwich you must be hungry after such a long flight'. 'Just coffee would be fine Claudette the in flight food was ok', she disappeared into the kitchen. I remembered her filter coffee 'Folgers' black and sweet as a nut while relishing the thought. It came in a fine bone china cup and saucer with red roses against a white background and a thin gold line round the china cup rim and saucer just how he remembered it She sat beside me on the sofa the dog at her feet between us shaking its head, with his ears comically drooping like a worn duster shaken from constant use. So tell me your plans Paulie'? Claudette looked at me quizzically before I replied laughing 'the painting is here just as you wanted. 'Oh I leave for Europe next week 'Jesus, you only just gotten here what's the big hurry? as she finished her last drop of Latte and put her cup down on a place mat on the polished side table leaving the saucer on the floor as 'Buster' had to finish his coffee too. 'I kind'a hoped you could stay a little longer Paulie' followed by a sigh before she rose from the chair to clear away our empty cups. I felt guilty for being so crass 'I'm sorry Claudette but duty calls', pausing for a moment 'I suppose I could re-arrange my return flight a day or two if needed, 'great, so I will contact Dominic after you have had a rest we could go round for dinner tonight if you're not too jet lagged'. She smiled 'You know what a great cook he is and we can catch up on old times'. It was settled we did go and spent most of night listening to Dominic Hoffman expounding for hours about the new play he was staring in Then eulogized about his new girl friend Jasmine Guy a dancer with the Alvin Ailey Dance Theatre of New York, now actress playing the lead Miss Whitley in 'A different World'. I remembered her being a warm interesting attractive vivacious lady. I had been invited by Dominic a year before to lunch at her bungalow off Hollywood Boulevard where I had enjoyed meeting parents for dinner while she was with Dominic as he spent much time with her, as they worked on 'A Different World 'series. He also had stories of his newest glitterati Lawyer girl friend in the firmament of the New York corporate scene his latest Paramour, as he kept busy in the kitchen tempting us with his culinary talent. In truth he was a better actor than a friend. Over the years he extricated himself what was left of our rare meeting, when he was either in the IJK or working on 'Grays Anatomy' or Appearing at a Theatre near you in the States. At his request I had booked him the East end of-London Studio Theatre in Mare Street for his one man show for two weeks which did not apparently impress him. We enjoyed our time less and less of what became for both of us tenuous during his peripatetic existence. He worked regularly with Claudette on the sound stage loop team in California. His last comment to her was 'I suppose I have not been much of a friend to Paul.'

Driving back from Dominic's apartment with Claudette to Venice beach my response was 'Bloody hell I was sick as a parrot listening to his ego he gets worse'. We went to bed after talking for hours before first light. We woke late the following morning and decided to go to

Spago's on Sunset Boulevard for a celebration lunch for the signing of her new contract on the 'Shrek' production voice over team on the studio's sound stage the following week. 'Keeps the wolf from the door honey She said 'and I get to go to Paris after its release'. Claudette went all dreamy and I remembered visions of the choir and of her singing with me in the Notre Dame Cathedral in Paris. Walking along the river Seine at Christmas we ended up at the chocolate shop, where fresh double cream was folded into dark rich bourbon chocolate to be served hot in elegant fine bone china while we sat in gilt chairs at tables covered with starched white table linen and crisp napkins under crystal chandeliers.

The reality of my returning to London was with inevitable sadness, it was fourteen years since Dominic I had met in Paris had introduced us. Our platonic friendship blossomed with fun and laughter uncomplicated by sexual tension. It had sometimes been fraught with stress and moments created by my bizarre exploits when she did not entirely approve of due to my eccentric and at times bizarre behaviour. Our friendship endured and had remaining rock solid, a week later after a kiss and hug I was gone. See you soon Bubba' Claudette waved until I finally lost sight of her through the departure gate, long farewells were not our style.

My arrival at Heathrow went without a hitch as I strolled through customs with hand luggage and a small flat parcel, no problem through UK immigration entry. The taxi drove straight into London on the M6 the traffic was light, within thirty five minutes I paid the off the cab and closed the inner door of my apartment, carefully sliding out the package from the valise, I un-wrapped a single sheet of brown paper containing a document folder to extract a framed painting within. The cheap plastic frame was serviceable I pulled it gently from the manila envelope revealing the picture printed on canvas of a caricature cat with a squint. On the litho print Your feline friend' was, I thought it a bit overdone but convincing. The frame was taped on the reverse of the picture I pulled the tape from the back of the litho exposing the true painted Canvas underneath and examined it with great care as of the Vermeer school. The original provenance was sealed in my wallet separately attributing the master and his studio. The brush work executed with confidence in the style of the period and of outstanding vision, a perfect example by an .important school of the period. This would be the most recent contribution to a growing private collection I Was creating for a legacy no one would ever see. I returned it to the package sealed it, and locked it in place under the cover of the security safe embedded in the floor, pondering whether to confide in Claudette. The impulse faded after all she had been involved unwittingly having purchased the picture from the dealer for me at the 'ART MART SALE' on the corner of Sunset and Third Street. It had been arranged prior to my visit to California. She would not have approved of such shenanigans, but I would always refer to it as the perfect heist on the market for $10,000, now off the market in my possession which had gone without a hitch.

I would never have taken up painting if women did not have big breasts. - Pierre Auguste Renoir

THE BIG PLAYERS

I watched the upward trajectory of the global art market a tryptic painting by Francis Bacon sold at auction in 2017 for an estimated $150 million dollars originally bought by Roal Dahl for six thousand pounds. The Art market rose during 2014/15, rising another 26% in value to $15.2 Billion. A Qatar buyer had paid $300 Million for a Gaugin. The Iconic Andy Warhol tryptic of Elvis Presley sold at $82 Million, Mark Roth sold for $76 Million. A Francis Bacon work went under the hammer for $1 Million with many more paintings to private mega rich collectors and new buyers from Asia 20% and Hong Kong 30%, Europe and North America 50%. Jonathan Stone the Asian Chairman of Christie's auction house enthused about the explosion in the upturn of investment in art in all categories and could hardly contain his satisfaction, even though in post recession the world economy was on a downturn his company was seduced by the commission on high turnover and no reason to doubt its continuance. It was as if the global recession had never happened. It actually never did for around 2% of the global population of plutocrats. In retrospect, to realise that losing $300 million on the stock exchange in shares for a trust fund is a relative form of risk. When whole family members to lose their livelihood and home it is a disaster, it is the disintegration of the economic backbone of working families when population migrates to where the work is: the expectation of trust between employee and employer is in question. Whole communities suffer the loss of fathers and Mothers, but relatives accept the fact that relatives have to send money home as they need to survive.

Billionaires only have to sell a painting and they are home and dry He or she does not have to take their daughter out of a Swiss finishing school, or a son out of Princeton, Harvard or Oxford. They do not have to pawn their wedding ring, or sell the family jewels to survive Oxfam noted that the 2012 income of the world's richest hundred billionaires was $240 Billion enough to wipe out extreme global poverty four times over.

In the Years since the 2008 crash has anything changed? Rules and regulations have changed little. A few super rich have seen their investment portfolios drop in value. Some have fallen by the wayside but most have weathered the storm with ease. Yet no one of any significance in the bank's or elsewhere has faced prosecution. Economies have shrunk, and people have lost their jobs and had to tighten their belts. politicians show little enthusiasm for bringing those responsible for the crisis to account, hiding behind legal complexities designed for and often by the wealthy. Almost all governments are in a race to attract the super wealthy, and their lucrative micro economy, if not London or New York, why not Singapore or Mumbai, all welcome venues for the super-rich.

In October 2013 Claude Monet's 'L'eglise de Vetheuil' was the subject of a legal case in New York-based Vilma Baptista, one time aid to Imelda Marcos, wife of Ex Dictator Ferdinand Marcos after she sold it and another painting for $32 million to a Swiss buyer. The said Monet painting with two others were acquired by Imelda Marcos during her husband's Presidency allegedly bought using the nation's funds. Bautista's lawyer claimed that the aide sold the paintings for Imelda but did not have the chance to give her the money. The Philipene government seeks the return of the paintings as part of the Monet water Lily series.

OUT OF THE SHADOWS
August 1898

The woodman arrived after 11 am the sun had not yet reached its zenith. He was of short stature about fifty years old weighing around eighty five kilo. A beret was pulled over his balding head as he perspired profusely. He stood to survey the trees large girth which had been rooted to the ground for over ninety years. He climbed onto it with the aid of a bamboo ladder up a side branch slow as an arthritic monkey, and continued up a thirty foot branch to tie a long rope. In a while, after several conversations about the proposed angle and rate of ascent with an assistant helper, he hacked away at a branch with a saw blade. After listening patiently to vocal directions from the swelling crowd of spectators the woodman ascended the tree and ran from the perilous branch, in trepidation to a sufficient distance from the shaded bowery he was about to claim. A crowd of spectators ran to his aide pulling at the rope in an almighty effort to control the direction and angle of a screeching branch descending to earth. With a heaving groan the timber fell to the ground onto a bed of wild thyme sending rotting leaves and verdant detritus into the air. It plunged into a bed of herbaceous wild flowers after hitting lichen covered rock and came to rest on the woodland floor. The pungent aroma filled the air with a fragrant botanical offering. The now denuded stump was left to rot in the open space in bright sunlight, where once the damp dark secreted home of the fauna had been nestling in looked on in silent solitude. Through bright rays of dancing sunlight a lone dragonfly flew from dark shadows into the light above the pool of water reflecting a Cerulean blue sky, this was the image Monet wanted most urgently to create on canvas.

MONETS GARDEN AT GIVERNY
(February 1900)
Letter of Instruction to his gardener

Sowing: around 300 pots Poppies - 60 Sweet Pea-around 60 pots white Agremony - 30 yellow Agremony- Blue sage - Blue Waterlilies in beds (greenhouse) - Dahlias - Iris Kaempferi from the 15th to the 25th lay the dahlias down to root; plant out those with shoots before I get back. Don't forget the lily bulbs. Should the Japanese pieaonies arrive plant them immediately if weather permits, taking care initially to protect bulbs from the cold, as much from the heat of the sun. Get down to pruning. Rose trees not too long except for the thorny varieties. In March sow the grass seeds, plant out the little nasturtiums, keep a close eye on the gloxinia, orchids etc., in the greenhouse, as well as the plants under frames. Trim the borders as arranged; put wires in for the clematis and climbing roses as soon as Picard has done the necessary. If the weathers bad, make some straw matting, but lighter than previously, plant cuttings from the rose trees around the manure in the hens huts. Don't delay work on tarring the planks and plant the Helianthus latiflorus in good clumps night away. If anything's missing such as manure, pots etc., ask Madame if possible on a Friday so as to have it on Saturday. In March, force the chrysanthemums along as the bud's won't open in damp conditions; and don't forget to put the sulphur sheets back on the greenhouse frames.

Claude walked away impatiently returning to his studio in eager anticipation of an early start. He had ordered fresh canvas from the Atelier a day earlier but could not wait as it had to be primed now and he was driven to get this down on canvas. His eagerness overtook him to be compelled to sort through old canvas he had bought at auction a year ago which was available to hand to work on instantly as primed. Quickly he Worked his Palette knife with intaglio strokes, colour tumbling from his palette with swirling brush

strokes directly, fingers stroking the paint lovingly as if in a dance of
pleasure with sensuality known only to the with the talent to create
light from inspiration of chiaroscuro onto canvas

GIVERNEY
France 1899

In the dawn chorus the green wooden lattice shutters of the house
had been opened by Celestine the housekeeper, which she had
done over the last nine years, allowing first light to enter a series of
pleasant rooms occupied by the growing Monet family in residence
Claude's first call was to the tiled kitchen cool to the midday sun not
yet come. He breakfasted at the scrubbed pine wood table on fresh
black coffee and warm croissant with hand-churned butter from the
meadow cows, the strawberries picked by the cook for conserve from
the greenhouse in the garden at the foot of the stone wall dividing
the main house from his new studio. He lingered a moment listening
to the sound of a dragonfly entering the garden then walked through
the tall framed glazed doors of his studio with high window lights
facing north. He threw them open to let the fresh breeze from the
garden in as the room's rancid air was permeated with Linseed and
old turpentine resin, with pigments stored on long trestle tables lined
the peeling walls. Canvas were stacked in rolls of different height
with brushes of every size and number, sable hogs hair, even a quail's
tail he used to sign completed canvas. He mixed pigments by hand
in a crucible of rusted metal lined with a white ceramic bowl taking
care lovingly, placing each one on its shelf as if a priest at high mass
would offer Eucharist to his congregation. The true alchemy was to
teach his students to show courage and spontaneity with colours of

each hue and shade inspiring them to take risk with conviction to capture light.

Claude painted 500 canvases. Inspired by his lily pond series of 60 canvases at home in his garden, he landscaped the water meadows in 1904 with five gardeners working under the head gardener from his daily instruction. Claude spend hours just gazing into the pool under the Japanese bridge, each lily floating a fresh nuance of inspiration starting to choose the moment and exact refraction of light before bringing paint to canvas. In 1926 he gave eight of his lily paintings to the French Nation now hanging in the oval L'orangery in Paris, as a result of a request from his lifelong friend President George Clemensau as a gift to the French nation.

Claude Monet's work was approached by his dealer Paul Durand-Ruel in London with a mixture of awe and reverence tinged with pecuniary advantage. The agent's greed had no boundaries, with the talent to attract rich clients in Europe and America by invitation to his Gallery to show the artist's paintings, where wine and canapés vanished from silver trays offered by pretty juvenile boys to rich clientele: Women daintily picked up petit morsels in their jewelled manicured fingers. The older men holding Cuban cigars in one hand the other a crystal glass surrounded by the rich aroma of Havana cigars from fragrant clients. Their dowdy wives with miniature poodles paid visits to pawn brokers, trading their south sea pearl necklace for hard cash in payment for intimate afternoon's of vigorous horizontal exercise between the sheets in quite hotel rooms: pleasured by vigorous young virile doormen who rose to the occasion to satisfy their lustful pleasure.

Later, after frantic reparation in fragrant showers of 'Miss Dior' the dowdy wives feeling invigorated, dressed in Chic Channel couture to sit on velvet stools at the Savoy cocktail bar. Their exotic plumage arranged like birds of prey, rhinestone court shoes sparkling in the evening glow with their chignon coiffed hair shining under the candlelight of crystal candelabra, sitting at elegant dinner tables beyond reproach.

Flickering candlelight was reflected in crystal 'Baccarat' glasses as waited for Champagne 'Brut' to be poured to grace tables with elegant guests, during social intercourse with family and friends. After the meal and brandy, wives and their husbands reminisced over their recent covert carnal complicity before retiring to separate beds, as the marriage bed remained empty as they slept in separate rooms.

At the heart of the physical lies the metaphysical.

Friedrich Nietzsche.

ITALY
1969

Professor Vitorio Montabano from Milan del Arte antiquity restoration department examined the painting scrupulously with experienced eyes through a magnified eyeglass. He had decided finally after exhaustive scientific tests, that undoubted authenticity was attributed to the Renoir on which he had completed examination, as beyond further doubt of provenance.

The young Begum Khan had been informed immediately at her summer home in Sardinia that she was the fortunate purchaser of the Renoir painting, from a reputable New York Auctioneer recently her bid was accepted by telephone at $5.3 million dollars. She had to be assured by an impeachable source the provenance of her investment and true value, as she was of her aging husband. This information was contradicted by an art historian who had the canvas scanned. Taking samples from the picture lining underneath he discovered the original work preceded the Renoir by 40 years by an X-ray examination as an earlier work of Der Stiel the German expressionist. The Pigment used was a Lapis Lazuli only available at the time from Afghanistan found in igneous rock formations surrounding a perimeter at over 20,000 ft. north of Kabul. The fight was now on of unimaginable proportion not only to win confidence to reassure the nervous art market, that reputations had to be kept intact internationally by Sotheby's Art department to name but one. Unless it was proven to be absolutely genuine she would not take delivery of the painting. Cancellation would cause consternation and scandal with wide repercussions beyond the incestuous art World.

MONET and the state

Claude kept away from human detritus and loathed attending his openings as he was nearly eighty he rarely went. But duty called, as an occasional President or Prime minister came to view his work. He had arranged to give eight of his paintings to the French State, proudly exhibiting them in the two oval rooms at Musee De L'orangerie with the direct help of Clemanceau.

Monet often amused himself by offering Industrialist's investment advice of a transient nature, regarding the rearing of quails for their eggs and method of farming them. Bored as he was with the flotsam, and past the age of eighty had cataracts, he noticed an amusing feature about himself. To make up for his loss of hair under the trilby he always wore, he exhibited a magnificent luxuriant white beard noticed in passing fancy by pretty teenage girls who innocently stroked it, while he enjoyed erotic fantasies in a state of bliss with them during occasional visits with their accompanying aunt's. As the flesh is weak and the passion strong, memories are all he had of a fulfilled and middle class French life. He had never been unfaithful after his second marriage, but that did not stop the urge for experiential yearning after the unattainable. His own passions had been fulfilled in his work which he dedicated to the future.

For a creator, nature is a pretext, a springboard- a pond, a pool, a leaf, are enough to allow him to dream of the world to recreate it

James Joyce.

PINKIE THE 12 YEAR OLD Lamani girl had finished giving fellatio to the old man behind the wall at the back of the toilet, He Anthony Gomes, a middle aged Goan from Saligao was on a regular weekly visit to the barber shop in Mapusa market for his weekly shave. His thinning grey hair was cut short with black dye applied judisciously. Heavy beads of sweat appeared on his scalp in the midday sun, it sent blackened beads running down his face which he mopped away with a freshly laundered white hand kerchief, while Pinkie ran off into the market after spitting the entire contents of her mouth onto the mud floor. She wiped her lips with the back of a grubby hand as she put stuffed the five rupee note Gomes had given her in to her pants. She was the daughter of an itinerant masseur who sold strawberries to foreign tourists on the Calangute beach in the tourist season. In the monsoon he returned to his village in Andhra Pradesh with his nine children and a wife to a small plot to sow a rice crop and muse over his water buffalo. He waded in the mud in the blazing Indian summer heat, waiting to reap the crop to feed his family before migrating to Goa annually to repeat the cycle.

After adjusting his freshly laundered underpants Anthony fumbled with his trouser fly to regain composure and wiped his tepid brow with the freshly laundered handkerchief from his shirt pocket, refolded it, returning it to the pocket from where it came. After this detour Anthony joined his wife for lunch after her weekly shop of selecting fresh vegetables and spices outside the 'Café Romantica' where they arranged to dine together most Saturday's. They purchased market produce bought in Preparation for a Sunday dinner with her brother the Priest in the church vestry. Every Sunday morning before mass they took a freshly plucked chicken provided by Anthony the dutiful husband of Millagrina as offering to his brother in law Father

Domini Assunte the local parish. The Priest officiated at the regular confessional with his congregation and attended the boys choir practice every Saturday eve with his punkah walla in hot pursuit in the cool night air outside the vestry. After choir practice black cassocks were hurriedly discarded by juvenile boys in his refectory who flirted with him, they lingered in the changing room to expose their juvenile tanned legs in brief tight shorts, while they smiled in the direction of their spiritual advisor. The Priest with suppressed fervour and excitement looked at the discarded cassock and surplus as they disrobed attempting to avert his gaze but remained transfixed to the impulse of sensual delight and the forbidden lust of the pubescent choir.

Millagrina had her eyes on the choir master in whose secret passionate embrace she had been in coital lust for years with consummate zeal. Her unconsummated marriage to husband Anthony which was without passion, Anthony spent most of his nights grappling with the barman's young wife. His brother in law Police constable Surendra Naik had obtained the alcohol license to enable them to sell tax free toddy made from coconut or cashew tapped from the illegal distilled crop. The inebriated farmers of Don Vaddo drunk in local bars to the chagrin of their wives' whose beds were seldom warmed by their malingering husbands until closing time in the early hours. staggered home pounding on the flimsy door of their hut for entry to sweet dreams' within minutes loud snoring vibrated the tin wall and roof of a corrugated tin shack.

1909
Hamburg in winter

The painter Herr der Stiel had been up all night with nothing but two candles to warm him and light the dim basement, he fell against the bed and on to the bare stained mattress where he lay motionless for three hours, he had been feeling unwell. Suddenly awoke to a tumultuous sound of marching feet in heavy boots stopped outside in the street. A loud rap on his door held terror before the crash of a heavy blunt instrument shattered the wood panel splintering it from the frame. The winter gale blew snow directly onto his bed from the blizzard raging outside the old building used as a ware house previously, where he lived alone near the dock side for over five years.

'Deutschland Uber Alles' the heavy coated sergeant holding the open door bellowed as the wind and snow swirled around him wrapped in the double breasted woollen splendour of a German army uniform. 'Hey you' come with us. 'Schnel', we do not allow pacifists to linger when Germany is at war with its enemies.' In a sudden violent movement der Stiel was grabbed, chained and cuffed still struggling dragging his feet now dangling, into an old cart drawn by the weary mare whose metal shoes slid on the snow covered icy surface of cobbled stone trotting slowly to the garrison Jail. After preliminary registration at the chipped wooden desk, he was interviewed separately in the Commandants office. 'We understand you are a painter Herr Stiel' the Garrison major said with an ominous edge to his voice 'your artistic talent could be put to better use' by painting the camps 994 meters of barbed Wire perimeter fence and double gates in alternate barbs of red and white. 'We would be pleased to have you as our guest for the duration of the War, he emphasised each word with significant pleasure.

So it was until 1918 when released, he came to know that 10 million horses and twelve million people had been slaughtered and perished in the war first-world war with nothing gained but a loss of face to the Kaiser and his war machine. De Stiel returned in 1918 to his dusty room with rats for company and washing dishes in nearby beer cellars for a living. This allowed him some comfort while enabling him to PUrchase canvas and wood to frame his paintings with pigment, brushes, and linseed oil for his 'Fabriken Machina' series. He assuaged the guilt of being a pacifist first and a non combatant second. His art now hangs in auction houses shown in International galleries to expunge the darkness of human destruction. It is ironic that the industrialist Herr Von Krup who gained most financially from the production of armament and tanks for the second world war purchased several of the paintings from a dealer. Von Krup enjoyed showing his Der Stiel art collection in the company boardroom to the Third Riech's Fuhrer Adolph Hitler who admired his taste. During 1938 to 1947 six million Jews were transported to concentration camps systematically gassed and murdered in the holocaust across Europe by SS Nazis State policy. The victim's fine art collections confiscated by the Nazi high command for their personal gain with provenance of title stolen from prisoners. Object D' Arts and artifacts of gold and fine jewellery secreted away in mines by the Nazis released years later onto the International art market they had stolen from their captor's. After the second- world war in 1947, Auschwitz, BurchenaU' Dachau, Bergen and Buchenwald concentration camps, liberated by the allies found to their horror lamp shades fashioned from human skin with looted gold teeth and the personal possessions taken by the German guards of deceased prisoners. Art created in human expressi0n to illustrate destruction in the Gestapo orchestrating the nation's continuation of the Holocaust.

Goebel's, the master propaganda of hate, arrested fifty six thousand homosexual victims forcing them to wear a Pink Triangle sewn on the sleeves of their upper garment. The SS gave them the tattoo identity on their limbs for recognition in the concentration camps for before they were gassed and burnt. Human life was valued at less than the art that mirrored it. Mass production of systemic murder was executed with unquestioned efficiency by a German master plan. Before Europe and the world entered into a state of war declared by Mr Chamberlin the prime Minister of the United Kingdom of Great Britain as German troops marched into Poland.

THE NEW MILLENIUM

The Talibans influence increased in Afganistan, removing millions of men women and children from the face of the earth in the name of God. The Cambodia killing fields of blood removed millions of educated dissidents in the name of the State. Afghanistan, Congo, Zambia and Ethiopian millions in the name of tribal ethnic difference selective lives of innocent civilians by ethnic cleansing, One million people were murdered within five days of killing in Ruwanda genocide, 500,000 thousand women raped, and as a result 25,000 unwanted pregnancies.

In Iraq Kurdish people were killed by the State, millions more in Bosnia. In Europe 20,000 civilian deaths in East Ukraine, 40 million in Russia under Stalin, Egypt, Tunisia, Algeria, Iraq, and China under Mao. Figures estimated at over 70 million human souls murdered just for being a minority not deemed suitable for inclusion by autocratic despots of the state and oligarchs of the world, motivated by religious fervour, politics and human greed. In Syria the war of different factions gained support from International power in 2017, as the population of women and children were annihilated.

87 per cent of all people in professions are incompetent.
John Gardner

OFFENDERS

Young offenders were institutionalised after a court hearing for a minor misdemeanour by USA Judge Chivarella who detained the youth without having been given legal Council. These and other young offenders were held in a government contract offenders rehab centre by Judge Conohan with Chivarella and the government contractor. They had colluded to accept bribes from the contractor after a 2009 investigation instigated by the parents brought a Court action for indeterminate periods of extended confinement of their children by the miscreant Judges to the attention of the federal authorities. Forty eight counts of cash bribes of $4 million dollars and unlawful sentences of young offenders were all adjudicated, and their cases dismissed and expunged from record as a result. The Judges were ordered to pay retribution of $95,000 and were imprisoned with the colluding contractor for two years.

If thou art rich, thou'rt poor; for like an Ass whose back with ingots bows, though bear'st thy heavy riches but a journey, and death unloads thee..

Shakespeare, Measure for Measure

CALIFORNIA 1968

The Begum Khan had been a Hollywood star of some magnitude in the fifties. Her previous marriage to Orson Welles and rise to fame provided a high degree of intrigue. Born Conchita Del Rio from a small Mexican town, angelic and pretty as a child, her full beauty flowered when her debut in the movies presented her as the glorious redhead renamed Rita Hayworth who danced and sang her way to celluloid history. She was little unstable and suffering from Bi-Polar, her hyperactivity hid severe clinical depression and degree of social ineptitude. It was a miracle that her second marriage to the Aga Khan had occurred just as her popularity was waning in the late 50s. After her subsequent divorce from Orson Welles, the Aga Khan had been smitten by her winsome smile which appealed to him greatly. At a party he asked her for a dance it happened to be the Tango and so it was, their relationship formed. Their private marriage ceremony was held on his magnificent luxury Yacht 'Con Amore' berthed in Nice Harbour on the Cote D'azure before their Honeymoon to the Adriatic. She had signed the Prenuptial agreement at the Advocates office while on a trip to Paris to visit a friend at Christian Dior on the Place de la Concorde. At this time her suite at the Ritz Hotel in Paris was being refurbished completely at her insistence. While viewing antique furniture at her favourite auction house she saw the bed, it was magnificent; indeed it had been slept in by Napoleons mistress Josephine it was duly installed in the suite, this gave Cache to an otherwise pastiche décor of no distinction. She had fallen in love With the Renoir painting she knew she had to have it. She had seen it in a private collection at a house in Beverley Drive, Beverly Hills in Hollywood at Greta Garbo's Chateaux behind the swimming pool in her cabin. After an early morning swim in Garbo's pool they used the changing room at the same time with Greta not then in a reclusive mood they expressed pleasure in each other's company.

The Begum was now on her way to notoriety with a reputation which soared subject to her elevated social status. With funds not exactly in short supply, she bid by phone for the Renoir without quandary or question as the doubtful provenance had put her in a bad light with her husband who had gone off in a huff to play Polo with friends in a bad mood. He was uncomfortable with controversy of any sort as he represented the Muslim sect of his people globally. He could not afford such wayward behaviour even from his wife the situation demanded authenticity of the painting to be absolutely beyond reproach for her acceptance in receipt of purchase.

SARDINIA
Sunday - Late afternoon

The Begum decided to go to the beach alone dressed in a Chanel shift over a white silk culotte followed by her favourite Saluki puppy on a lead. Lunch with her husband had been a tense affair with his reproach over the painting, as it had been a week since the Renoir provenance had not been clarified and the world media published the story. Sliding off her Gucci sandals tossing them to one side she sank her bare feet into soft sand stretching cat like unfolding her arms slowly, and dropped into a canvas chair near a rock for shade. A Hermes scarf covered her titian hair and oversized sunglasses set on her pert nose. She reached for the house phone plugging it into a socket in the rock and ordered Evian water and cigarettes to ease her tension. Sixty two white painted stucco steps carved into the volcanic rock winded down through the subterranean rock caves ending onto the private beach cove Enrique the butler arrived at her side announced by his asthmatic staccato cough.'

Oh I'm sorry Rico I thought Assunte would have brought it down'.' No senora she is feeling so tired, sleeping in siesta after the lunch' he wheezed. Bowing, he left her side with the same smile he had worn every day for the last forty years in service with the Aga Kahn. She poured a glass of ice cold Evian cooling her hand with the glass and lit a menthol filter cigarette exhaling one billowing cloud into the soft breeze, in a few minutes her eyes were closing to sleep. The Begum Kahn heard a voice the other side of the escarpment. He came round the rock face slowly, to stand in front of her causing a shadow to fall across her face. Where did you come from she spoke softly and focused on his youthful face and tanned torso. 'Oh, I guess I got lost while taking my boat fishing from the other side of the Island'. He looked intently at her smiling, 'Don't I know you from somewhere', not unless you went to an old movie of mine'. Removing her sun glasses, she could see how handsome with amazing muscle tone to his legs and arms. She remembered seeing this kind of beauty in Rome viewing the 'David' in San Marco Piazza. Swimmers trunks fitted perfectly over his sculptured torso, as he turned round she could see he was well endowed. Breaking the silence after a long minute she said, why don't you sit down the sun is hurting my eyes, he did so without hesitation. She gazed with intense interest at his broad shoulders and six-pack. You are a beautiful woman he said, 'You're not so bad yourself she laughed softly holding his gaze, 'but in your case its better coming from a younger man than hearing it said by an older woman'. She picked up the cigarette pack taking one then offered him a cigarette which he took with long slender fingers. He picked up the lighter from her chair Offering the flame cupping his hand round her cigarette touching her fingers, she felt aroused as an excited shivered went down her spine. They gazed into each others' eyes, his olive green, hers turquoise blue, their pupils enlarged with mutual interest. 'Why don't we walk and talk. 'Ok' she said stepping out of her culottes revealing a Schiaparelli pink G string that briefly followed the contours of her still shapely dancers legs.

The tense interval of silence between them ended, 'amazing' he murmured slowly and she giggled. We could take the dog for a walk 'Ok, He breathed rapidly as they reached the end of the small private beach small waves lapping round their ankles he turned to take her hand in his asking her name. Against the rocks they brushed lightly against each other she smiled, 'Conchita,' mine is Marco,' he pulled her to him. Her surprised reaction caused by his strength of purpose and her passive acquiescence produced a rapid palpitation in her breast. In a feint of expectancy she stumbled on a running crab as he bent forward to break her fall, she fell into his arms, surprising him with a lascivious kiss her tongue thrusting his searching in passion. He threw himself against her 'Oh god that's wonderful' she cried. The pent up frustration of a week swept away by lust he entered her against the hard rock. It seemed an eternity until a symbiotic orgasm caused them to cry out in primal scream changing to gentle sobs with tears of joy welling up in her eyes after their coupling. He said 'OK' as if it had been just another Sunday stroll on the beach. The Sun now setting in a cloudless sky against an inferno of orange light changed rapidly to a deeper pink in minutes. They parted wordlessly she went back to the house as he dived into the sea swimming back to his boat. They never met again but she always remembered those moments of passionate intensity. When her husband sought intimacy it was more of comfort than passion. Years later the Begum sought refuge in asylum after her divorce from the Aga Khan as she had lost all contact with reality, Alzheimer's had been diagnosed, as the condition had slowly deteriorated, taking her mind away with the essence of her personal identity leaving only a husk to contend with. Fame has many admirers, but few friends when you are left in splendid isolation from a disease of the brain that robs you of all memory and knowingness of self by dementia, to live in a twilight zone until death claims you.

PACIFIC PALISADES California
1986

This rustic canyon is the neighbourhood east of Chataugua Boulevard, borders Topanga and Medio Mesa, nestles where Sunset Boulevard meets the Pacific coast highway. The Medio bluffs are on a high ridge overlooking the Pacific Ocean. The neighbourhood affords beautifUI Ocean views and Ocean air. Underneath this veneer of rich upward social mobility residents aspire to familial ties and sometimes fraternal confrontation, I found myself in such a web of deceit. My agency had recommended the client to me and a meeting between us. The client, an elderly bed ridden lady with health problems required a butler for her pacific Palisade Estate. At our first meeting, I considered her offer as it met my needs and I liked her noted a certain charm, with an eccentric dress sense, wore a turban and suggested a starting date the week after our meeting. The apartment offered to me came with a swimming pool. Hesitant as I was at living on the job, I decided it did give me a chance to increase my depleted savings and I started duty. A week later I was formally introduced to her private nurse who administered daily from a library of prescribed drugs for her patients health needs. I attended to her home comfort included the preparation of a menu. The lady waited for the nurse to be out of earshot before she whispered in my ear pleading for a 'Bloody Mary' with ice and asked me not to inform her nurse. I understood this beverage was for her consumption as nightcap after the meal. The nurse often asked me to collect her medication prescription. One day while in the pharmacy with the prescription I was alarmed to find she was Prescribed a double dose of 'Prozac' followed by 'Demarol' as and when she asked for them from her day nurse. In conversation with the Pharmacist he also indicated his concern but suggested I contact the FDA to report this, as he could not without raising concern with her MD which he did not wish to do, Instead in my naivety I reported this to her son on one of his rare visits to the house. I also understood from his mother he was beneficiary of her $6 million estate and will. Within a week of my informing him of my concern I was locked out of her room and found the police had been called to escort me from the premises without notice, the reason was not given, but I was put in the back of the police car until I was allowed to pack my possessions to enable them to be collected later. As I was leaving, her son loudly proclaimed to his wife 'It's like getting rid of gum from your shoe', as his respectability was maintained.

In 1985 Jack Nicholson and Kathleen Turner filmed 'Prizzi's Honor' on location in a private house at 15025 Corona Del Mar, it belonged to Joyce Proctor since demolished now only exists in film history. The first season of 'The Golden Girl's' was shot in a home in Pacific Palisades, for subsequent seasons of 'The Golden Girl's' a facade house was built on the Disney/MGM back lot. Brian De Palma directed the best film of 1976 'Carrie' when he rewrote Steven King's book into a film script shot in Pacific Palisades high school built on land owned by Debbie Reynolds and Eddie Fisher, parents of Carrie Fisher, before the school was built.

Pinky, now twenty two had emigrated with her adopted parents from Goa to Brazil and had become a street smart beauty. She had run away from Rio de Janeiro with an itinerant American sailor after a brief civil marriage ceremony, a month later she left him on a cruise ship and disembarked at Long Beach California with papers and her application for a Green Card, having saved money from her earnings from prostitution. As luck would have it a senior citizen homeward bound disembarked from his yacht had found her company exhilarating and delightful on the poop deck one sultry night. He promptly offered her a berth at his Beverly Hills mansion she accepted with charm and showed him her gratitude by moving in immediately at his suggestion. Within days after arriving at his Beverley hills home she had discovered her niche both as confidante and as madam. Her talent for pandering was employed by the old boy at Movie parties to attract the movers and shakers whose enticed hands wandered in her direction. She had access to other stunning ladies of the night who were fresh and ready to party at any time on demand. One weekend her patron Bob Evans Paramount studios legendary producer of Iconic 'Rosemary's baby', 'The godfather' and 'Love Story' snorted his night away on the mirrored bath room floor, his cocaine addiction in the 80's led to catastrophic decline, drug trafficking charges and a brief stint in a psychiatric hospital. Evans life was simply another slice of Hollywood noir. He came out to the terrace and pushed her into the pool waited to see her nipples through the wet see through bikini. In a fit of pique she retaliated by drinking him under the table with the last bottle of his favourite 'Blue Sapphire' Vodka, she remained Unavailable and comatose for the rest of the party. Bob true to his reputation found solace in the winsome loveliness of a newly arrived English girl who wanted to be a starlet selectively exposed then dumped, as was the modus operandi in the dream factory called Hollywood. Evans story lends itself to a dash of caricature -- Polanski, Evans nemesis; Ali MacGraw his wife, Charlie Bludhorn, Evans persistently enraged boss contributed their story chronologically to his. Paramount studio had a new head Sherry Lancing a fierce lady in charge, running the studio for the Chairman Sumner Redstone with an iron fist in a velvet glove. Bob had his day but did retain a token office on the Paramount lot with his parking space as a hand shake. Bob and his brother George had sold out the Global 'Evans' fashion empire their father had started in New York at the beginning of the sweat shop era. Their liquidity bought their way into the movie business. Bob into film production, his brother trained race horses and securing finance for Bob's production company via the New York syndicates through Mr Brown.

Bob employed an assistant in his office to archive his career which had faded from the firmament after his bio-book publication 'Keep the kid in the picture' had been in the New York best sellers list for 12 weeks, Bob's periodic attempts to revive his relationship with his son from a previous marriage with Ali McGraw was tenuous, she had divorced him to marry Steve McQueen and settled in New Mexico. Bob tried to revive his flagging career, but as Busby Barclays said 'There's no comeback for a- has-been' in tinsel town. Pinkie continued to revel in debauchery and corruption as a fish to water. She maintained her 'pandering' to a geriatric crowd spreading her popularity generously to all takers who could afford her high maintenance for their intimate gratification, and their eleven seconds in paradise. She was always available to the party crowd being a wiz at the tango on the dance floor and reputed to be an angel in the boudoir.

It all started in the 1970's, producer Robert Evans offered Robert Towne the noted screen play writer $25,000 to write his own story the film ' Chinatown ' to which Evans accepted. 'Chinatown' is set in the year 1937 and portrayed the manipulation of a critical municipal resource water in Los Angeles USA It was to be the first part of Towne's trilogy about the character J J. Gittes and the subjugation of public good for private greed. Roman Polanski directed Jack Nicholson and John Huston and Faye Dunaway. Towne wrote the screenplay with Jack Nicholson in mind. Robert Evans wanted Roman Polanski to direct this dark and cynical subject. Polanski a few years earlier in 1969 had undergone a personal trauma- the brutal murder of his wife Sharon Tate as well as that of his unborn child by a group known as The Manson family- he lived up to the producers expectations. He made the Villain live and the victim of circumstance die at the end. The casting of the iconic director John Huston- Maltese Falcon (1941) The African Queen (1951) in the role of the villain —Noah Cross was a master stroke. John Huston created one of movie history's most formidable bad men. Producer Robert Evans accepted Jerry Goldsmith's music score recorded in 10 days. Goldsmith's Academy Award nominated score with haunting trumpet solos by I-Jan Rasey. Paramount Picture studio released the film June 20, 1974 which was a box office success, earning $17 million outside North America, millions more earned in North America in 1991. The film was selected by the Library of Congress for preservation in the United States registry for films that are culturally, historically or aesthetically significant. It is listed as among the best Film Noir genre in the world and all time success.

For a while Robert Evans appointed me in 1994 as Butler and major Domo to run the property and staff of his Beverley Drive residence. It had been the original home of Greta Garbo through large gates at the end of a private drive built in the style of a French Chateau in landscaped grounds, with tennis court, and a separate guest house whose walls and ceiling were lined in mirrored glass. Sir Lawrence Olivier stayed in the Guest house as Bob's house guest while shooting on the set of 'Dr Mengeler' the movie' in Hollywood. The actress Beverley D' Angelo a close friend of Bob Evans ordered afternoon English tea while on an extended visit, and asked me if my apartment in the house was to my liking. At least someone cared, but the demands made were impossible and the guest list endless at all hours of the day and night without offering me any respite working from early morning to nearly midnight, with one day to sleep. I had left San Fransisco in north California moving from a dream client in San Fransisco to a neurotic tyrant in Hollywood but I had been warned. The anti-social aspect of my position played havoc with my aspirations and without time off for friendships or any recreation. Robert Evans ephemeral expectations of my constitution fell short of his impulsive objectives as we parted company after nine months, it was a gestation period I could do without as Big Bear Mountain beckoned me as I took my leave of Beverley Hills and the menagerie of Hollywood tinsel town.

What do you think China should do about Tibet?
Who cares what I think China should do? Im'e a fucking actor
Im'e a grown man who puts on make-up

Interviewer and Brad Pitt.

GO TELL IT TO THE MOUNTAIN

Driving through the valley up through the San Bernadino Mountain highway to big Bear Lake I stopped for a break outside a roadside cabin. In the yard was a sale sign on the windscreen of a pretty good flat bed truck, I walked over to the timber framed garage to take a good look, reaching the vehicle as the owner stepped out in the path toward me. 'You wanna buy fella' I said 'maybe, 'a half hour later after a test drive I returned the keys and we struck a deal agreed a price. I drove it away the next day to Los Angeles and home.

The next week I put three lines in the classified section of the Los Angeles Times. It read 'YOU CALL WE HAUL. ' From the first publication the phone never stopped ringing for enquiries to shift a rapidly mobile population to wherever they desired. The first telephone call from a lady enquirer was very taken with my British accent 'Oh my god your Bridish please say sum'n' her vowels played havoc with a selection of clipped consonants rendered in a high pitched scream. I said 'Something,' she screamed again with delight. I got the job at twenty seven bucks an hour minimum two hours plus extra for the first floor lift. I never stopped moving peripatetic members of the 'Angel' community until I reached eight thousand dollars saved in my account and that's the truth folks. Sometimes it was a breeze, always full of surprise as there's no Primate like the human for strange requests and the world is one big stage when it comes to the dream factory of Hollywood. It taught me that you can put Your hand to anything if you have a mind to do it.

After a while I came up with the idea of 'The mad hatters Tea Party,' it became popular with the baby shower and mum set for high tea, a theme which captured the mood of the moment: if you like angel cakes and afternoon with friends. It went down well with

Tracy Nelson and friends. Enamoured by the Beverley Hills and Bel-Air community on the manicured dyed green lawns and potted red poinsettia. The tricky part was when they forgot to turn off the water sprinklers, their lawns mikeq into bright red and green stripes became a shower party par excellence It occurred to me that it may work better in a home setting, so a Hatters' tea party was organised at Claudette's. That weekend we invited her forty movie friends mixed with the acting fraternity in her swish Beverly hill's apartment. I printed engraved invitation cards with a Lewis Carol design. We draped her baby grand piano with Pashmina shawls and exotic gemstone pieces to sell to her guests available at informal tea parties. Guests turned up at 4pm to take English tea served on silver trays with petite fours and cucumber sandwich dainty's. At the end of the afternoon our takings were seven thousand dollars.

My experience of American's are, that they have a generous nature with wit and posses sociability, but surprisingly on the conservative side and a tad naive. Claudette's generosity was rewarded and I had a new take on the party crowd. If anyone says that they can't find opportunity in them there Californian hills they should look to their own creativity for solutions as it's all out there. Stop to think what you can bring to the table, you could surprise yourself, come down from your ivory tower and bring it on. I really believe nothing ventured, nothing gained, so once in a while it ends up arse over tit so what, just pick yourself up and start all over again. Attitude and affirmative action make the day go great.

Ozzy Osborne was invited to the white house to meet President Bush. Just goes to show that if you do a lot of controlled substances and talk like a three year old you can go really far in America Ozzy's doing OK too.

Gregg Proops

LONDON

In June 1995 at the age of fifty eight I decided to look after my mum full-time, who by now was a septuagenarian approaching ninety and temporarily in hospital. My siblings were incapable, disinterested, or both in taking care of her. After discussing it with mum I took the lead and left for London to find an apartment for us to share and take care of her needs. This took a while to find, so she chose a convalescent home while she waited until I got suitable residential ground floor flat. Three months later we moved her in a Wheel chair out of the Hospital bed, with her bits of furniture into my north Finchley London home. I can say that it was the best move I made and We did get on really well, rather like a couple of good friends which was the best part. When she felt up to it I would drive her to Hampstead Heath on a sunny day for tea, to leave her for a few minutes sat in her wheel chair while I brought the tray, to discover on my return she was surrounded by dogs, her canine friends would be petted and talked to as if she was the 'Dog whisperer. ' She obviously loved it, and they made a team of admirers. I loved my old mum and though she passed away five years later in February 2001 1 still miss her smile Her health had deteriorated and she could not walk any more her only mobility was a wheel chair, standing was not possible. Everything had to be calibrated to her existence which was for a previously active working life, had become a difficult and frustrating situation that she never complained about. At the age of ninety one she passed away in her sleep. She is now at peace and so it should be, she gave me the chance to spend the time with her I had lost as a child. Her other children missed the best years Whether they understood it or not. It can't be much fun wiping kid's bums and making sure they get to school on time with four of us. Loving us, even when we did not understand the 'Angst and Straum' of her existence, even when we gave her very little in return she stuck with it. I like to think I have got some of her humour and determination and maybe a little of her patient wisdom, or am I am just wishing. Never the less she was a great act to follow and there will never be another like her. She said to me 'l don't know what you've got but if I were you I would bottle it and sell it' I said well you would say that wouldn't you. Another time, she exclaimed 'If you fell into excrement you would come out smelling of roses'. Maybe Mum but you are not here to enjoy it with me. Her sweet smile and voice still lingers in total recall. 'Jesu joy of mans desire' was played at her funeral service as I had promised her and the priest officiated in accordance with her wishes. After her funeral service I returned to the apartment with Babafemi a friend as I did not feel up to returning alone. We entered the front door passing into the hall walking to the kitchen. Before we reached the door to pass her room we stopped abruptly at the entrance as an overpowering fragrance of Tuberose overcame us at the door to her room, and as sudden as it had come it was gone. I understood this to be her last farewell message as the fragrance faded I stood weeping. I remained stricken with grief on the edge of an emotional abyss as none of my siblings had attended her demise or funeral service. After the cremation I placed her ashes under a rose bush in the gardens of Islington Cemetery in Barnet north London in the spring of 2001.

HUMAN COMPASSION

In a passage from Albert Eisenstein letter written March 4th 1950 in his reply to a 19 year old girl who was grieving over the loss of her younger sister:

'A human being is part of the whole called by us as 'Universe' pad limited in time and space. He experiences himself his thoughts and feelings as something separated from the rest, a kind of optical delusion ofhis consciousness. This delusion is a kind of prison for us, restricting us to our personal desires and to affection for a few persons close to us. Our task must be to free ourselves from our prison by widening our circle of compassion to embrace all humanity and the whole of nature in its beauty. Nobody is capable of achieving this completely but the striving for such achievement is itself a part of the liberation, and a foundation for inner security. '

I demand a second opinion.

Spike Milligan

Bel Air
California USA - Fall 1969

California had lost its appeal for Edward G Robinson a long time ago. Inside the compound of his Bell Air cottage up in the hills he settled into his favourite overstuffed chesterfield chair surveying the sunset. The last picture he had just finished had become a chore. With long boring journeys to the days shoot that brought on his sciatica and an even longer way from Europe. He travelled extensively during each movie project and visited the world's fine art galleries with auction houses, between scenes on location in different European capitol's he Viewed Obje'dart at auction sales, bought and shipped his prize back home. Sitting in the stuff-over leather chair he reached toward the humidor that graced the marble stairwell of his ground floor Mansion. He leaned to pull his chair toward the ormolu inlaid rosewood cabinet sliding the doors to reveal cross banded inlay, and the maple leaf interior doors of his well stocked humidor. He selected a hand rolled Romeo & Juliet cigar from a metal tube in its cedar wood lining laid down some four years ago, and cut the hand-made cap. Lighting it with a steady hand he held the match for a moment before leaning back relaxed into the chair. He never tired of enjoying the first draw as the aromatic fragrance permeated the room, he smiled in quite indulgence. Opening the new edition of 'Art International' and startled by the news of the recent Renoir controversy. It was in fact a proven provenance now available on sale after Aga Kahn had called on a cancellation the year previous.

Edward G. Robinson, the Hollywood actor with his homburg trademark owned one of the finest collections of modern art in the United States of America. Equally famed he dealt with a connoisseur's knowledge and wanted the Renoir in his collection. Carefully calculating the time zone he booked a call through his trusted Philippine secretary on the east coast entering the date into his diary for action. The auction house suggested offers of a King's ransom. He grinned with pleasure at the possibility of adding it to his growing investment not realizing a long time ago that his position in the scheme of things was determined not by the magnitude of his thespian talent, but by his appreciation of fine art. This would be his legacy to date, he settled back into the soft hide sofa contemplating his next move While his cigar ash dropped perilously on the waxed parquet floor as he dozed fitfully into the early hours.

The moment had come, for eternity had taken over as he passed into the next dimension of universal equanimity. Edward G was found dead by his houseman at seven am the next day in his chair. He had passed peacefully away into the big sleep in full evening dress. His Romeo & Juliet corona had burnt out on the nearby Onyx ashtray as dawn broke over the Sierra Madre Mountains. A month later in New York his lawyer read his last and will and testament of his collection of art signed by his hand Compos mentis to be gifted to the nation, not only to avoid death duty but to thank a country that allowed him as émigré to become what he had always wished for and allowed to be. It resolved his peripatetic leanings by returning those gifts he had earned from his talent and energy to give to his chosen homeland in gratitude of a busy life now ended.

Stardom? I never touch the stuff.

John Lithgow

SAN FRANSICO
July 1994 - California USA

At dawn, the golden gate bridge thrust into the early morning fog. Diaphanous webs of spun metal glistened with dew drops as in joining hands they were closed in joyous prayer of a new day. Two white sails of a distant yacht appeared slowly returning from the Ocean, her deck sparkled in the suns first rays in wake of the rolling surf against the bow in the dark blue sea followed by twin white plumes. The Sun rose as the Pacific Ocean breeze gently lifted the clouds exposing the leeward inland. Early morning traffic thundered across the bridge highway into the arterial inner roads, slowing up into a clogged pedestrian crawl before entering the beating heart of the city.

Across the 'Presidio Park' the bird song echoed in morning chorus through the Trajan column arch of the palace of fine Arts, I walked the daily route with the family's irritating toy white poodle for his constitutional. My tenure at the household in Green Street was run with firmness and precision, administering the staff with a kind but sensitive authority for the convenience of the delightful couple who doted on each other. I had been flown down by previous request through my agent to Palm Springs for the meeting. My flight tickets to Palm Springs had arrived by Fedex courier with an invitation from Mrs. Robert Naify to meet her at the golf club restaurant on the Fairway. I was picked up on flight arrival by her chauffeured limo which transferred me to the clubhouse where we were to meet. I was shown to her table by the Maitre'D. After mutual introductions we ordered a lunch of wild Pacific salmon accompanied by a bottle of Californian Riesling and noticed the without any resistance the chocolate mousse desert. She was a warm and charming sophisticated beauty which had faded over middle age years• After coffee, she told me she had met her husband at Neiman

Marcus while at a fashion show while she was working on the cat walk. Born from Italian parents in Bakersville, California; their conjoined family of siblings from the previous marriage from his first wife, and hers from the second marriage had produced familial blessings and a divorce, while questions were directed at me as to my credentials. After our discussion she offered me the position, I was pleased to accept and joined the San Fransisco household two weeks later after background security checks on me had been confirmed through my agent. Later in Northern California while planning a visit to her Palm Springs cottage on Frank Sinatra Drive, she advised me not to allow the eldest son from her first marriage to enter the family home while they were away, confirming if he called he was to be accompanied by me at all times. This alarmed me and I quickly enquired the reason, it was simple. Several valuable impressionist paintings had been taken from the house during their absence and secreted away by their son. A particular valuable Matisse hung in the dining room had disappeared, later it was found to have been sold at auction to fund his drug dependent lifestyle between frequent visits to the Betty Ford Clinic as an inpatient on a rehab programme. They had not informed the police as this would have caused a deep divide between his duties as a father and his allegiance to the state as an appointed USA Marshal. So I was instructed to follow the son around and not be left alone in the house, this onerous task proved a valuable lesson as later on he would find out the resolve could be worse than the crime. His half sisters visited on irregular LAX flights with the intention of keeping family ties securely tied

SAN FRANSISCO - 1912 spring

Their grandfather a Lebanese emigrant had endured a long and hazardous journey by sea from the port of Beirut. His primary purpose was to escape chaos after the first-world war and its impending destruction after the French had been appointed a mandate by the league-of-nations to run the government. Secondly, and more important his journey was to find a new beginning and a better life for his family. Few personal belongings were allowed on voyage, he brought a hand cranked film projector. The first moving images in 1768 were projected from slides in the dark with candle light onto a white background by travelling showmen called 'Galantes' in England and Europe, as a matter of historical fact.

In the 19th century four minutes of silent moving film was shot from the northern city of Leeds in the United Kingdom by the camera's inventor. On the heritage site of the bridge of the first moving image showed a pair of Shire horses pulling a cabriolet carriage over lower Briggate in Bridge Street on the river Ouse in 1804, pedestrians walked in the fashion of the period. The hand cranked camera had been taken to France by its Yorkshire inventor, but mysteriously a few months later the Lummiere brothers claimed a patent application in 1895. The rest as they say is history. The invention became the new medium of communication bringing informed entertainment and news to the world. The immigration officer on board was amused at his choice of luggage wrapped in wax paper for protection against the damp sea air on board.

Sailing into port past the statue of Liberty into a vibrant New York skyline, he marvelled at the size of a city the new world offered It stretched as far as he could see, the skyline unfolded before the captive passengers disembarked through emigration at Elis Island process centre on entry to North America. Name please ' the Irish immigration officer asked' 'Naify' came the reply, well pal, you need one in the new world how about Naify, and wrote it down, 'as you came by boat it's a lot easier to say my friend' this was said in a Dublin accent. It was duly stamped on the emigration card he now treasured while entering the United States of America. He felt elated With a surge of expectant joy as he walked into the crowd with his small parcel into the jostling human tide and hope in his heart. A few months later his wish came true at the pawnshop in Atlantic City. He had taken the moving projector returned by the pawn broker and later repaid a cash loan. Walking away with the little cash left from washing dishes at an all night coffee shop he returned to his dingy room, he assembled the machine wound the celluloid spool through the gate waiting a few seconds. He cranked the handle to see the flickering image of 'Fred Karnos army' the first silent movie he had ever seen projected onto the wall of his apartment produced and filmed in Hollywood california. He was enthralled, after a few minutes his new adventure had begun.

The idea of live piano accompaniment offered drama to the new experience of the silent moving image to entertain the masses. Long lines formed outside waiting to pay a nickel for their experience in a darkened room watching the moving picture. He decided the 'Nickel Odeon' was his to carve a future with, his two infant sons Marshall and Robert had mouths to feed. He gave a hard shove to the double carved doors which opened into a darkened room which had been a pool hall. He negotiated the lease at the lowest rent he could find. It was a beginning his venture would cover room rent and put food on the table.

He opened his 'Nickel Odeon' in Atlantic city to the public with the first silent movie 'Gay Times' a forgettable but excellent entry into a family audience. He invited all the neighbour's their families and friends for an audience to the premier opening. It worked as he had little budget left for promotional advertising he needed their good will by word Of mouth. The size of his audience grew rapidly as he got bolder by hiring school boys to carry advertising boards over their shoulder through the city streets to a surge of delinquent children running amok in the isles during Saturday morning shows. In 1920 to 1924 the silent comedy shorts and news reels ran back to back, increasing the intermissions by repeating reels of a Charlie Chaplin and Mickey Mouse and a cartoon interval. The advertising revenue from local business, with ever longer lines around the block realized his dream. Putting the entire investment of cash flow revenue into each new nickelodeon moving picture house, coast to coast his entertainment starved audience stretched in lines round the block beyond the capacity of his first pool hall. The smell of roasted popcorn during the intermission with snacks and ice cream supplied by his old friend the Italian gelato merchant, business looked even rosier each passing year. He was on his way to his first fortune generating sufficient turnover to motivate him to enter into an agreement with United Artists originally started by Mary Pickford, Douglas Fairbanks and Charlie Chaplin who formed a motion picture production company named United Artists theatre, This was the moment he had been waiting for realizing his ambition to buy and build screens rather than rent real estate for his picture house empire gave his corporation stability. Growth came with bigger financial gains followed during the silent years as the screen went to talkies he brought sound to his theatre screens. In October 1927 with Al Jolson's first talking picture shown with astounding box office receipts. Success followed with Busby Berkeley screen choreography, and in 1928 Disney's 'Steamboat Willy. Later, Greta Garbo as the screen siren with a husky voice sent shivers down the spine, as her sensuous lips and beautiful photogenic face filled the silver screen. Charged with emotion the audience reacted in awe, he had found his metier and revelled in his success to entertain the masses through his theatres 2,050 silver screens.

On his death Mr. Naify senior left United Artists studios and distribution network to two his sons Mr. Marshal Naify and Mr. Robert, Robert then moved into the mansion built by his father in 1920 overlooked the Golden Gate Bridge in San Francisco bay. The west coast of California and the states beyond was the stage now set for riches beyond imagination of the eastern seaboard conjoined with New York to Main with all the USA. The nineteen sixties set the scene for new enterprise and innovation with Mike Todd invention the Naify's took TodAo into post production studios on the east and west coast of America including London UK. He acquired large tracts of the San Fransisco bays waterfront and dock area with commercial developments of the city centre with swathes of industrial real estate. With surplus funds he bought shares in the developing Cable TV and telecommunication industry together with foreign exchange invested in golf courses on the Spanish peninsula in Europe. Forbes 400 listed his estimated worth at $4.3 Billion Dollars.

Robert Naify made Shrewd Investment in Art over the years which proved a prudent pathway to beat inflation, with impressionist paintings of twentieth century art as a lucrative investment in the early years. Displaying wealth in private residences was nothing new, but bringing it to notice of the Media could antagonize the poor divide and attract rich pickings for the criminal.

Mr. Robert Naify's son knew the price of everything but the value of nothing, hedging his future trust fund with handouts and deals, to feed an addictive habit after his multiple inpatient therapy sessions at the Betty Ford Clinic proved unsuccessful. He apparently had a talent for evasion and pecuniary advantage. His two half sisters also engaged in the Los Angeles life of co-dependency came infrequently on Visits to assure a continued familial connection. I stayed for almost two until the isolation and long hours overtook me. After much soul searching I gave in my notice to Mrs Naify who did want me to stay by offering to increase my salary as inducement. I was happy to be treated with such belated respect but decided to leave, as the few friends 1 had neglected were in souther California, and I wanted to return to Los Angeles as there was so little time to develop a social life in the isolation of San Fransisco, with less chance to meet new people due to being on duty for such long hours with only one day a week to rest up. My day off was spent in a Gallery or Library in the Presidio Park. Mrs Naify generously offered me her private circle box in the San Fransisco Theatre to have a better view of the stage, as she was a member of the board, she suggested I use her Bentley limousine and invited me to park in her private space on the opera house lot as inducement. This may not be a usual experience but I was often asked to keep the fleet of vehicles serviced and driven regularly, with one particular week a request came to keep the mileage up between services, I was told drive the Bentley car to 'Vons' Supermarket to pick up a bag of sugar, surely an eccentric move. For what it cost to purchase the two kilograms of sugar, it could keep a family in food for a week with change left over to send their kids to school in South America. This does appear to be excessive and over the top, but it is the American way of keeping on top of the game.

*Don't confuse fame with success, one is Madonna; the other is
Helen Kellen - Irma Bombeck*

AGNUS DEI

'Agnus dei qui tolis pecata mundi miserere nobis' Max and I looked at other to see if we had the answer to this liturgical question. If the answer was unavailable what was the point of the question. Later after leaving the church congregation in a heightened state of confusion Max explained to us that the Latin translated to ' lamb of God who takes away the sins of the world forgive us O lord ' was the meaning. In our case it only added to the confusion, I was eight and Max only five year's young but advanced for his age. I asked Max what sin had he committed as mine had passed me by. I supposed smacking someone over the face did not count but he wasn't sure. My ability to cause pain and suffering to someone else had not been fully developed only the intent I wondered if it counted. Max however was a different kettle of fish by the age of four he said he had broken all the commandments bar the sin of adultery as he had not taken his marriage vows yet. I was not sure what he meant but he was always in advance of his age it was as if he had been born in another time and place. I could not hide my amazement when Max took out a note from his tiny wallet which read 'l promise to pay the bearer 'on a regulated currency note of the Queen. He then told me he had taken this note from mummy's purse, I was horrified and he just giggled, by now he had stopped gurgling. He explained his act of criminal intent was intended to explore the meaning of sin. I said he had plenty of time for that in the years to come and he should put the note back where he found it as mummy will need it for shopping.

The idea of sin as we know it applies to those who know the true meaning of lies, not to babes in arms and infant children suckling at their mother's breast. Max and I took a long walk home in deep thought in silence through the park before Sunday lunch. It had rained the night before and the grass was greener with banks of flowering tulips and hyacinth lining the path home, somehow it felt brighter too.

I had not seen Max for several months due to the confusion over train timetables on Leeds platform as British Rail decided to run the 'Flying Scotsman'. This information 'was announced over the speaker in muffied bursts of flat vowels in a broken dialect of west Yorkshire aided by the microphone being slammed against the counter for guaranteed listening potential. By the Scotsman'. This information was announced over the speaker in muffied bursts of flat vowels in a broken dialect of west Yorkshire aided by the microphone being slammed against the counter for guaranteed listening potential. By the time it was established there was not enough platform left to run on another term went by without contact with Max. No phone was available at school it was only for explicit emergency such as births, marriage and death. My intention would be for social purpose and therefore it was barred. Letters were restricted to immediate practical use and parental affection was not encouraged. I was relieved to leave this bastion of religious fervour and unloving environment at the end of winter 1948, Mother thought my tears were of sadness but they were tears of Joy of departure. On my return home from school I was despondent but Brother Max soon encouraged me to enjoy his company and I was entertained by him. I warmed to the occasion and found myself at the deep end of the pool on Saturday mornings with instruction from the father to learn to swim without enthusiasm. My Father was a distant figure there was no bond between us. As his child it became apparent that the gulf between us became a chasm and never developed into a close bond. I think we both recognised our relationship would go nowhere so we gave up on each other. What was an eight year old supposed to do I would never have given up on my child at any age. His macho mentality reflected intolerance at my wish to continue ballet class while my intolerance at his demand for me to take up boxing became a battle of wills between us. The years rolled by before I started to become more independent. The few friends I cultivated overtime had gone their own way, by the age of eighteen I moved to London. My contact with Max became infrequent as our lives had changed with the pattern of youth and discovery it was a loss between almost as if it had never happened.

I HAD A BROTHER

I had a brother born February 1943 but he lived only a few hours. If he had survived what would he have become, would he and I have been friends. What path in life would he have chosen to take, would he and I have always been there for each other in life as my other three siblings had not, these and other questions would be answered in the fullness of time. Mother hid the fact of his birth and only told me of this before she passed away at 92. It took some years for me to fully absorb the fact of his demise and acceptance of his being here if only for a visit.

Firstly his name was Max short for Maximilian named after mother's favourite uncle. I imagined his stubby fingers sticking out from his cot covers gurgling and jerking his little legs as if in a hurry to go nowhere. I was three and walking by that time and able to climb stairs if we had some as we lived in a bungalow at the time. The small garden gave a place to park the pram by the begonias on a postage stamp size lawn. It offered a tight fit for our family dog an Irish red setter to patrol and guard Max his charge. Did this memory provide detail of sound, sight, taste or imaginary landscape of the mind, it did happen as described.

There is no mystery in birth but death has a head start and sudden or lingering finish. In a race we can fall at the first hurdle but the finish line presents us with a problem as there is no photo-finish to review the passing when it's over. Imagine your surprise at a visit from your favourite uncle who recently passed would this deter you from giving him a whole hearted welcome or would you ignore his visit, the choice is yours. I would be delighted if mine made a visit as he made so few in his lifetime and it would make up the deficiency. Whatever the answer it can do no harm in drawing on reserves of happiness. There is enough sadness in the world to open a reserve Bank of misery where you could open an account to take interest free loans to spread a little misery to those who need it. Your generosity would be two fold. First you could enjoy your own misery and second spread it around with good intent. If you believe that you need to smile a little. Back to Max the brother I had, he just gurgled in happiness because he had just opened his own account with the reserve Bank of happiness and intended to spread it around generously to those in need.

Icing on the cake

Max had his first birthday at home surrounded by those nearest and dearest including grandma's parrot brought to reinforce the numbers. His cage resplendent with dramatic black curtain's drawn in an attempt to tone down the loud screeching emanating from the folds of 'Dolly's beak. Grandma herself sat in a high back wing chair looking rather regal. Max smiling and gurgled over the starched white linen table cloth with his little hand trying to reach his oversized white iced birthday cake lit with one candle lit on a crystal cake stand borrowed for the occasion. In red icing the message Max Birthday boy' had been applied lop-sized so as to give it a jaunty look. This did not mean a thing to Max, all he wanted was to stuff his fingers into the confection in an effort to transfer it to his little mouth while screaming in competition with 'Doll'/ the parrot who by now had enough of being ignored.

Mother distributed paper hats and jelly to my cousin Antoinette as she needed to improve her appearance. She sat on a stool with a plastic straw stuck between her fat pink lips sucking on a bright yellow concoction with harmful additives. She was painfully aware of the impression she gave of an unruly toad but this did not do justice to her kind nature. Similar niceties relating to the other invited toddlers were given as they sat back in awe of the organised chaos. It finished with birthday cards and wrapped gifts given to birthday boy Max as was the custom. Some of the hand-made gifts took hours to make were destroyed in minutes. A last chorus of 'happy birthday to you' directed toward Max who by now completely ignored the ensemble was stuffing his face with what was left of the icing on the cake after being demolished by departing guests on paper plates.

Later that evening after school I looked in on Max if he had enjoyed his birthday bash he replied by regurgitating the menu on to my new school blazer with a splendid Rorschach blot followed by a smile and even more gurgling before his bedtime, who could blame him I never did.

The months turned to years while I had become more reticent, Max had developed a lively concern for others and gave him-self to the point of being selfless. To illustrate the point I was sent to boarding school at the age of five with my other brother David who was two years older than me. I remember writing letters home at the age of five which were taken to the post office in Alton Village by the nun's, in which 'I wrote asking Mummy for some more tooth paste and coal tar soap'. Max had asked for the letter to be read to him. Believing that I could not wash myself and have clean teeth until the parcel arrival he cried and had to be consoled before bed time. The nuns at boarding school as brides of Christ functioned as teachers for the older boys and nurses to the younger infants like me. At bath time they hovered like black ravens at the tap end of the bath to administer a scrubbing brush and lathered soap on a face cloth which was applied with vigour as the ritual of cleaning in my case was critical. In 1945 the summer holiday my daytime was spent on the beach at Blackpool a north of England seaside town enabling my tan to deepen to a dark brown where the sock ended at the knee in a neat line. 'Oh you are a dirty little bov the old crone dressed in black wheezed 'why doesn't your mummy wash you '. I was so ashamed, to this day years later I remember I wished I could have been swallowed down the plug whole instantly strangled on the way down. At mass in Church on Sunday's the Priest would wail in reverential tones swinging the incense on a long chain hypnotically like a giant pendulum in the direction of the congregation narrowly missing a supplicants head. As if the hand of God pointed him out for the multiple sin's being commited for penance left unsaid. At the moment of Eucarist he raised the shining golden goblet high over his head holding the blood of Christ while I imagined he had plucked it from heaven above. Max was not there to share the memories he was too young to appreciate these moments or so I thought. At Christmas he and I would be ecstatic over stories of his weekends spent with grandma. She was the only Irish Rose I knew, while I provided him with the intricacies of spring picnics by the river at Alton trailing over fields of shamrock and daises. What else was there to do in the winter of 1946 the future was unknown and the second world war was about to finish.

Chapter 11

CHILDHOOD in Post war
Britain 1940 -1948

'Twenty two tramps trotted through the town', I was made to say this over and over again. With, 'are you copper bottoming um mum'. 'The quick brown foxes jumped right over the lazy dogs'. Or 'she sold sea shells on the sea shore'. Or, the cat sat on the mat as a war of attrition raged between me and my father at the age of six, he made me repeat the elocution lesson daily. Fearing his wrath believed if I did not perform this would result in severe beatings from his brass buckled leather belt that left bright red welt marks on the cheeks of my buttocks, then sent to bed and banned from eating meals made to drink water and dry bread. Mum would wait for him to leave the house and slip into the bedroom I shared with my older brother on holiday's who was away at boarding school for deaf children to learn outside the mainstream education system. I missed the playful company of my brother David the thought of this made me sob with tears and frustration. My Mother Maude had her own problems with her partner a husband who beat her physically with malicious intent consistently to cause bodily harm and mental torture over forty years of marriage. This resulted in her multiple ambulance visits to the hospital trauma ward during years of a miserable married existence without respite. With strong spirit she bravely executed her wifely duties with courage, but without conviction. 'Mummy do you love daddy' I waited for her reply she answered with a sigh 'I used to' and held me close before leaving my side on hearing the front door closing on father's return. She had developed a siege mentality to protect herself with no support from her family she had left, the Catholic dogma she was exposed too from Childhood forbade divorce and offered her no safe harbour. Night after night I lay in the dark listening to screams of painful physical beating from the next bedroom room. When mother cried out against his physical assault, I ran to the cause of suffering to be shouted at by father to 'clear off. I stood in the door frame in my pyjamas thinking how to help her but unable to give assistance watching her receiving bruised cheekbones and a broken jaw. I was petrified as these severe beatings were usually followed by ambulance to the emergency ward at the city hospital where she had to stay days to get medical treatment. The emergency service called the police to intervene. They came to take his statement but left without bothering to refer to me as the only child as witness. Crying and confused at the pain of being part of the nightmare on her return then it would start again. I hated him with a palpable loathing not Wishing to speak with him wanting to grow older and bigger to fight the monster that rampaged through our lives. He would often shout 'Just like your mother sharing a bloody vendetta from Corsica'. Without a safe house to go to she had to stay knowing he would start the cycle all over again.

A RED LETTER DAY

While mum cooked Sunday meal on the stove she turned to my father to answer his question, he struck her forcibly with his fist across the face she fell to the floor. I saw red and jumped on his back, I could not remember how I got him to the floor grabbing hair at the back of his skull I jumped on him, stamping with my feet on his face and body, beating his bald head repeatedly on the concrete flagstone until blood ran from his nose. I was fifteen years of age and my brother in law and uncle pulled me off as I hit him hard during the fury of hate I understood the emotion. I could smell the fear this instilled in him, deciding not to retaliate, he did not fight back. I felt empowered, this compelled me to shout 'Try someone your own size next time you bastard' I bellowed at his retreating figure someone pulled me away from attacking him further. A retreating coward of a man who made our life a living hell, at this instant I decided to leave home at the earliest opportunity, 'You don't like me do you' he would say 'no I never did and never will' was my reply, a wary existence existed between us. In 1958 on my eighteenth birthday I left my maladjusted between family home never to return as the journey of my independent life had begun.

Mother separated from Father on her sixtieth birthday, on her retirement as a civil servant With the UK Department of highways. I would often visit her in her small flat in Yorkshire with Keith my partner and stay over in her apartment on our visits from London. To our amusement she would fuss round us with home baked cupcakes, jam tarts and tea. 'l wish would come more often.' 'l would mum but we have to make a living don't you come down for a few days to see the sights in London' the smile spread over her sweet face she beamed all the way to the kitchen for another pot of tea. She did as we suggested many times in the years that followed, we had laughter and fun she felt included and worked in our office as shorthand typist, telephonist and secretary. She would often say 'please stop it', 'I'm hurting from laughing so much' as the tears of joy ran down her face during one of my silly monologues. 'Well it's better than being beaten up mum' she nearly fell off her chair in peals of laughter the happiest I had ever seen her for a long time.

WINTER 1944

My early years, from the age of four in a private public school as border was a desolate period. Britain was on its economic knees after the second-world war in September 1945 Germany had surrendered Anti-air craft guns and the searchlights were dismantled from the roof of battlements from St John's preparatory school designed by the Architect Pugin built on an imposing high bluff point overlooking the village of Alton North Staffordshire. Before the Easter holiday's during the great thaw of the 1944 winter, cattle drowned as the river burst its banks. I remember watching from the battlements the dead livestock and their bloated carcass of sheep and heifers in calf floating on the swollen river covering the valley below.

I ran to the kitchen below stairs after lessons to see Sister Anne the Irish Nun whose gentle kindness allowed me to sit on a stool beside her while she worked. I watched her remove hot ginger biscuits and angel cakes from the oven with a smile on her face. She noticed my gaze as she offered me a biscuit warm and crisp as toast. She would hide me under her black voluminous garment when other nun's entered, passed as unwanted guest down stone stairs to the kitchen. Fresh strawberry jam tarts with warm crusts of pastry melted into buttery crumbs as they went into my hungry mouth while I hid in her petticoats. This memory of her kindness was an image I will always keep of Sister Anne and my days away from home as a five year old toddler.

My journey's home on the 'Flying Scotsman' the steam locomotive train was the highlight of my return from summer holidays. The box fireman allowed me to pull the whistle chord before we departed the Uttoxeter station as the smoke filled platform slowly disappeared into clouds of steam, with the clanging of released buffers moving after a porter's whistle and a green flag. A great whoosh of sparks from the open coal firebox threw misty clouds of vapour high into the sky. The groan of metal wheels on the wet track in straining movement of slow turning wheels, and urgent slamming of heavy carriage doors as last minute passengers waved goodbye with tearful eyes until the Station disappeared from view of loved ones in the distance. Returning home on the 'Flying Scotsman' was exciting, the train travelled through the war torn midlands with weary Britain's post war bombed out rows of terraced houses. Rail tracks wound through English cities laid waste with bombed acres of rubble and miles of roofless buildings. Street markets had sprung up next to torn out shop windows. Scarred and charred office buildings next to roofless churches with blown out lead glass pictures of the divinity lay in devastation with great loss of lives and a sad reminder of the uselessness of war and the trauma of the returning hero's civilian life to the family home to rebuild a future. My father in the civil home guard waged war at home without respite, his private rage and the siege to resist the enemy within became a reality. On my return the first morning I woke to my sister Celeste standing beside my bed shaking me by the shoulder and tickling my nose with a banana. She was only three but climbed on the bed starting to jump up and down giggling and smiling while aiming her feet at my head. I turned over quickly to avoid impact and pulled the sheet up to my chin as she disappeared from the edge of the bed landing on the bare wooden floor boards that had no carpet. The splintered wood surface made hard contact with her derriere as her screams subsided later after the sobbing all was forgotten on her welcome to my homecoming. At home twelve years old I wet the bed, the shame of this happened during my sleep was followed by father's abusive words of discouragement. In contrast Mummy's soothing concern confused me even more as I gave in to recurring asthma attacks and bedwetting. The unholy alliance of extreme psychotic behaviour from my father, followed by the patient care of an understanding passive mother created seventeen years of frustration and misery. After my eleventh birthday I escaped at weekends and long summer holidays from school to work at 'Crag top' Farm, reached by my walking 400 feet high on Rombalds moor in the Yorkshire dales where I had been an evacuee in 1941 from six months old during the war. From ten years old I laboured hard from first light until dark, muck spreading or driving the sheep into the pen with 'Old Bob' the Welsh border cross at my heels gathering sheep for annual wool shearing. When the family returned from the fields at dusk to paraffin lamps with supper cooked from the wood burning Aga stove on the scrubbed wooden table, listening to off shore illegal Radio Luxembourg. Sometimes the weekends Saturday was an exciting trip to the Ilkley Cinema to see 'Annie get your gun' and other epics is now sadly closed. Return to a four mile walk over the moors after a two hour feature film with cartoon short's. In September a treat of an invitation to beat grouse on the moor for the gamekeeper in the shooting season was the highlight of autumn. We walked in a straight line at the end of the day over coverts and rough moorland with sticks making noise so as to drive the game over the line of waiting guns, with grouse screeching in flight toward the guns held high, the retriever working dogs would carefully pick up the game in a soft muzzle and drop them to the ground on the roadside. At the end of the day the invited guests of City Gun Syndicate had first pick of the birds arranged in brace on the heather before dispatch to the cities grand hotel menus. This natural world gave me insight to choose between the country and the city during post war boyhood. I learnt to drive on a 1954 Massey Ferguson tractor driving over field's haymaking and muck spreading in the spring lambing season the sheep sheared fleece was bundled for collection by the Wool marketing Board. The audience threw empty cigarette packets at the screen adding drama to the event, then a slow walk over the moors back to a warm bed to be up at daybreak during hay time after lambing season from dawn to dusk. In September a treat of an invitation to beat grouse on the moor for the gamekeeper in the shooting season was the highlight of autumn, We walked in a straight line over coverts and rough moorland with sticks making noise so as to drive the game over the line of waiting guns, with grouse screeching in flight toward the guns held high, the retriever working dogs would carefully pick up the game in a soft muzzle and drop them to the ground on the roadside. At the end of the day the invited guests of City Gun Syndicate had first pick of the birds arranged in brace on the heather before dispatch to the cities grand hotel menus. This natural world gave me insight to choose between the country and the city during post war boy hood. I learn to drive on a 1954 Massey Ferguson tractor driving over fields haymaking 9 redact and muck spreading in the spring lambing season the sheep sheared fleece was bundled for collection by the Wool marketing Board. Waking up at dawn with Bernard my childhood friend at Crag Top farm to scrape a winter frost inside the bedroom window shivering to dressing hurriedly before breakfast, loading up the 'Land-Rover' with clanging buckets. Breaking the ice surface of the frozen spring water collected in the bath outside the barn in winter with forks to carry bales of hay and bags of feed to the store cattle in the barn. We had breakfasted on duck eggs straight from the hot sizzling pan cooked on an open wood fire in the black leaded grate. Fresh baked bread from the oven with a golden crust appeared straight from the hot Oven, with home-made butter dripping onto the warm plate.

CALIFORNIA HERE I COME
USA 1985

Earlier in Spain I had bought gold assayed in Toledo when it was seven hundred US dollars for ten grams during a visit to Lanzarote spain in 1984. In 2012 1 sold the gold for two thousand six hundred dollars a gram in India the biggest importer of gold in the World. I realised that one bullion gold bar was now worth $64,000 rising in value reaching new highs in 2011. As the perfect transferable currency without borders it melts down to liquid in a crucible and can never be traced back to any source. Twenty five percent of the world's gold bullion deposits worth three hundred and eighty billion dollars are in the safe at 33, Liberty Street in New York. Fifty percent of the total is deposited in Fort Nox, Kentucky, USA in the world's largest gold vault. The Federal Reserve distributes dollar currency backed by its promise to pay the bearer the amount specified on both sides of numbered paper. Printed in Federal Reserve government press by the Intaglio process from master engraved plates in four separate layers of ink, two identity stripes one holistic and one metallic through cotton and linen paper used to deter counterfeiters. Each new engraved image takes ten years to perfect. It really is a matter of conversion from gold to paper, trading in the commodity then transferring it back to gold as a simple commercial formula for business enterprise. Nations engage in this exchange mechanism, some foolish people believe otherwise, it's not rocket science. My habit of folding bank notes face up In Sequence face up before placing them in a wallet was born of necessity due to a condition affecting my sight from cataracts. I can evaluate weight Without the help of a machine by lifting it in hand, an ability to work out Percentages and interest rates without recourse to a calculator to multiply and subtract for percentage margins. I realised prosperity increases by) observing opportunities as they presented themselves.

Quick to respond in making decisions it gave me the edge in sizing up the prey, with the added bonus of me having an IQ of 170, but my emotional profile needed a long time to catch up. The day after another very late dinner at the Trattoria, the Chianti had flowed liberally with friends after the midnight hour I stumbled into a cab homeward bound in the early hours. My depression sufficiently anesthetized to consider conceiving the idea of calling it a day. The recent confirmation that the house I had a mortgage on had been repossessed as my Nephew Anton had not paid the rent to cover the mortgage cost during his last few months of tenure. I found out the bailiffs had taken the contents and furniture with all my personal possessions to be sold at auction while I had been away in the States. Anton, my brothers son had left the house paying no rent, with his musician student group. His father David took no action to assist me despite his promise 'Don't worry kid ' I will take care of it. 'He ignored the matter without any intention to inform me of the critical situation which would have enabled me to put it right in time. His assurance that he would monitor the situation while I was away became an empty promise. My house had been sealed and repossessed by court warrant which had been attached to the door I lost my home and I could not enter it to clear my few personal possessions but worse was yet to come.

YORKSHIRE

My phone rang While was making an espresso in my bijou kitchen. The stifled sound of sobbing traveled across the line, 'l can't take it any more Paul I really can't,' recognising the voice of my sister in law was in a confused state as her voice broke between heartfelt sobs. 'Hello Hazel what can't you take?' After a long pause the sobs died away she blurted out the depth of her unrequited feelings with my brother she had married. She loved him but felt he was no longer expressing his love for her, I let her ramble on. After ten uninterrupted minutes of this turgid but true account of her married relationship he interrupted her at intervals You should not be talking to me about it why don't you talk to him he is the one to resolve your intimate situation Hazel' Oh! 'Please come tomorrow Paul he has been away all week and I have not heard from him. I waited a moment before finally saying 'Ok Hazel, get some sleep I will come tomorrow' with some latent composure she said 'Thanks Love, goodnight' and rang off.

I pondered, was this how marriage was for most people, a Tolstoy tragedy of 'War and Peace.' I shuddered and thanked my good fortune I was single by choice and inclination. I could not see how important it was for reason of survival of the species that I plant my seed in wedlock to create a new life in my image that would continue a genetic line. This equation would always be my understanding of the issue since my tryst with Jeanette. I considered marriage to be serialised promiscuity in the form of a legalised contract with added tax benefits and the Possibility of procreation and a recycling of expectations. Religious and traditional acceptance of the roles I consider unequal in every way. I cogitated on this cultural tradition, with the demands of peer pressure and the nocturnal cogitation exhausted me. I managed to get to bed after ablutions. Taking out my dentures dropped them into a bedside glass they smiled back at me non-judgmentally. I turned off the light to muse in the darkness before sleeping with dreams of Utopia, an imagined perfect world deciding I would make my own.

OLIGARCHS
2015 - year of the sheep

China is the biggest investor in the economy of Africa's infrastructure development they tender contracts to Governments by providing capitol and credit for projects which are conducive to the investor. Seventy percent of the work force is Chinese and the essential materials are also imported from China, circumventing local labour and resource available in Africa. This policy gives little to the local economy and regions of those countries who currently participate in this new expansion. This attracts political and economic motivation to the power brokers of the African continent and State Governments. The United States of America invested $1.2 billion dollars in equipment and military training in the African continent, a huge investment creating security forces and the supply of equipment for military regimes to keep those governments in power under the legal pretext of a Global war on terrorism. This claim is a threat to ethnic forces who oppose the American invasion of boots on African soil. Somali gunmen in a revenge killing in the Westgate mall in Nairobi Kenya murdered 67 people in a state Of siege against the US involvement in Africa, who view China in opposition to their presence. This did not bode well for the future peace and security of the civilian population. The continents natural resources are made available by the new sophisticated de-colonised

Independent African countries to the few contracted corporations, causing a major corruption in the National interest of its people. Oligarchs who control the economies Of the continent allow the merging of political and military regimes causing instability and ethnic contest to keep in power. Professor Jeremy Keenan of London University confirmed with research, shows the claim from the USA that 'Terrorism is prevalent in the Sub-Sahara region and as a swamp of terror' is exaggerated, but the mindset of the spectre of ISSIS and Hamas is firmly established. The African union held its 24th annual meeting in Addis Ababa without an anticipated overdue report on human rights in the region regarded as negligent by neighbouring countries.

What's large and hard and pink in the morning?
THE FINANCIAL TIMES crossword

ECONOMIC SANCTIONS

Russia started 2014 to 2018 with a planned expenditure cut of 40% of to their economy due to sanctions imposed by United Nations in response to Russia supporting the pro-Russian rebels in east Ukraine, by supplying military aid and equipment and training to the rebel army over the Ukraine border. In addition the 50% drop during 2015 in oil and gas price globally combines an economic catastrophe and GazProm had an 86% loss in profit in sales. Mr Putin stopped buying foreign currency but   imported epic proportions of gold bullion $70 billion in 2014 which impacted on the Russian economy. The reduction in the standard of living holds the potential of political and social cataclysm as a future reality for the Kremlin and Putin's political future. I had memories of my own experience of isolation during childhood, and on a subjective level Understood the mistrust of people for politicians and Government as power corrupts, absolute power corrupts absolutely. The Crimea had been taken over by Russian asserting that it was historically their original heritage. Ukraine went to war and United Nations voted for sanctions as a deterrent against the Russian state.

SEIGE
Terrorism

Watching BBC TV in 2014 the report of an interview with so called Islamic state (ISIS) without a country, of their fighting to control vast swathes of Islamic states achieved a currency of publicity in the International media, illustrating their brutal inhumane and horrific executions of blood being spilled from civilian decapitation of their hostages on camera. Amassing a war chest of 20 billion dollars this media scenario played out directly with the Jordanian Government who wished to negotiate with them for their air force Officer taken as hostage by ISIS who was burnt alive on screen later by so called ISIS. Japanese journalist Kenji Goto captured in an attempt to help another colleague escape was beheaded a week later on video. Journalist Christian Amanpour the anchor from CNN news channel reported President Assad of Syria had ordered poisoned Gas bombs to be dropped on his civilians causing 100,000 deaths. This adds the oxygen of publicity to a volatile cocktail of violence; a heinous crime of murder in the quest to promote politically Islamic radicalism. Their tactic has reached maximum publicity value, ISIS have destroyed priceless antiquity and works of art recognised by UNESCO as of world heritage sites. Irreplaceable value created millennium ago for an expression of the human endeavour to create, and bring an element of control to their political cause for continued violence against civilians. Worldwide news media has coverage of these atrocities I headed for the bathroom and vomited into the water closet, was this really the world to realize indeed it was in the here now. I ran the shower stood under it for fifteen minutes, wrapping a towel round my waist to out of the bathroom and paused before lighting sticks of Agar placing step them on my desk, sat down and cogitated. In my reasoning, the concept of reality is a limitation with regard to its completeness reflecting an individual mind set opinion or perspective. Cause and effect is founded on a premise, as such it attempts to bring reality down to mundane experience. If effect is a self expression of the cause there is no reason why the two should be regarded as distinct. Reality is both being and nothing as Buddhist logic tries to denote it as " point instant of reality" as „pure object" or "own essence" "neither zero" or "non zero" what can one say about it just nothing, silence. To stake an intellectual explanation is futile: life is an illusive transient journey.

Small fish darted under the clear surface of water in bright shards of colour in endless movement. The aquarium held them captive in a stone jardiniére under the cover of an upturned surboard protecting their closet nursery against intense heat of the sun which stood on a border of carefully swept sand against the edge of neat cut grass. I sat under a cool canopy of mango and coconut fronds reading my book as a soft breeze gently lifted the edge of a page I was reading. During a paragraph I was disturbed by an ant crawling up my forearm shaking it away as the sound of a nearby train thundered past the bottom of the garden on the ribbon of hot metal toward its dusty destination on the south coast of Galle. Bala and I were in pursuit of the late morning sun on Bentota's beach which lay golden fringed by the shading palms inviting us to a surfer's embrace in the warm tidal waves breaking into a gentle murmur.

The next day a palpable climate of fear descended on the island of Sri Lanka from the blast of bombs exploding in three Christian churches simultaneously and two luxury hotels within seconds, bringing death to two hundred and fifty human lives from an ISIS terrorist attack creating destruction of human life of mothers, children and elderly relatives attending Sunday morning mass. Five hundred of the congregation were seriously injured and hospitalised. Sixty Muslim's known to be extremist ISIS were arrested and investigated by special commando military units in the days that followed, several were found to be without Visa's. Special commando military units investigating forensic evidence brought the bewildered government and frustrated police force to suspend the social media internet service and impose strict curfew for over a week. The President of the Republic called for the resignation of the Minister in charge of security. Public order was tentatively restored in the belief that retaliatory action would take place in future with further violence.

Rain, Rain, go away the monsoon is here to stay. Flash of lightening and crack of thunder breaks the heat asunder, bringing open heavens with heaving clouds to fill empty river beds flowing into the sea. Birds take cover and lovers hide under leafy trees to brace against the storm on wings to fly. There beating hearts with love not hate against the human race.

REFUGE OF REFUGEES

The human race has apparently learnt little through self interest from the individuals and institutions who use force with residual violence. Political and religious factions give little concession to the civilian population. The collateral damaged of children behind prison bars share the same fate with thousands of their mothers who have no rights, or receipt of an amnesty. Their future is dictated by politicians in tribal Afghanistan. Over sixty million refugees are without a home on the planet, 32 million children do not attend school in Africa of those only 10 % go to further education and College. 358 million people on the planet don't have access to clean drinking water. Families are destroyed by the very people that they elected to act in their future interest now regarded as collateral damage. The visceral and traumatic impact of their human ordeal will remain with them for life, while the ineffective UN and NATO hold talks debating their plight without deciding effective means of implementing or Providing a clear and secure future for its own people. This reflects on us as human beings, and questions whether we are able to be truly humane and live in a just world. My depression took firm hold at this dreadful impasse as sleep beckoned me I went to bed. Prayer without conviction is an act of symbolic contrition without involvement in deed in the slow Syrian massacre of women and children.

HOLOCAUST

If there is a God we should all pray for salvation of the human race from extinction as on the third of February 2015 the International Court at the Hague judged no case to answer to allegations of Genocide in Bosnia and Serbia due to lack of proof, after six years of evidence had been provided from the Victims communities and their Advocates to the court. Germany's final solution referred to as a national policy in 1938 to wipe out an entire race and replace it with the superior one aided by Doctor Mengler excluded minorities was unsuccessful. The apparent hidden agenda promulgated by the SS and Hitler youth movement majority. In the new millennium right wing fanatics in Europe•are gaining political ground swell in the notion that immigration control is the new buzzword used to manipulate their agenda motivated by ignorance and bigotry, the politician Le Pen leads the national front way in France, the UK National front parties numbers represented in Parliament by an MP with a new generation whose experience has no empathy of the holocaust and genocides but do have a vote, reminiscent of the Hitler youth. Maddame Le Pene of the National party became the Vox Populi in France.

Everything went right for him until the day he was born.

Victor Borge

I am looking at a sepia photo of Mum and me on my desk at the time of writing. She in 1941 a pretty twenty six year young woman holding me, a six month baby in her arms dressed in glamorous white lace facing the camera. My head turned to the left listening to some off camera instruction assembled in a wartime photographic studio. Now ninety years later to the present time at home, 360 degree circumstances were complete. Mother ninety two and incontinent waiting for her shower before the district Nurse comes to examine her for bed sores or other marks which there are none. A brisk towel dry after her shower, with 'Wild Jasmine' talcum powder applied liberally she stands in a cloud of floral aroma much to her liking before returning to clean crisp bed sheets. The ignominy of her being treated as a child now is something I had forgotten, however she grinned and bore her second childhood with remarkable courage. She waited for her treat of getting dressed in a white polka dot navy blue dress, under a woollen boucle navy double breasted overcoat as her choice, to match the wide brimmed navy blue hat set at a jaunty angle for her audience of dogs. On our arrival by car at the Hampstead tea room she waited in her wheelchair at a table she had chosen out of bright sunshine. On my return I placed a tray of cucumber sandwiches, Battenberg cake (Her favourite) and Ceylon leaf tea finding her surrounded by an adoring crowd of dogs of all sizes. She could not have been able to move out of this circle of appreciative canine fans, and they had no intention of leaving her audience just yet.

Another memory of my not sleeping well at age twelve coming downstairs in the early hours, to find her darning my grey woollen socks before I returned to school. Other times she had to go out to work to keep going after the financial crisis post war 1945. Life in

post war Britain was pre-NHS so private medical bills were paid
by private loan at ever higher revolving interest rate as it started a
cycle of debt spiraling out of control. This went on for years. Even
now I save rather than borrow. We are what circumstance and
environment shape us to be with a dash of some genetic item to even
out misfortune. She passed away in 2001 after living with me for
five years I still remember her voice after all these years as if it were
yesterday. In the grand scheme of things it is only a moment away.
She is now at peace away from harm, injury or malice. God Bless her
memory she gave me life, I hope in some small way to have returned
some to her in the universe.

MY ANCESTORS

My maternal Grandfather immigrated from Marseille in France willing to work for a better life for him and his family, they settled in England London in the 19th century. My maternal grand-parents were viniculture growers of grapes into wine, from Corsica but left for a better life in Marseille, France. My great grandmother on our maternal side was a french speaking Belgium Walloon who married a Parisian. After four years study their two sons entered as Escoffier students to attend Lille Ecole de Cuisine. Maximillian and Alfred Liotard graduated to Chef de brigade with a blue ribbon tricolour of France, the cuisine equivalent of an Oscar. My maternal grandfather's marriage followed, to Helen de Groote a Belgium actress with a penchant for stage performance in Theatre, she danced and sang as soubrette on the stage in Paris. My great Grandfather later moved to London, he never became a British subject appointed as Chef de Brigade with cordon Bleu ribbon, to her Majesty Queen Mary Queen consort to Albert George VI from 1910-24 on the Royal train. As an immigrant domiciled in London he had to sign on every week at Pimlico police station. From choice he did not renounce his French national status. On his death bed he found the energy to sing the Marseilles' national anthem loudly with great pride before his last breath surrounded by his wife and two sons. My mother's paternal Grandfather born in Bow the east end of London a cockney followed the family tradition as Chef de brigade. His father was an emigrant from Marseilles originally a wine growing family from Ajacio, on the isle of Corsica. My Grandfather was appointed Chef de Brigade, at the Hotel Majestic in Harrogate, his son Gaston Liotard moved to the North of England after his marriage to Rose McMann, a spinster from the Gorbals in Glasgow. Her parents immigrated from a farming community in Eniskillen County Fermanagh Ireland to Scotland in the Gorbals, Glasgow after the Irish Potato famine to work as housemaid in service before her marriage, their second daughter my mother Maude Liotard was born January 1912.

Previous reference of my descendent heredity in this book to my ancestor Great uncle Thomas, prompted me to investigate my genealogy through Wakefield local history museum, National Archive, Census and York University. It revealed a paternal line of ascendancy to my eight times great Uncle Thomas Clarkson 1760 the Abolishionist with continuity to our shared Grandfather John Clarkson born in Thirsk 1610, North Yorkshire. This information was retrieved from British National archives and examined with great enthusiasm of the 400 years included clergy records, which helped me understand my own life journey with wonder and excitement.

THE ABOLISHIONIST

My paternal ancestor Thomas Clarkson born 1760 Wisbech Cambridgeshire ordained as Dean and Anglican minister was the abolishionist of slavery. His name is remembered next to William Wilberforce, laid in Westminster Abbey attended by Queen Elizabeth 11 at a memorial service.

He was the son of Thomas Clarkson a merchant, born 20th December 1710 baptised in Thirsk 25th in the East riding of the county of Yorkshire in December, entered in the Bishops transcript and parish register. His father also named Thomas Clarkson baptised 22nd October 1684 was son of John Clarkson who married Mary Allenson 7th June 1642. In 1653 John Clarkson was elected register of the parish nominated by act of parliament. Between them my Clarkson ancestor's recorded in the Thirsk parish were augmented by 41 siblings. My family extant of the first recorded George Clarkson is buried in the parish Church graveyard of Thirsk on 28th April 1610 in the reign of James the 1st. Thomas Clarkson's siblings married into other local families. William Henry Clarkson 1725 travelled between town and countryside looking for a new stat. Difficult journeys were stimulated by railway traffic or barge on the new canals, as the agrarian population travelled by foot or equestrian means on roads in very poor conditions due to heavily rutted surfaces sometimes impassable from mud in heavy rain and flooding in winter subject only to local village repair. In 1700 a structure based on oligarchical complacency and lasser-faire was soon to be shattered by widespread industrial revolution. After several false starts William clarkson settled as parishioner of St Peters and St Leonards Church in Horbury West Yorkshire in 1796, his children attended the Village School in Tithe barn Road. The population migrated to developing towns and cities which offered work with the industrial revolution. The almost complete disappearance of rural crafts and village industries contributed to Thomas Clarkson's migration to Bradford in the new woolen weaving trade. The family finally settled in Hunslet Leeds to work in the heavy engineering industry as recorded in the 1841 Census to Holbeck in Leeds. Thomas Clarkson born 28th March 1760 in Wisbech Cambridgeshire in the reign of George the third, was recorded in the clergy of the Church as a student at St John's University College, after his original schooling at St Pauls college in London, he received some form of assistance such as meals lower fees or lodging during his period of four year study for his Cambridge Alumni, He was ordained as Anglican Minister. His father also an ordained head master of Wisbech free grammar school Cambridge, his Sadler born 1735 - 1799 was the daughter of Alpe Ward a physician of Royston Hertfordshire; her mother was one of the Banyers, a leading Wisbech family of Huguenot descent with connections in the gentry of Essex, including the Naval Rowley family.

Reverend John Clarkson's son's believed that through him they were distant cousins of the English social reformer Granville Sharp one of the founders of abolitionism. Reverend John and his wife nee Anne Ward born 1735, were parents of a daughter Anne, with two son,s Thomas Clarkson and Lieutenant John Clarkson RN. After their fathers death 23 September 1766 the family continued to live in Wisbech paid frequent visits to their Essex relations. Thanks to the Rowley's, after completing his schooling John joined the Navy in 1777 as a 'young gentleman' in Captain Joshua Rowley's ship HMS Monarch.

Thomas published twenty three works, most of which dealt with slavery. The Essay had a great success and lead to the creation of an informal committee to lobby MP's. It's most important achievement was the recruiting of William Wilberforce MP in which Thomas Clarkson played the chief part. Thomas took on the essential job of seeking out every possible source of information with an eye to an impending inquiry by the privy-council and later proceedings in Parliament. The years between 1808 and 1823 were largely taken up to ensure the abolition act was enforced, and after the defeat of Napoleon in forwarding the cause internationally, lending his pen and prestige to the cause of abolition in the United States. He was in Paris in 1814 and at the Congress of Aix-la-Chapelle in 1818 he rode over 35,000 miles on horseback in seven years since 1872. By the summer of 1824 petitions had been sent to Parliament demanding gradual emancipation. In 1830 the society adopted a policy of immediate emancipation, Clarkson and Wilberforce appeared together for the last time to give their support. The Act finally abolished slavery in the British Empire in 1833. On 12 June 1840 Thomas presided at the opening session of the grand anti slavery convention when he blessed the proceedings. He died in 1846 and was buried at St Marys Church Playford 2nd October.

Thomas Clarkson the first historian of the abolishionist movement wrote an account of the triumphant campaign to end the slave trade. The book was in print by 1808, Clarkson understood the historical narrative but after 1833 he became victim of a new history written around Wilberforce whose two sons, in their five- volume biography of their father demoted Thomas Clarkson to a hired functionary, they did not return the letters presumed destroyed of his correspondence with their father, an act of historical vandalism. The contributions of black abolishionists, Olaudah Equiano, Mary Prince, and Otto Sanchbah Cuguano were also redacted. Phillis Wheatley, James Gronniosaw, Ignatious Sancho through their letters, poems, memoirs and of their speeches in Britain. In the Victorian Galleries of the National Gallery in London hangs a portrait painted by Carl Frederick von Breda 1760-1846 of Thomas Clarkson president of the society spoke of the British Empire and of her many millions of Indian peoples bondage outlined. He spoke of the atrocities and horrors of a system of bondage in his speech he told the convention, of more than two million fellow human beings in most cruel bondage by slave holders in America. He warned such men lived in daily habits of injustice cruelty and oppression as having no fear of God.

Olaudah Equiano,
or
GUSTAVUS VASSA,
the African.
Publish'd March 1 1789 by G. Vassa

BLACK LIVES MATTER

June tenth celebrates emancipation in the USA freedom day and the end of slavery 19 June 1865. Black lives matter founded in 2013 as a global decentralised movement advocating non-violent civil disobedience in protest against incidents of police brutality and all racially motivated violence against African American people. There are 40 chapters around the globe promoting a vision for black freedom committed to liberation work. In July 2020 the movement found it's voice after the murder of African American George Floyd by a white police officer in the street after kneeling on his neck for nearly nine minutes until George expired, Several other police officers stood by and watched the crime, they were later indicted for second degree murder. International news media exposed this and other multiple episodes of endemic police brutality over the last seven years to date brought to light this injustice as yet still unrecognised by congress as a matter of inequality and breach of human rights in the USA.

In the UK desist economic inequality by supporting black British business 15% of shelf space to black enterprise for products and services, by promoting economic equality to entrepreneurs enabling them to qualify for Bank loans for expansion of independent black business in the mainstream economy.

During Clarkson's 4 year study for his Cambridge Alumni, he took Deacons orders and was ordained an Anglican minister. His father also an ordained Vicar was head master of Wisbech free grammar school Cambridge, his wife Anne Sadler born 1735 1799 was the daughter of Alpe Ward a physician of Royston Hertfordshire; her mother was one of the Banyers, a leading Wisbech family of Huguenot descent with connections in the gentry of Essex, including the Naval Rowley family. Reverend John Clarkson's son's believed that through him they were distant cousins of the English social reformer Granville Sharp, one of the founders of abolitionism. Reverend John and his wife nee Anrie Ward born 1735, were parents of a daughter Anne, with two son's Thomas Clarkson and Lieutenant John Clarkson RN. After their father's death 23 September 1766 the family continued to live in Wisbech paid frequent visits to their Essex relations. Thanks to the Rowley's, after completing his schooling John joined the Navy in 1777 as a 'young gentleman' in Captain Joshua Rowley's ship HMS Monarch.

Thomas published twenty three works, most of which dealt with slavery. The Essay had a great success and lead to the creation of an informal committee to lobby MP's. It's most important achievement was the recruiting Of William Wilberforce MP in which Thomas Clarkson played the chief part. Thomas took on the essential job of seeking out every possible source of information with an eye to an impending enquiry by the privy-council and later Proceedings in Parliament. The years between 1808 and 1823 were largely taken up to ensure the abolition act was enforced, and after the defeat of Napoleon in forwarding the cause internationally, lending his pen and prestige to the cause of abolition in the United States. He was in Paris in 1814 and at the Congress of Aix-la-Chapelle in 1818 he rode over

35,000 miles on horseback in seven years since 1872. By the summer of 1824 petitions had been sent to Parliament demanding gradual emancipation. In 1830 the society adopted a policy of immediate emancipation, Clarkson and Wilberforce appeared together for the last time to give their support. The Act finally abolished slavery in the British Empire in 1833. On 12 June 1840 Thomas Presided at the opening session of the grand anti-slavery convention when he blessed the proceedings. He died in 1846 and was buried at St Marys Church Play ford 2nd October.

A FRIEND TO SLAVES

Thomas Clarkson born 28 March 1760 at Wisbech in 1775 was sent to St Paul's school London gained a first at St John the Evangelist at the University of Cambridge in 1785 for his prize winning essay 'the merit of originating the triumph of the great struggle for the deliverance of the enslaved African 'as a violation of human rights. In his biography by Ellen Gibson Wilson Thomas Clarkson a Biography (1989) he with the MP William Wilberforce persuaded the British people and government to end the slave trade and slavery in Africa. Thomas Clarkson was elected the first President of World Anti-Slavery convention in 1840.

William Wordsworth, Thomas's neighbour in the Cumbrian Lake district was moved to write a sonnet in honour of his friend:

Clarkson! It was an obstinate hill to climb;

How toilsome-nay, how dire-it was by thee

Is known by none, perhaps so fleetingly:

But though, who, started in thy fervent prime,

Didst first lead forth that enterprise sublime,

Hast heard the constant voice its charge repeat,

Which out of thy young hearts oracular seat,

First roused thee-Oh true yoke fellow of time,

Duty's intrepid liegeman, see, the palm is won by all nations

Shall be worn! The blood stained writing is forever torn:

And thou henceforth wilt have a good mans calm,

A great mans happiness; thy zeal shall find repose at length,

'Firm friend of human kind'

Thomas Clarkson was described as one of the noblest of Englishmen, a pioneer with a life-long commitment to the abolition movement. He was the first President of Anti-Slavery International (ASI) which has consultative status at the United Nations. His life is commemorated on a plaque 'Friend to slaves' in Westminster Abbey 26th September 1996, my great and good ancestor raised his head above the parapet in honour of the human race. He was a friend of Wordworth, Coleridge and Southey, the former a neighbour in Ullswater jn Cumbria. William Wilberforce MP in Hull sons wrote their father's biography omitted that Thomas Clarkson as the Architect of human rights they mentioned only an agent. They subsequently apologised (Not officially in writing). 'We were wrong in the manner in which we treated you in the memoir of our father. We are conscious that to jealous a regard for what we thought our fathers fame led us to entertain ungrounded prejudice against you and this led us into a tone of writing which we now acknowledge was practically unjust.'

In 1787 after Thomas wrote his thesis essay entry for Cambridge University it was accepted with alacrity, He formed a committee, as he was one of the twelve that formed 'The society for effective abolition of the slave trade.' He travelling thousands of miles in great danger throughout Britain and was nearly murdered in Liverpool, on the continent he met the Emperor of Russia with whom he gained support, (five months in Paris in 1789-1790) trying to persuade the National assembly to abolish the slave trade. His health was collapsing and he decided to retire from the work as he had spent his capitol in the cause.

Led by William Wilberforce, his friends raised fifteen hundred pounds in 1794 to compensate him for his financial loss, and he bought a small thirty four acre estate at 'Eusemere' at Ullswater near Penrith in the Lake District to take up farming. His retirement was transitory he used it to reestablish his health and married Catherine Buck (1772-1856 of Bury St Edmunds in 1796. She shared Thomas's radicalism (they got to know each other through anti-slavery work) they had an only child Thomas who died 1837. They returned to the south of England and lived at Bury St Edmunds from 1806 to 1816, and thereafter at Playford Hall, halfway between Ipswich and Woodbridge, leased for a nominal rent from a friend the Earl of Bristol. After recuperation he returned with his old vigour to fight against the slave trade, when in 1804 the cause revived until the act abolishing the trade was passed in 1807. On his death at the age of 86 his whole life had been dedicated to ending slavery and the inhumanity of man. In 1996 to mark his sesquicentenary a tablet was placed in Westminster Abbey next to the Wilberforce monument. Jamaica created a settlement in his honour Clarksonville at St Anne.

In 1791 John Clarkson was appointed to lead recruitment of the Nova Scotia black loyalists and establish a new colony of black settlers in society, he was to be answerable to the board of Directors of the Sierra Leone Company who promised to develop settlements of the grain coast and return a profit to the investors from the settlement crops. so long as the principle of liberty remained without resorting to the selling Of inhabitants as slaves, and become a model community of the province Of 'Freetown' the capitol of Sierra Leone. To ensure the colony lived up to its creed the man chosen twenty-seven year old John Clarkson and younger brother of Thomas Clarkson the moral leader of the British abolitionist movement. John Clarkson left his fiancée Susan Lee behind in England and began a tour of the regions in which the black loyalist settled. Within three months 1,196 black men women and children had abandoned their life in British North America, to a future in Sierra Leone Africa a province of Freedom. Crossing the ocean with Thomas peters a former slave now a free man from North Carolina travelled with John Clarkson, they toured all the regions in which the black loyalists had settled, speaking from the pulpits of Churches in the black community and in their homes promoting the new Sierra Leone scheme. Thomas peters reputation for integrity won over the black loyalists and within eighteen months John Clarkson left 'Freetown' to return to England and rejoin his fiancée, he named the harbour he departed from 'Susan Bay'.

William Wilberforce MP delivered his first speech against the slave trade to the House of Commons in May 1789. He was able to support his critical introduction against the slave trade with the enormous body of damning evidence compiled by Thomas Clarkson. The first bill brought to the house by Wilberforce as Member of Parliament was watched by Thomas Clarkson from the viewing gallery. Wilberforce introduced the second bill in 1792 supported by a petition of over four hundred thousand United Kingdom Citizen signatures but even this did not persuade Parliament to support the bill. Wilberforce continued introducing further bills for the abolition of the slave trade every year until 1799. At this time the war with France and wide spread distress among the poor with rebellion in Ireland made it increasingly impossible for Clarkson and his allies to bring the abuses of the slave trade to the front of the lawmakers mind. Abolishionist publications with fiery speeches were delivered at meetings countrywide yet the bill still failed. The general election of 1806 brought newly elected parliamentarians encouraged by the

Prime minister. The opportunity came and the bill was passed by both houses which received royal ascent from King James 2nd. The British slave trade had begun under Charles II in 1668. Granville sharp the social reformer estimated that between 1789 and 1807, 767,000 African were enslaved and transported to slavery in British ships, slavery remained legal in British colonies until 1830.

Women denied the vote or a meaningful role in British politics brought scorn from journalist hacks as they boycotted sugar in the domestic home, it was the women that brought anti-slavery politics into the home. The abolishionist could not have achieved much without their existential involvement.

To demonstrate the brutality and educate the audience at meetings, activists acquired tools, the shackles, metal collars and whips, chained manacles in evidence of violence. Wilberforce demonstrated thumbscrews with shackles. Thomas Clarkson had two models made to scale of the slave ship 'Brooks' built from the original in Liverpool, fitted to carry 451 captives as typical example used in the slave trade. The scale dimension was given to Thomas Clarkson by Captain Perry of the Royal Navy. Clarkson took one of his model ships on tour and gave the other to Wilbeforce to show to his fellow MP's in the House of Commons. In 1783 the 'Brooks' sailed with 609 enslaved Africans, 158 more than she was fitted to accommodate. Alexander Falconbridge, bodyguard to Thomas Clarkson as his life had been threatened, gave his description of 'The hardships and inconvenience suffered by the enslaved 'Africans during their passage are scarcely to be enumerated or conceived of. They are more violently affected by sea sickness than Europeans. It frequently terminates in death, especially in women. The air below deck is excluded and the rooms soon grow intolerable hot, confined air rendered noxious by the excreta and effiuent vomit exhaled from their bodies, and being repeatedly breathed in soon produces fever and fluxes which generally carries them off in great numbers.' Falconbridge wrote the account and withstood four days of probing questions from Parliamentary Privy Council committee in the House of Commons on the matter of the slave trade.

In 1807 the West Indies became a target, on the Islands hundreds and thousands remained subject to the many horrors of plantation slavery, in Britain abolitionism was dormant. In 1814 a mass meeting was called in London and the National abolishionist movement sprang into action. One and a half million people signed a petition in Britain registering opposition to any restoration of the slave trade. Thomas Clarkson believed the abolition of the trade would be a death blow to plantation slavery as slave owners were unable to buy new slaves Thomas Clarkson at sixty three was energetic in gathering data. In 1814 Clarkson continued to criss-cross the country conducting meetings with those involved in the trade, and their victims. He embarked on an epic journey on horseback around the country mobilizing the faithful. In 1831 the Jamaican slaves rebelled with a sit down strike in the sugar cane fields. Over 23,000 slaves rose up in the fields to set them ablaze, with houses of the slave owners put to the torch, in the new year of 1832 the British Parliament realized unless the slaves were emancipated there would be greater rebellion with loss of life and tension grew. The newly elected British government introduced a slavery abolishment bill into Parliament that enabled the bill to be passed in 1833. Slave owners were compensated for their loss of property and 20 million pounds was set aside to compensate the forty six thousand slave owners, this represented half of all Government spending in 1883 equivalent to seventeen billion pounds from the exchequer today. The Government capitulated and emancipation was brought forward to August 1838 Thomas Clarkson the first historian of the abolishionist movement wrote an account of the triumphant campaign to end the slave trade. The book was in print by 1808, Clarkson understood the historical narrative but after 1833 he became victim of a new history written around Wilberforce.

In the National Gallery in London hangs a large painting of the group, over one hundred identifiable figures in an enormous portrait. The painting by Benjamin R Haydon is a depiction of the world anti-slavery convention of 1840 in which Thomas Clarkson stands with his raised left arm pointing in his opening speech for the country to lead a global moral crusade against slavery. It is a panoramic view that captures a moment in history of human affairs. It had been commissioned by the British and foreign anti-slavery society, an organisation born from British abolitionism, the movement still exists today as NGO anti-slavery international. Thomas Clarkson the first President of the society spoke of the British Empire and of her many millions of Indian peoples bondage outlined. He spoke of the atrocities and horrors of a system of bondage in his speech he told the convention, of more than two million fellow human beings in most cruel bondage by slave holders in America. He warned such men lived in daily habits of injustice cruelty and oppression as having no fear of God.

In 1791 Thomas's brother John Clarkson was appointed to lead recruitment of the Nova Scotia black loyalists to establish a new colony of black settlers in society, he was to be answerable to the board Of Directors of the Sierra Leone Company who promised to develop settlements of the grain coast and return a profit to the investors from the Settlement crops. So long as the principle of liberty remained without resorting to the selling of inhabitants as slaves, and become a model Community of the province of 'Freetown' the capitol of Sierra Leone. To ensure the colony lived up to its creed the man chosen was twenty-seven year old John Clarkson the younger brother of Thomas Clarkson the moral leader of the British abolitionist movement. John Clarkson who had left his fiancée Susan Lee behind England began a tour of the regions in which the black loyalist settled . Within three months 1,196 black men women and children had abandoned their life in British North America, to a future in Sierra Leone Africa a province of Freedom. Crossing the ocean with Thomas Peters a former slave, now free man from North Carolina travelled with John Clarkson, they toured all the regions in which the black loyalists had settled, speaking from the pulpits of Churches in the black community and in their homes promoting the new Sierra Leone scheme. Thomas Peter's reputation for integrity won over the black loyalists and within eighteen months John Clarkson left 'Freetown' to return to England and rejoin his fiancée, he named the harbour he departed from 'Susan Bay'.

William Wilberforce MP delivered his first speech against the slave trade to t House of Commons in May 1789. He was able to support his critical in duction against the slave trade with the enormous body of damning evidence compiled by Thomas Clarkson. The first bill brought to the house by Willberforce as Member of Parliament was watched by Thomas Clarkson from the viewing gallery. Wilberforce introduced the second bill in 1792 supported by a petition of over four hundred thousand United Kingdom Citizen signatures but even this did not persuade Parliament to support the bill. Wilberforce continued introducing further bills for the abolition of the slave trade every year until 1799. At this time the war with France and widespread distress among the poor with rebellion in Ireland made it increasingly impossible for Clarkson and his allies to bring the abuses of the slave trade to the front of the lawmakers mind. Abolishionist publications with fiery speeches were delivered at meetings countrywide yet the bill still failed.

To demonstrate brutality and educate the audience at meetings, activists acquired tools, the shackles, metal collars and whips, chained manacles in evidence of violence. Wilberforce demonstrated thumbscrews with shackles. Thomas Clarkson had two models made to scale of the slave ship 'Brooks' built from the original in Liverpool, fitted to carry 451 captives as typical example used in the slave trade. The scale dimension was given to Thomas Clarkson by Captain Perry of the Royal Navy. Clarkson took one of his model ships on tour and gave the other to Wilberforce to show to his fellow MP's in the House of Commons. In 1783 the 'Brooks' sailed with 609 enslaved Africans, 158 more than she was fitted to accommodate. Alexander Falconbridge, bodyguard to Thomas Clarkson as his life had been threatened, gave his description of, 'The hardships and inconvenience suffered by the enslaved Africans during their passage' are scarcely to be enumerated or conceived of. They are more violently affected by sea sickness than Europeans. It frequently terminates in death, especially in women. The air below deck is excluded and the rooms soon grow intolerable hot, confined air rendered noxious by the excreta and effiuent vomit exhaled from their bodies, and being repeatedly breathed in soon produces fever and fluxes which generally carries them off in great numbers.' Falconbridge wrote the account and withstood four days of probing questions from Parliamentary Privy Council committee in the House of Commons on the matter of the slave trade.

In 1807 the West Indies became a target, on the Islands, hundreds and thousands remained subject to the many horrors of plantation slavery, in Britain abolitionism was dormant. In 1814 a mass meeting was called in London and the National abolishionist movement sprang into action. One and a half million people signed a petition in Britain registering opposition to any restoration of the slave trade. Thomas Clarkson believed the abolition of the trade would be a death blow to plantation slavery in the Caribbean as slave owners were unable to buy new slaves. Thomas Clarkson at sixty three was energetic in gathering data. In 1814 Clarkson continued to criss-cross the country conducting meetings with those involved in the trade, and their victims. He embarked on an epic journey on horseback around the country mobilizing the faithful. In 1831 the Jamaican slaves rebelled with a sit down strike in the sugar cane fields. Over 23,000 slaves rose up in the fields to set them ablaze, with houses of the slave owners put to the torch, in the new year of 1832 the British Parliament realized unless the slaves were emancipated there would be greater rebellion with loss of life and tension grew. The newly elected British government introduced a slavery abolishment bill into Parliament that enabled the bill to be passed in 1833. Slave owners were compensated for their loss of property and 20 million pounds was set aside to compensate the forty six thousand slave owners, this represented half of all Government spending in 1883 equivalent to seventeen billion pounds from the exchequer today. The Government capitulated and emancipation was brought forward to August 1838.

My ancestral lineage to Thomas Clarkson the abolishionist and our shared grandfather Thomas Clarkson born 1684 in Thirsk North Yorkshire and his father John Clarkson c. 1610 reflects a different human experience. Providing me with a sense of historical reference resonating with my own existence in time and place, as if by genetic or conscious effort it influenced my own thinking toward an inclusive world of equality and LGBT human rights I am grateful for having had the opportunity o take action with conviction to make a better world in the 21st century.

Chapter 12

ECONOMIC MIGRANT

It is wrong to discriminate based on skin colour, when there are so many other reasons to dislike someone.

Dennis Miller

In 2011 Mrs Teresa May as UK Immigration minister capped skilled professional's foreign entries from outside the EEC at 21,700 annually. Application for entry would be waivered if a minimum fifty thousand pounds was brought in as an asset to the UK. Once again a cynical twist of the rich being treated differently from the poor is nothing new. Britain's immigration policy signed with other NATO countries declares to protect and preserve human life to accept those who want to enter the UK and become pan of a British nation which offers compassion, without dishonesty as in a special reservation category. It has not reneged on its promise to date, but denies enrichment of the nation with new talent and expertise in every field of endeavour to provide a net contribution to the wealth of the Nation. A working life in Great Britain is seen as enrichment to the British economy as migrant entries are dictated by politics and implemented by the politician as specified under the mainstream xenophobic cover of politics for votes.

ART OF SEDUCTION

In February 2015 the Art world was stunned when the Swiss collector Rudolph Staechelin sold Paul Gaugin's 1892 'The two Maidens' at auction for $300 million to a museum in Qatar. It had been on long term loan to the Basel Kunstmuseum since 1950. Gauguin was born 1908 into a wealthy family. He had disengaged with Europe, after his decision to immigrate and live and work in Haiti during the 20th century it became his metier, he flourished in this tropical paradise on earth. The local native population accepted him as one of their own, his liberal behaviour and ease of social intercourse gave him status he never had in Paris sophisticated society. From the banking background of strict etiquette he elected to abandon this for economic uncertainty to paintings of the life he had in Haiti of his vision reflected in the application of a fauvist palette as a visceral moment as fresh as the dawn of each new day. With the human elevation of inspiration from the physical he was challenged by his emotional discharge to give new energy to each canvas which became his sanctuary as an oasis of spirit. Thus his genius for conveying his personal vision resonated in the mind and emotions of the viewer. History holds many surprises, none more than his yearning for new horizons with the unknown. This set the stage for his role in Art as the Fauvist movement gained momentum in the 20th century. Abstract form in painting as an idea of presentation over representation became a dimension of his innovative expression an important component of his artistic freedom of choice. Paul Gauguin was intellectually studious, well read in academic thought; His insatiable curiosity compelled him to break away from the stricture of bourgeoisie life with his background of duty to family and friends. He left France and those he cared for. Kind in nature but less concerned about his own ego he valued integrity and honesty in his work applying a fertile imagination in aesthetic creativity of a subjective vision.

Picasso remarked that 'all art is a lie but useful in getting to the truth'. In 2015 Picasso's painting 'Head of a woman ' value at over $4 million was seized from a yacht berthed at Ajacio in Corsica bound for Switzerland. The painting had been refused an export license in 2012 by the Spanish government. Mysteriously, the yacht was owned by a Senor Hymie the President of Santander International Bank, who owns a 20% share in the UK Company registered as the operator of the ship. Police are investigating those responsible for its covert illegal exit of the painting from Spain across her border.

Western retail corporations play lip service as stated in public relations policy against slavery in the workshop but mandatory monitoring is absent. Western viewers in the 21st century in the developed world sit in front of their sanitised news watching reports edited for family consumption know nothing of this practice. Retailers producing cheap garments in demand realize that their antislavery production values protecting viewer sensibilities should not be upset or outraged to this inhumanity on a daily basis or with tabloid fodder for their disgust. I write this subjective account for future reference. We may forget that crime in the middle ages, was reported by public announcement and the miscreant locked in shackles in the dock. This practice could be reinstated in the 21st century as men of greed manipulated modern slavery in collusion with Governments through International Court of Human Rights in the Hague.

2017

MONEY GIVES US CHOICE and creates its own energy. The holder can manipulate it and convert it as a commodity into the cruelty of slavery or kindness of a saint. As we own nothing we ourselves are the currency becoming convertible in choice determined by the expectation of self interest. Economic slavery is the extreme case illustrating the point in the endemic use of child labour which is illegal according to UNESCO. Poverty and illiteracy is the enemy. In the UK modern slavery exists in the form of workers brought in to Britain by 'human traffickers' who take the workers passports away after entry to forced them to work as agricultural labourers, cleaners, and sex worker's. Human rights Lawyer Cherie Blair stated in August 2017 'we have the legislation to enforce the law and the tools available to eradicate this illegality' but it still remains. In August 2017 eleven people were convicted for slavery in the largest modern slavery trial in British legal history in Lincoln UK.

MODERN SLAVERY

Ms. Fatima CEO of the bonded labour federation in Pakistan reports that between three and eight million landless families are itinerant labourers, take cash loans offered by rich owners of brick kilns. In exchange for repayment they become indentured to the owners who consistently rely on the complicity of the police. No contract specifies an interest rate which is arbitrary charged, and not understood by an illiterate labourer as a result of poverty and illiteracy who has no choice or understanding of the consequences, forced into the agreement due to their lack of education. This is ignored by political Pakistan members of assembly in government as a cheap and convenient method of available labour for a guaranteed block voting from the literate owners of the kiln operators. When the helpless labourer and their families want to leave after the season they are forced to stay until their overextended loan is settled. Police tip off the owners as the complainant goes to them for help and make a report of their owner's intimidation of the labourers. Owners strip the women and beat the males and apply additional interest to the already inflated loans. Police accept bribes from the kiln owner and violate the workers human rights and thus keep the system in place. Whole families of men women and children are kept in labour camps for a life of bonded servitude. This inhuman practice is acceptable socially as explained by the Human rights commission office in Lahore, as the Pakistan government see no wrong in this feudal practice as they hold complete power over life and death of their bonded slaves.

Western retail corporations play lip service as stated in public relations policy against slavery in the workshop but mandatory monitoring is absent. Western viewers in the 21st century in the developed world sit in front of their sanitised news watching reports edited for family consumption know nothing of this practice. Retailers producing cheap garments in demand realize that their ant-slavery production values protecting viewer sensibilities should not be upset or outraged to this inhumanity on a daily basis or with tabloid fodder for their disgust. I write this subjective account for future reference. We may forget that crime in the middle ages, was reported by public announcement and the miscreant locked in shackles in the dock. This practice could be reinstated in the 21st century as men of greed manipulated modern slavery in collusion with Governments.

The Human rights Commission in Pakistan apparently acquiesce in their acceptance of this inhumane practice. Responsible action by the UN taken against the authority and government who fund heir office in accordance with their brief, to pay lip service from the comfort of their official office sanctuary as tools of the government act with platitudes, but no active agenda or implementation of law: Seduced into submission by ignorance which is no defense in law as published in the public domain. Human rights are clarified as 'the framework and foundation of individual right of the freedom of choice'. Ineffective and paralysed by circumstance forced upon them, the labourer and their family imprisoned in permanent debt and illiteracy must be made aware of their individual right, not left in ignorance of the potential of their talent and ability to rise above circumstance forced upon them for a lack of opportunity in education, disabled to share in the wealth of the Nation who allows this to continue by condoning it.

Seventh February 2015 watching the news on Al Jazeera of the UN General Secretary Ban Ki Moon interview referred to the current political climate of the joint members as 'a narrative of hatred' divided by politics and intolerant of human dignity. ' Those countries respond with brutality and violent acts instead of respecting human dignity. He confirmed that Mr Putin President of Russia ordered the annexing of the Crimea which is part of the sovereign state of

Ukraine in Europe since 1933 was an illegal act of forced entry into that part of a European (EEC) member state. The General Secretary of the United Nations did not draw a conclusion as to how this would be resolved other than by suggesting dialogue at the table between the parties. I had another sleepless night following a full moon in the ascendant. I understood United Nations was formed after the second-world war in order to harmonise the differences Of nations and offer a way forward in the hope of avoiding war between the member states. Little trust exists between the member states but maximum attendance with minimum effect in providing window dressing to view the global transition of generating power of the few, over the many who remain in blissful ignorance of tomorrow.

BEDTIME STORY
On the circle line

I hesitated to get dressed one morning. My habit of rising early broke the nightmare of reality giving me no comfort. Over a late breakfast the cell phone bleeped an Ad-message answering by a prerecorded digital invitation to buy games on-line prompted me to curse. The irony made me aware of a useless game as I dressed and left the building to spend the whole day riding on the circular tube-line as a symbolic gesture of distraction. Not taking an umbrella as rain was not forecast as inside the carriage I would preside in for the entire day. I could think of any better way to waste time and demonstrate a futile attempt at passive protest. Taking a notebook and hastily prepared club sandwich I observed similar pathetic passengers, I even imagined starting a National campaign for time wasters with the objective of forming a National competition with the prize of a diagrammatic gilt framed map of the tube. The time chosen was significant at 8:33am as most people in London seem to be in a dreadful hurry but with no great purpose to get to the office. Where they spend globs of time standing around the office water dispenser arranging polyurethane cups in a waste bin, later to rush home in a domestic emergency to a high tea of fish and chips with mushy peas on the on a tray, sitting in front of the television with their loved ones to share the urban world through sanitised News channels before bed Sleeping separately or collectively to rest in slumber land. They rise early in the same frenzied attempt to carve a niche in their world of work but with no repose.

ARTIFICE

With relief the next day my subscribed monthly 'Art world' magazine arrived and I opened the publication. I knew the high rollers spend millions of dollars on big ticket items realizing art is one of the many avenues to explore When laundering high end dollar items as a means of converting black money into white the surplus covert funds. The objective of their investment is a hedge against future inflation. The International art market is a guarantee of current trajectory rising in percentage value. A high profile artist such as Damien Hurst prefers cows and other animal cadavers to be injected with formaldehyde as his expression of 20th century art, supported by the Saatchi Gallery and his one hundred million pound collection.

Picasso's 'Minator' series posthumously secures high returns way beyond the volatility of a stock market share certificate or financial Director on the Board of a public company. Art is a useful and covert method for arms dealers and drug barons to put their black money into without too much scrutiny from the authorities. Telephone bids are accepted paid by international transfer of funds cleared through off shore accounts. Once filtered through the Interpol Net list of stolen items customs clearance is arranged with legal documentation and provenance provided. Interchangeable and flexible Galleries owners know their client as well as any stock broker and in this rarefied environment they clear billions of dollars of inventory in the blink of a cursor on the screen of a laptop with their commission on billions of dollars inventory in collusion with International clients. The art work 'if subject to a private sale' becomes untraceable if stolen, and if claimed on Insurance the loss adjuster has a hard time to justify a crime of theft for a value replacement. Unique works of art with a prime market value on demand cannot be replaced. Insurers having accepted the risk, after investigation must pay out to the insured as specified in the terms of cover, a nice little earner

The CEO of Sotheby's auction house international spent time in prison for a term appropriate to his crime, his reputation was shaken but not stirred. His friend Mr Blackstone the Chairman of a public company and an ex member of the UK house of Lords defrauded shareholders and received sentence from the high Court in London for a long period of imprisonment. Other mortals conspired in incredulous circumstance over the years to dupe the public successfully.

ONE PER CENT

The top 500 Forbes billionaires invest in Art collections as does her majesty the Queen, but she leaves hers to the British nation. Millionaires need not apply to enter this esoteric list. Horse racing is the sport of kings and the UAE Sheiks joined this elite club rich with their oil money billions. The Dubai racecourse attracts International owners and trainers to enter a race with the knowledge of winning a $10 million purse. Owner Syndicates can launder vast sums of black money from a client's profitable venture without attracting too much investigation from tax authorities as a source of revenue through International transfer funds. The Cayman Island, Mauritious, Switzerland and other offshore banks offer safe tax havens with additional benefit for clients to avoid tax liability. The Banks corporate clients are kept happy with clearance codes and inflated bank charges for their overt and illegal transactions. In the UK serious crime agency SOCA national crime intelligence service NCIS permanent staff is unable to handle 20,000 cases in 2018.

Three monkeys sat on a wall named: See all, hear all, and say now't.

The single bell of the 500 Years old John the Baptist Church tolled twelve times in D Major, it was midday in Furtado Vaddo found me in a T shirt sitting at my laptop having respite from the heat of the garden. Noel Coward wrote: Only mad dogs and Englishmen go out in the midday sun, how true. The buds had shriveled, their curled leaves burnt under the constant 35 centigrade tropical heat outside.

From the smell of strawberries that I had put on the stove inside I could tell they had by now turned to delicious jam ready to be preserved in jars of fresh luscious fruit from Mahabaleshwar in Maharashtra, hand- picked in the dawn of the day before in the cool of a February evening. Spreading butter on thick crusty rolls fresh from the local bakery at 7am before anointing them with the last pot of preserve I had made a week ago placed next to my pastry. My cafattiere of fresh ground coffee waited by the stove to compliment my breakfast, these simple pleasures gave an antidote to the maelstrom of activity I had gone through in the last decade.

My peace of mind was disturbed by events in the morning paper brought the news engaged with bigotry. The local Goan's display xenophobic bias against foreigners, with lies deceit and corruption as normal currency with the lack of integrity offended me. I had waited ten Years and my patience was rewarded with full clearance from the Reserve Bank of India (RBI) and gave license for my venture Reso Ipsa Loquitor. This is what happened de facto. 'Slowly, slowly catch the monkey'.

It is not impossible to perceive that you could define a person by their limitations or horizons. Limitations accepted by the individual are dependent on strength of will. I accepted this and was prepared to pay the price of integrity, but in no doubt that truth is stranger than fiction. In my experience most people accept that a lie was often more palatable than the truth. This anomaly is a cause of most criminal cases and allegation brought against a defendant. Lawyer's clients lie, as do their client but the truth is not always evidential. Beyond reasonable doubt is sought as a measure of justice, the miscreant may not get what they deserve but can get what they want. Forensic evidence is licit in advocacy and appropriate in law.

Probatum. Justice delayed is justice denied when you smell a rat there is usually a rat. There is no smoke without fire, but it is not sufficient to bring a case to Court with circumstantial conjecture to win the action unless beyond reasonable doubt is established.

ARTISTIC LICENSE

The Curator and the archivist sealed the room with their keys to the double mortise lock, and the security chief used his code number to activate an internal grill to hydraulically lock the heavy double doors which closed the vault in the basement of the conservation department Of the Louvre Paris. The restorer and his assistant had left for the day.

Two floors up the five security guards paused to check each position they would take during their shift on duty in the reception area Of the Gallery. The visiting art historian from St Petersburg had signed Off the Faberge collection to their safekeeping, after Brink security had delivered their vehicle accompanied direct from Orly airport under heavy guard without incident. As a matter of National pride the Franco-Russian exhibition would be well attended and open to the public the next day. The Russian ambassador and his opposite number the French ambassador would lead the cultural exchange with cordial smiles followed by the usual statements of mutual appreciation of their precious cargo with the great and the good at 9am sharp to allow the great unwashed public in to view at 10am.

Before the stroke of 4am the bells of the Notre Dame Paris had died away as mist rolled off the Seine to reflect a ribbon of blue light moving at speed. The doppelganger siren of the Gendarme Citroen DS19 bounced off the walls of the Notre Dame Cathedral. The blue beacon light announced its arrival at the Louvre as two officers jumped out of the front doors prematurely. Waiting anxiously on the steps of the entrance, stood the receptionist and three security guards. They had set off the alarm, announcing details of the missing painting. 'Mon Dei' one whispered as they entered the silence of the sepulchral interior. 'Merde' said the senior officer who was listening to the receptionist who had woken only ten minutes earlier from a deep sleep to the chaos now unfolding before him.

Later the same evening the president of France Giscard D'Estaing held an emergency meeting with the Chef Security minister to update himself with new any developments, he finally intervened on behalf of the French Nation to return the Monet painting. It had been found by a cleaner, stuffed behind a toilet cistern later in the day inside the ladies WC on the ground floor access near the exit, a planned heist to be completed by the miscreant foiled at a later stage, they were never found. The Curator was ecstatic and the Nation grateful and security was tightened. Not all art gains an ignominious reputation however. Renoir's Bal de Moulin de la Gallete' painted in 1876 was sold in

1990 to the Japanese industrialist Ryoei Saito for $78.1 million. He died in 1996 and the painting was taken by the bank against loans to his company, its current whereabouts is unknown.

In 2017 two Van Gogh paintings stolen from the Van Gogh Museum in Holland was put back on display after they had been found in a private safe. The paintings had been stolen years before, and had been taken from the Exhibition by miscreants who had dealings with the Cosa Nostre in Naples.

Bolton Abbey, North Yorkshire | UK 2010

A break in a moving shadow of the cumulus cloud revealed the afternoon sun's rays scattered over the distant landscape exposing a moving figure on the horizon. The discernable female form striding toward the dry stone wall straight as the crow flies. My friends sat on the patio Geoffrey with irritation in his voice said 'Dirk who is this?' I thought we could enjoy the peace of a lazy Sunday afternoon and have a quite tea in the garden'. Within a few minutes the figure came into view as a short slight woman striding through the moorland grass came toward the garden wall. Geoff moved to the perimeter gate and noticed the she wore a tattered raincoat flapping in the wind held together by baling twine tied round her small waist. With a Hermes silk scarf loosely over her short cropped silver hair, tiny feet in rubber boots suitable for the farmyard rather than a visit to her neighbour, now arrived at the foot of the gate.

'Ime' so sorry to arrive unannounced', Im'e Deborah Duchess of Devonshire', she extended her tiny hand toward them in cordial greeting 'may I come in, my estate manager told me you were at home.' They were taken aback as surprise registered on their face and stood aside allowing her to enter the garden. She stood for a moment her rosy cheeks shone as if polished by the wind like other countrywomen and spoke with a Sincerity that stirred like a bright light. 'You see as a child I used to dream of living here one day but Chatsworth House is so far away, these rare visits to the Bolton estate don't often allow me as much time as I would like ' gesturing Geoffrey spoke first 'would you take tea with us in the garden? 'You are so kind thank you' the Duchess following they entered the low beamed farmhouse. Dirk said 'Do you want to see what we have done to the place? Margaret replied 'if it's not an imposition. Not at all just feel free to wander' and they went into the kitchen to put the kettle on the Aga and Dirk opened a tin of fruit cake left over from Christmas. A few minutes later she entered breathlessly, 'my husband the 11th Duke would be thrilled it's not changed a jot I hope you will both be very happy here' as they all took tea on the window seat in the courtyard. The Duchess turned and rose to her feet, still in army socks she pulled them up to her calfs starting to put her boots on. Standing up straight she smiled and said 'do please come to our annual garden party at Chatsworth in June' and after a few moments she had gone , returning through the Kitchen garden over the moor and striding briskly to eventually disappear from whence she come. 'I don't suppose she does that every Sunday afternoon, do you' said Geoffrey, and they both laughed in relief when she had gone.

The gilt edged invitation card arrived a week later in the Royal mail in a hand written Italic script announcing the request of their Presence, with the Devonshire family coat of arms and the Heraldic crest from Chatsworth House in Derbyshire. Respectfully they replied and Placed it on the drawing room fire mantle as a reminder as if they needed it They left for Chatsworth House on a wild and windy day in June. The journey down the Ml motorway was buffeted by force eight winds as they followed a lurching convoy of caravan revellers for three hours throwing their empty beer cans out of the window at regular intervals Jeffrey and Dirk arrived at Chatsworth estate where they were directed toward the car park and marquee entrance to a sudden windy squall. Pristine white David Mlinarac chairs were scattered on the lawn by guests in hasty retreat to avoid the heavy cloudburst. It was decided to evacuate the landscape grounds and move everyone to the long gallery of the main house. Guests congregated for a viewing of one of the finest collections of Art in the UK still remaining in private hands. The Butler stood at the entrance to announce gracefully that tea would be served in the sun Logia.'Very ironic' said Dirk. Geoffrey grimaced and said 'Oh god I think it's a sort of aristocratic version of 'muzak,' he pointed to the assembled string quartet 'no one is actually listening' 'vell dey vud not all fit in a lift elevator vud they' said Dirk, Geoffrey wandered off to look for sugar cubes who pointedly looked displeased. Bored with the usual antecedent portraits they wandered into the library suddenly coming face to face with a Renoir portrait hung against wild silk at the side of a shuttered windows half light. 'Blody ell' said Dirk 'Du last time I saw dis vas at the Rijkmuseum in Amsterdam a few years ago when I was home.

'Well actually it was included it in a touring exhibition from the Louvre arranged by the British Council'. The voice emanated from a high back bishops chair swiveling round in their direction, to reveal the eleventh Duke gently smiling at them his balding head shone like an eagle's polished egg his hands fidgeting with the piped edging of his chairs arm rest. His kind smile made them feel less embarrassed at their crassness. A hidden door opened suddenly in a painted mural on a wall Of hand painted Chinoiserie through which the Duchess made her entrance as in a Faydeau farce from behind towering gilded columns. Her court shoes echoed in syncopation on the marble slabs down the long room heard but not seen appeared suddenly 'Really darling you can't hide yourself away like this we do have guests' She hesitated a moment, as an element of surprise registered on her face noticing 'the two boys' as she referred to them. 'I thought you were alone my dear but I see you are denying our friends to meet other guests, it is a party after all' She said this with much affection as if she and the Duke were alone. The Duke rose slowly from his overstuffed chair shuffiing off following them into the main salon, a bit sheepishly they thought. The four of them descended the elegant double staircase lined with Rembrand, Holbein and Titian, jostled side by side with a Vermeer in the Grinling Gibbon entrance hall. They crossed through the main doors to the portico entrance. Margaret Duchess of Devonshire opened them wide standing on the steps pausing for a few moments gazing beyond the now sunlit gardens: 'Capability Brown new a thing or two when he designed the fountain don't you think' she sighed and noticed the rain had stopped. Without waiting for an answer she smiled her farewell and turned with a gesture of her hand to the Duke who stooped toward them in a gentle bow as they left through the rose garden waving, and they drove back to their north Yorkshire dales and 'Laund House'.

AS LUCK WOULD HAVE IT

At first light the sound of the horn bill called in the early morning mist, I discovered the track that had been overlooked the evening before. This encouraged me to look further for the wallet I lost a week ago. Amazingly I found it by a bush on a bank under the shade of an Ashoka tree, the leather pouch was camouflaged in green algae among the new shoots growing around it. The paper money was missing but the Passport was still folded in the plastic envelope where it had been thrown I was relieved to find it. Returning to the apartment through the rice paddy fields to brew fresh coffee I sat on the terrace gazing out on the first flower buds of the mango tree and heard the thud of a coconut falling on the mound of red earth under trembling palm trees. The rising Sun cast deep shadows over dry leaves of the tropical February morning. My thoughts strayed to the day ahead disturbed only by the barking of a puppy-dog and a peacock screaming in the distant jungle. The mongrel puppy 'Sweety' lay licking the toes of my bare foot stopped to lift her head alerted by the sound and growled, she decided to abandon any plan to move or take action which could intrude upon our dual reverie. The dog 'Sweety' returned to sleep between my feet without looking up wagging her tail in recognition of my writing on the laptop. Mid morning I made tea and toast and we shared the crumbs as is our custom while planning the rest of the day.

At the same time back in England Celeste and Marie lifelong friends since school, were hatching a plot to escape on a brief winter holiday in the winter sun which would take them away on an Art week together. Marie had taken the initiative and phoned the number in the Ilkley Gazette advertising a competition for amateur painters who wanted to take a class for landscape water colourists in Goa as holiday, to a studio in India for a week in a hotel with sightseeing as a side attraction. 'What's not to like Celeste,' I think it's a great idea let's do it while the kids are away with Arthur on that fishing trip in Norfolk he has planned'. 'I can book it and so we should go'

Celste nodded her approval 'Well, all right then and smiled let's do it.' Two middle aged Yorkshire ladies not of the Women's Institute persuasion, 'on an escape from the domestic scene and really most welcome said Marie' as she picked up the phone and her credit card to confirm their planned adventure.

A week later the two intrepid ladies arrived at Bambolim airport in Goa to a blast furnace of hot air as the plane's doors opened to the hot midday sun in a cloudless sky, brighter and more intense than they imagined. After going through arrivals exit they found a crowd of taxi's one sign with their names hand written on a board held high by a friendly smiling face to welcome them. 'I am Anthony pleased to meet you to I will you to your hotel in Saligao'. They passed through sleepy villages and brightly painted red roofed villas, the occasional tantalizing glimpse of a brilliant turquoise blue sea appeared through white and pink bougainvillea nodded in the breeze, over the closed wrought iron gates to the green paddy fields beyond. 'Oh Celeste it looks heavenly' as she turned to ask the driver how far it would be to their resting place. 'Only a minute more Maam and we will be there', they arrived at Casa Tipri a two story white painted Portuguese villa set in a small banana plantation. A large woman in a pink jump suit ran toward the gate stretching out her ample arms smiling warmly, embraced them in the cool courtyard of the pretty entrance of the country hotel in Saligao. A Jacuzzi tucked into the corner of the garden stood on a tiled floor against the white stucco wall offered a hint of glamour after a day on the easel. 'Antonia Hurford-Jones I am your tutor' she clasped their hands ' pleased to meet you both' in a vigorous shake after moving into position slowly as an ocean liner coming into port she waved them on into the foyer to disembark. Nim the Nepali room boy took their bags up to their light and airy bedrooms. Each room had huge four poster double beds with pretty drapes blowing in the breeze of the open window, the bathrooms as big as their terrace outside extending to panoramic views of the Countryside, surrounded by the green lush flora and fauna. They sat in faded rattan chairs in the garden to have a welcome herbal iced tea with Antonia. 'We start class in the morning after an early breakfast so please do get some rest until then I bid you a good evening', with a wave of the hand she was gone.

They had both slept well, and after seven Marie knocked on Celeste's door was already dressed. 'Are we good to go I think a coffee Would start the day' as they joined Antonia who wore a dark blue apron over a sky blue tea shirt and faded jeans fashionably frayed, at the breakfast table. Fresh Marigolds were placed in a ceramic bowl on a marble top with three bamboo place mat sets. 'Very rustic' they chimed in chorus with a giggle they all sat down. 'Today my dears it's all about scale and perspective in the courtyard' Antonia swayed in her chair, her ample proportions vibrated with excitement and chatter, 'then an early lunch as it gets too hot after one. Nim the young Nepali waiter appeared with a tray from the kitchen before they all trouped off to the first lesson, as a cool area had been prepared under the Banyan tree for shade as the first rays of sun came over the horizon. With pencils sharpened and cartridge paper pinned to drawing boards they assembled with a brief talk from Antonia and started to draw. After a leisurely lunch Al fresco they took siesta until late afternoon when a light breeze had cooled the midday sun. Later walking through hedgerows and paddy fields to take photo's and sketch books as reference in the sunset, watching water buffalo with the attendant heron on their host's back wading through the water as the white birds picked insects from the gourmand feast on their beasts broad backs. The week went by in fun and laughter, on the last day they were invited to create a finished painting of the landscape from their own choice. To their surprise Antonia proclaimed they were all worthy of gallery space and asked them to sign and date each one before they were framed. 'Not so much the journey more the freedom of expression' she exclaimed. Their week of independence in a new environment gave them renewed energy before reluctantly returning to the conservative bosom of their urban familiarity.

Boasting about modesty is typical of the English.
George Bernard Shaw

In November after the first week of arrival Bala and I visited the Peace Buddhist Temple. The gold stuppa domed roof high up on the mountain crest reflected the first light of dawn. The profile glittered against the blue backdrop of the early morning sunrise. After a few hours we traced our steps further down the track as a strong wind started to blow in from the north east down past the Annapurnam mountain range into the Kathmandu valley below us. We shivered in the cold as we left the temple of peace early in haste as heavy snows were coming. On higher slopes the surrounding landscape lay in a mantle of frost, as an early mist shrouded the mountain village from the view below the Feva Lake appeared opaque as a misty mirror through breaks in low clouds. We descended further making slow progress over the rough path to the valley floor below returning to the warmth of the Hotel Ghurka and a an expectant welcome at the door from the wagging tale of the 'Pug' dog at lakeside.

A SEASONAL CHANGE

March twenty first day of spring, a new equinox brought fresh germination and a renewed growth from the Sun. Moisture dropped from rainclouds in resurgence of a new life cycle. This energy gives synthesis to tie creative mind. A complex of emotion's provided recurring images of a primitive characteristic present in our distant ancestors to a former type. Compulsion will go forward to choice of our own needs which should not interfere with others of a different persuasion to make their individual choice, I realised I often fell short of this ideal.

My niece Nicola offers unconditional love without entering into one other's space or making an agenda. This allowed our relationship to function without emotional baggage from our joint historical parameters. She was affectionate and fun to be with, shared intelligence and humour allowed us to express freely our thoughts. We both love dogs of the canine variety, hers 'Patch' a long haired cross dachshund she spoilt profusely, mine short haired terrier cross named 'Sweety I had found on an industrial state had been dumped and discarded as a puppy one windy night, at first I thought in the dusk it was a rabbit with a huge pair of ears in the cars headlights and almost ran the mite over. Stopping the car to take a closer look I opened the door and within seconds it hopped into the car climbed on my lap without a murmur and fell to sleep. So I took her h and weaned her on milk. Within a week she was running about the place with an air of familiar possession so she stayed and became my constant travelling companion. Fate had decreed our future together securing a long time friendship for many happy days together. I sometimes thought myself as Tin-Tin, and she was the mongrel companion, an image I was not entirely averse too in the days ahead, as we both sniffed the air for confirmation of any suspicious circumstance. We formed a bond that would last with shared walks on the beach in the evening sunset running into the water and swimming out into the waves. 'Sweety' returned home to sleep under a chair, while I wrote notes in my diary from memories enjoyed, made the days go better to smile and laugh with. Later a snakebite took her life.

MUNICH
1970

Prima Bel Canto Opera singer Hildergarde Kneff sang her heart out in her role as the mother in Richard Strauss Opera 'Oedipus, on the stage of the Bavaria State Opera house Munich in the autumn of 1970. I enjoyed the performance in the audience with IJschi Kaut Bagnall, during the intermission we joined the throng in the gilded mirror bar with orange spritzer. We were in a state of dharma dressed in full evening wear, she in a diaphanous sea green silk evening dress, I was resplendent in a white cummerbund and bow tie with black silk lapels, dressed appropriate to the glitzy occasion. After sixteen adulating curtain calls, we departed with the crowd before joining Keith and his brother Brian at a nearby Bar. Weincongruous duo caused uproar on entering the bar in which they had been drinking steadily for hours. 'Bloody hell you look like a couple of Christmas trees without lights' said Keith, I replied 'we cast pearls before swine' then paused to turn to order cognac in balloon glasses served with an elegant curtsey from the barman. Uschi the daughter of Elis Kaut the author of 'Pumeckle' giggled, and sat down on a stool at the bar adjusting a Pashmina shawl round her bare pale shoulders said softly 'what's the use of a sun dial in the shade' and we joined the crowd. We all left the bar in Brians old 'Amazon' Volvo car to return home at midnight ready to fall into our respective beds.

The following day a party invite came from Uschi's friends to might include Keith and I. Always ready for a party as Brian as consider looking elegant for the function as it was held apartment overlooking the English garden. The guest's came from the Munich glitterati artistic and media community the incestuous guests would know who was Who. Our arrival was a little late, but we were impressed as a sweeping marble staircase directed the large crowd upward to a dramatic double paneled door entrance where you could hear the hubbub of laughter and loud conversation. On opening the doors, the noise was palpable in the Way people sound in an intermission. As they wandered in Keith attention was drawn by his brother to a corner with Brian joining the amused artists in a private murmur, with overly anxious smiles welcomed their British visitors and the topic was adjusted toward the familial. We turned away from Uschi who darted across to a severe looking shaven head woman dressed elegantly in Chanel, whom we were told later was professor and head of department at Potsdam University, an old chum of Uschi and they played catch up from their last update. I walked on alone toward the end of the long salon where two gilded chairs stood side by side against a gilded mirrored wall. Ignored by the crowd as if I was not there, this suited me I was not the best small talker in town and sat in one of the chairs watching the crowd the other chair remained empty.

Suddenly an absolute hush descended as if in rehearsal. The double doors of the salon opened slowly as attention was drawn away from the collective clique toward the entrance where a tiny feline creature glided in. She ignored the milieu and without looking at the few grovelling in her direction the pretty and delicate young woman turned her long neck toward me moving graceful as a swan. Her porcelain skin with golden hair made up into a braided crown round her head poised in a bright halo of light With a radiant smile she walked directly toward me and asked 'please can I sit with you' I nodded smiling. She sat next to me as other guests astonished by her alacrity, and intrigued at her apparent disregard Of the crowd she simply ignored them without acknowledgment. My name is Ghuslinda' and offered me her hand without smiling, 'mine is Paul' I gently shook her tiny hand. She sat in her private space where she simply wanted to be in. I had no idea who she was fit's a pleasure to be here with you'. She had just returned from Rio de Janeiro, being feted by the Brazilian government on a National Tour. The prospect of her next tour to Australia and the far-east was daunting. She was exhausted and did not want to talk to anyone else so 'would I mind' 'not at all' I smiled she relaxed and asked me for advice. What was said and the thoughts we exchanged for the hour we spent together was illuminating for her and for me. She felt at the pinnacle of her professional career, though with a peripatetic lifestyle she felt isolated and alone. The audience adulation and sycophancy was not giving her what she wanted human contact which evaded her like a tree with no roots to nourishment, the branches of her life experience had been cut short as a child, her talent overcame her. Although the centre of attention she was not approached at the party, the disappointed crowd wanted some of the heat of her flame they focussed on our private tableau but they resisted being burnt. After our brief encounter she left with a glance to the crowd with a fading smile, nodding to a chosen few. It occurred to me that I was selected by her to expose a reflection in her that she had perhaps seen in recognition of herself. Several years later over breakfast in the English Garden in Munich with beer and liverwurst sausage on the table, my conversation turned toward my memory of Ghuslinda.

'Oh,' gasped Uschi, 'she became a heavy drinker, and after some time got too drunk to perform she became very ill.' She left the 'dance' and could not work she was offered a job in the wardrobe but did not always turn up we were worried about her state of mind and saw her less and less, she was found dead in her apartment some months later as no one had seen or heard from her' for a few days it was so sad. I recollected our meeting with the memory of her feeling unable to contain her talent. The experience of human contact was not lost, I realise that people want to be near you when it suited their motives and steered away as the flame dies. I could identify with this conflict as my own experience synchronized with hers but the difference is I wanted to go on. I do not feel the need to curtail what is in store for me and I do not think it necessary to justify my existence through other people, pain is to be endured as is the pleasure of joy.

I don't understand anything about the ballet. All I know is that during the intervals the ballerinas stink like horses.

Anthon Chekov

I received a frantic phone call from Keith one afternoon, he, not in the first flush of youth and of an erasable nature gave an historical account of his medical condition. I write this as a treasured memory. His most recent visit of many doctor appointments to the Medical centre was to establish the cause of his symptoms, bringing to the doctors notice that he had a problem in his groin area. The lady Doctor asked 'where exactly is the problem.' 'Well doctor I have two perfect matching pimples on either side of both testicles ' The Doctor said 'drop them,' on examination the doctor agreed with him after close scrutiny. 'Your testicles appear to have a probable case of herpes.' Shocked though he was by the doctor's diagnosis Keith informed her that he had not had sex for a long time 'since I can't even remember' was his assessment. The doctor concluded that he should see a specialist 'I suggest that you have a Pet scan'. Keith responded 'Do you mean I have to take the dog with me,' after a moment his reply prompted the doctor to collapse into his chair in laughter 'I don't think it's necessary to have a cat scan. Recovering from the faux pass the Doctor gave Keith a prescription, and Offered the opinion that 'if he took the cat it could make up a threesome.'

This bizarre situation illustrates a perfect example of his view on life. It is laughter and humour keeps us going but the shared existence of intimacy of our pets is taking it to the extreme.

TO MUCH OF A GOOD THING CAN BE WONDERFUL

Mae West

The writer Quinton Crisp asked by an interviewer 'what his mission in life was' the interviewee thoughtfully gave his answer, 'to become a work of art,' the interviewer decided to probed deeper. 'I understand you live on your own' a polite 'yes,' was given. 'How do you manage on your own,' the journalist enquired further. After a great deal of thought the answer came, 'l never dust I don't see the point, after the first year it seems to settle beautifully, 'I never wash my plate after meals with the exception of after eating fish' I can then concentrate on me as a work of art.

PROMISCUITY

Promiscuity is an indiscriminate act from a moral standpoint and open to debate as the moral stance is generally one of social disapproval observed hypocritically as a double standard, it follows when moralizing about others transgressions, if our own conduct is in question it,s a case of don't get found out or you could lose face and credibility. There is no monopoly on morals and no margin for error. A man who is colour blind driving a car cannot see the stop sign is red. Is it his fault that he cannot see what is apparently obvious to other drivers who can recognise the colour and likely to avoid the accident. Would a woman understand what it feels like to have a child in labour when she is without child, it seems that unless we have the faculty to experience what the person sees as a reality the feasible explanation is one of subjective experience and understanding.

Between 1% & 3% of the population are psychopaths in the prison population, with an average of 12% & 15% having no emotional response or compassion, or ability to understand the damage they cause by their actions. 72% have mental health problems their sociological and physiological emotional detachment through self obsession gives nil response. A psychopath has no compunction in murdering in cold blood or executing a plan of brutal action against another human being, seeking no solace in guilt or compassion as possibly criminally insane. Biopsy shows the emygdala an area of the brain indicates a deficiency or absence of the area responsible for the brains inability to discern the impulse to stop violent behaviour. This suggests the individual has reasoning but not necessarily empathy to bring a rational conclusion to bear on their actions from cause to effect through anti-social behaviour.

IN A DARK ALLEY

My Bipolar is a physiological condition caused by lack of the hormone Serotonin in the brain which enables the smooth syntax of neurones in contact with billions of cells to affect mood swings. The resulting erratic behaviour is referred to as extreme clinical depression. The body is unable to make enough of the hormone. One in 10,000 people having this physiological condition, it is not a mental aberration, but living with it is a challenge due to the behavioural symptoms both for the partner and the entire life of the patient. The writer knows this first-hand recognizing my genetic disposition to cause bizarre antisocial behaviour, from mildly disturbing to manic depressive. My MD provided a prescription drug therapy concerned with the symptoms, I as patient ingested the efficacious medication to alleviate the symptomatic behaviour it made mine worse there is no cure only intervention.

Carrie Fisher runner up bipolar woman of the year 1977, author and actor wrote 'One of the things that baffies her is how can there be so much lingering stigma with regards to mental illness specifically bipolar disorder. In her opinion living with manic depression takes a tremendous amount of balls not unlike a tour of duty in Afghanistan(though the bombs and bullets come from the inside). At times bipolar can be an all consuming challenge requiring a lot of stamina and even more courage. So, if you are living with the illness and functioning at all, it's something to be proud of not ashamed of. They should issue medals along with the steady stream of medication one has to ingest (September 1977)

Ruby wax the comedienne and writer sponsors the web-site 'Black dog' which offers the 'Sane' organisation a forum to subscribe to members to share issues concerning their experiences on the worldwide-web.

A LEGAL DEFINITION

A mental condition impacts on the individual social behavior, implies a legal question of prognostication. Without forensic medical evidence which causes the effect of the alleged action as a mitigating fact. I advocating a legal point of reference this would be outside the purview experience of a jury unless presented as forensic evidence as a necessary component which would be evident in their subjective understanding of the complex condition. In concluding a legal verdict, a fractured limb is an injury you can see, but a fractured mind you cannot and is easy to ignore. In the movies if Mickey Mouse slaps Minnie Mouse cross the face we feel immediate sympathy with her pain and suffering at hands of the transgressor, but when Donald Duck laughs at this aggression we laugh with him. Who then is the guilty party? The aggressor, or a passive reaction to Donald Duck, this is a question worthy examination should we need to answer? This is not a deep psychological treatise, but an example of our Complex human reaction to EVENTS beyond the general acceptance, and being ignorant of the facts. As an experience, madness is terrific I can assure you, and not to be sniffed at' wrote Virginia Wolfe to a friend in 1930, and in its lava I still find ore of the things I write about. Byron observed 'we of the craft are all crazy but more than all the rest.' Recent clinical studies of creativity and mental health conducted in Sweden and Iceland, confirms the link tween madness in families, mood disorders and those in creative professions. A man walks into the psychiatrist wearing only cling film for shorts. The psychiatrist says, well, 'I can see clearly your nut's'.

HIMALAYAS
POKHARA NEPAL 2007

At first light, sipping Massala chai at the lakeside table, the gentle lapping water reaching the wild shores edge. My eyes wandered to the landscape where the sudden glint of the first rays of the sun hit the gold roof of the Stuppa on the silhouette mountain top. I was with Zero who had arranged to take us both on a self drive motorcycle to the mountainous region. After we had collected the two wheeler bike we had to stop at the foot of a hill before we could reach our intended destination. 'This bloody thing is useless' was my understatement as the engine was unable to power us further up the steep gradient. We drove spluttering back to Kathmandu and dumped it at the door of the rental office, after demanding a refund which we got. After settling in to our seats at the bus terminal the ascending climb brought us to our intended destination. Zero, actually named Sher my friend Bahadur Shahi did not have much to say and without much conversation we were both quite during the journey. As passengers got off eventually the bus became empty except for one young guy who remained in the front seat by himself. He turned constantly round looking at us to chatter, wincing and blinking his eyes rapidly with an involuntary shaking of his head and shoulders seemed to be a permanent feature. Zero turned to me and asked why is he staring and talking to us like that he said 'he should not be on the bus' I did not understand his reaction and replied 'You should consider he has the same right to be here as we do.' I continued 'remember some people have a physical or mental condition they were born with. Zero scowled 'He looks like an idiot if you ask me'. This final comment brought me to recognize this other occupant's demeanour while I smiled directly and I acknowledged him. He smile back and laughed, as I did with him. Zero remained still in a state of wonder at us both.

I had named him Zero 'he responded with great enthusiasm to his new title, and to this day he is hailed by his nom de plume' in recognition, The peace and tranquillity of Pokhara added to the wonder and discovery of many visits to Nepal over the years and the friendship of Zero. His ascetic behaviour however denied an opportunity to get beneath his facade which remained a mystery to me. Eleven years later I sat at the same lakeside table with Bala and had no such doubts.

Singhala and Thamil | Saturday 20 April 2019

Small fish darted under the clear surface of water in bright shards of colour in endless movement. The aquarium held them captive in a stone jardiniére under the cover of an upturned surboard protecting their closet nursery against intense heat of the sun Which stood on a border of carefully swept sand against the edge of neat grass lawn. I sat under a cool canopy of mango and coconut fronds reading my book as a soft breeze lifted the edge of a page I was reading. During a paragraph I was disturbed by an ant crawling up my forearm and shook it away as the sound of a nearby train thundered past the bottom of the garden on its ribbon of hot metal toward a dusty destination on the south west coast of Galle. Bala and I were in pursuit of the late morning sun on Bentota's beach which lay golden and fringed by the shading palms inviting us to a surfer's embrace in the warm tidal waves breaking into a gentle murmur.

The next day a palpable climate of fear descended on the island of Sri Lanka from the blast of bombs exploding in three Christian churches simultaneously and two luxury hotels within seconds, bringing death to two hundred and fifty human lives from an ISIS terrorist attack creating destruction of human life of mothers, children and elderly relatives attending Sunday morning mass. Five hundred of the congregation were seriously injured and hospitalised. Sixty Muslim's known to be extremist ISIS were arrested and investigated by special commando military units in the days that followed, several were found to be without Visa's. Special commando military units investigating forensic evidence brought the bewildered government and frustrated police force to suspend the social media internet service and impose strict curfew for over a week. The President of the Republic called for the resignation of the Minister in charge of security. Public order was tentatively restored in the belief that retaliatory action would take place in future with further violence.

Rain, Rain, go away the monsoon is here to stay. Flash of lightening and crack of thunder breaks the heat asunder, bringing open heavens with heaving clouds to fill empty river beds flowing into the sea. Birds take cover and lovers hide under leafy trees to brace against the storm on wings to fly. There beating hearts with love not hate against the human race.

PATERNAL

In 1924 my father patrolled the north east frontier of what was the British Empire from Sikkim to the Kashmir border on horseback while in the army. It's impact on him as an inner- city boy with his middle-weight boxing championship medals provided pugilistic evidence of aggression and self esteem, later used in more intimate and less professional situations against his wife. The memory of his birthday gift of a pair of red boxing gloves presented on my thirteenth made him proud to give his lad a lesson in physical culture. I had been forced by him to stop classical Ballet at the age of twelve as 'no lad of his was to be involved in such a thing that was for girls.' His suppressed homophobia was the cause of his unease in expressing affection and unable to show paternal love toward me, probably based on his own youthful experiences coming back to haunt him.

'Me thinks he doth protest too much' in much ado about nothing.

William Shakespeare

MY WILD GARDEN

Parra 2015.

When I found it I could not see the house at first, it was well hidden set back off the road in tall weeds and clusters of trees With overhung branches. It stood within a crumbling compound the walls undisturbed. It had not been lived in for over three years, sad and uncared for, shrouded in a green mantle of overhanging conjoined shrubbery and branches in waist high grass created by the monsoon season. I could see the possibility of making it a home which could rise out of the chaos; after two months hard labour it was indeed finished.

After first light one morning, Bala and I sat resting on the garden step of the kitchen door watching the thin plume of our blue cigarette smoke. I imagined the hell fire of Dante burning beneath the garden as an early morning mist rose above the tree lined paradise. The garden was heaven to sit in with the dog at the foot of the wild unkempt grass covered in heavy dew, clusters of bamboo overhanging the rattan chair Bala now sat in. A past memory sometimes visits the present, but the future takes care of those willing to take joy in peaceful solitude. Listening to the peacock calling through the misty branches of the Bohdi tree, swaying from the fast track of the Gibbon monkey the family ran in a furious flight, rushing along the maze of the garden wall's for a breakfast feast of their favourite wild fruit. A primate family of twelve with the mummy holding the hand of baby and the alpha male chattered and with his bright red chest and grey beard surveyed his domain from sunrise on the apex of the neighbour's pan-tile roof.

In the distance a yellow hammer's birdsong in rehearsal for the morning concert of the daily performance, with the Lepidoptera in flight in a chromatic winged display and the buzz of the bee cruising for nectar in the bushes. This is the stuff of dreams and wild thoughts of nature's full force, an awakening of the spirit of animistic energy with nature's bountiful harvest as a tribute to creation. Just pure joy, and inspiration of the spirit and succour of a peaceful co existence: with an early sunrise changed from pink to gold with an ambient mist unfolding through the branches dripping with heavy dew, falling on the soft earth below. My puppy 'Sweety' unable to contain her state of excitement, dashed headlong into the deep grass lining the garden wall in the hope of challenging the gibbons on their return, in flight of the first sun's rays to hit the roof. She returned unsuccessful, her tail trembling in anticipation of another latent greeting. I tried to imagine the transition of what it must feel like to be beyond the limits of the garden but could not. The reality of seeking a change to transcend beyond the garden compelled me to leave this precinct, 'garden of Eden,' as a lost paradise still yearning for peace and wholeness outside the parameters to be in a state of my own self indulgence.

I waited all day for my cat 'Billy', 'Bila' in Hindi who saw fit to disappear. He ignored the bowl of fresh milk which was left t untouched the night before. 'Billy' had gone into the night, while I slept fitfully until the first light of day. When the dawn came I rose and padded in bare feet to the garden door, looked for him down the path beyond the long grass heavy with dew. I imagined his whereabouts stalking in the long grass licking his bloodied paws in the jaws of my daydream. Was he pecking the red coxcomb and attacking the hen's chicks in a flurry of feathers and fur, with a pounce of claws and sudden death the torn flesh now lay still after final strike. My state of anxiousness to find my feline friend, my mind lade up to search the stalking predator, I became his victim. The bond between us had been weaned in earlier years, now his presence was needed in the empty house. As evening fell and dusk began to gather in Corners of the walled garden, the gate creaked open and I saw no harm had come to 'Billy' as he cried loudly leaping up nuzzling his whiskered face in the palm of my hands, proclaiming his innocence in purred delight. Amplified in thanks of our mutual sense of need, his tail twitched in salutation exclaiming his conducted arrival home to a concert of sighs.

My view of the world is disturbed by the prosperity of one person which usually depends on the poverty or exclusion of another; when we get something that makes us happy we start to worry about losing it. We almost never see things as they are in themselves, our craving for gratification clashes with the greed of others. 'I want' often leads to ill will and enmity, fillings us with feelings of envy, jealousy and rage. Corruption leads us further to deny the normal response of human consciousness by distorting a sub-conscious anxiety in an alien world of the aspirant. Since recorded history began around 3000bc previous oral tradition handed down through generations, as there was little documentary evidence of the way human beings thought, only in remnants of imagery. Imagine what 20,000 years of prehistory would have been like. Fast forward to today and human greed still has no boundaries, but finally rendered meaningless by the fact of senility and our eventual demise.

THE HUMAN SPIRIT

A political Cadre works in a relative time frame to reinforce control over the masses. Minorities of every human being spreads the earth with a millions smiles of children in need of a parent to learn the way forward. The human spirit prevails and will be with us for millennium in times of strife, as will hunger. This is humanity and a prima facia case of survival. Political and religious constraint allowed by belief can fool some of the people sometimes, but not all of the people all of the time. It is questionable whether some mad person will one day extinguish the human race by pressing the red button of mass destruction and ending their own life in tandem with their peer group. Or by taking control of the mind by appealing to the masses through divine right and the flat screen IV. The ensuing maelstrom would annihilate the prospect of protectionism of the human species. We are all the same race that is the human race. From the first Cro-Magnons to the Homo-Sapiens we strive and struggle for survival. Each member of the human race contributing to the whole of mankind's evolvement, through genetics and knowledge as the future belongs to everyone not just to the chosen few. It may suit the politico's of the day to leave whole tranches of the population in ignorance by none inclusive educational disparity for reasons of economic and administrative constraint, but by the inaction of those few Nations will suffer, by squandering natural talent by ignoring opportunity to contribute to the greater good. We can enjoy the benefit of human endeavour by being responsive to others, and for the individual need of conscious self determination to explore inherent talent and skills, as a contribution to the greater good. This raises us beyond animal instinct and blind acceptance in ignorance, to a level of understanding without greed: guided by selfish aims and self gratification, Believing the pen is mightier than the sword as the reader responds with emotional intelligence. Being intelligent and having a loquacious turn of phrase is not enough to communicate with each other without humanity and the warmth of emotional depth to touch another being. I watched the other primates our near relatives, as they touch each other to establish their role in the family and wider community Mothers touch babies, not just their own, but the extended family the alpha male touches his mate to communicate not just sexually but with a need to contact the wider world. We can relearn what we experienced as a child to bond and empathise in sympathy, to be compassionate to one another. This is not weakness but a powerful strength in exposing our understanding of body language which is seventy five percent of human communication.

You a writer

Listen dear you couldn't write 'fuck' on a dusty Venetian blind,

Coral Browne

A SCRIBE

Writing 'is a strange and peculiar occupation as the pen writes on with thought in print. In my case until a power cut interferes with the keyboard process of my laptop as I am a self confessed technophobe. The compulsion to write is a necessary part of the tenuous order of my mind to focus on a mechanical and physical symbiosis, With this in mind, it is a balancing act between imagination and the reader. Reading implies the possibility of artistic endeavour through the writers imagination, the aesthetic process of an individual's perception itself has primacy creating a sort of satisfaction in a literate sense. Thought emerges into the light tattooed with the reader's emotional memory. Visualisation depends on the recognition of emotional circumstance felt by the stimuli of a narrative and the writer's imagination. It suggests to me an endless store of memories in synergy of consensual understanding of an illusory and transient world. All this is part of a journey to be taken until our last breath yet it is still a road to be discovered.

An editor said to me? 'You could be the next Dorothy Parker' I thought what, keep slashing my wrists and drinking shoe polish Lynne Truss

PROLOGUE

Human rights are rights inherent to all human beings, Whatever our nationality, place of residence, sex, national or ethnic origin, colour, religion, language, or any other status. We are all equally entitled to our human rights without discrimination. These rights are interrelated, interdependent and indivisible. Universal human rights are often expressed and guaranteed by law, in the form of treaties, customary international law, general principles and other sources of international law. International human rights law lays down obligations of Governments to act in certain ways or to refrain from certain acts, in order to promote and protect human rights and fundamental freedoms of individuals or groups.

UNIVERSAL AND INALIENABLE

The principle of universality of human rights is the cornerstone of international human rights law. This principle, as first emphasised in the Universal Declaration on Human rights in 1948, has been reiterated in numerous international human rights conventions, declarations, and or resolutions. The 1993 Vienna World Conference on Human Rights for example, noted that it is the duty of States to promote and protect all human rights and fundamental freedoms, regardless of their political, economic and cultural systems.

All States have ratified at least one, and 80% of States have ratified four or more core human right treaties, reflecting consent of States which creates legal obligations for them and gives concrete expression to universality. Some fundamental human rights norm's enjoy universal protection by customary international law across all boundaries and civilisations.

Human rights are inalienable. They should not be taken away, except in specific situations and according to due process. For example, the right to liberty may be restricted if a person is found guilty of a crime by a court of law.

UNTOUCHABLES

Slaves and surfs purchased or sold as commodities were made to stand 64 feet from a higher caste person section 29 Indian penal code. Later the British Government in India banned the stave trade in 1792 giving some protection to them in 1862. Castes were systematically listed in 1936 in a schedule government of India order. Only after intelligent and committed leaders like Dr.Ambedkar (a Buddhist convert himself and Dalit) did they obtain certain basic rights after the independence of India 26 January 1950. Constitution of India conferred on them the right to vote, article 17 in achieving some equality in politics.

Who are the schedule caste, namely Sudra and Avarnas, including many other caste groups who suffered social and economic inequality since 3000 castes exist in India divide themselves into four grades. A bulk of the untouchables were Buddhists, conflict between Buddhist and Vedic religion for supremacy lead to the destruction and degradation of Buddhism. They were deprived of the right of property, education, equality and opportunities during their lifetime they were assigned low status even in the womb and could not be changed even after they were in the tomb. Buddhist were in fear of declaring themselves due to the fear of oppression after the eleventh century. The schedule caste system governed by the Brahminical law was regressive in character and used as an instrument to subject the Sudras and Avarnas to perpetual poverty. An arrangement was made so that the subjected class could never rise in future by ways of depriving them of any chance of economic power. This continues even today, as a result the Avarnas/Panchama castes are deprived of the economic power Of property. The anti-untouchability act 1955 passed by parliament of India gave some to SC by the upper castes, but implementation by each state was unable to implement the act therefore it did not serve its purpose in alleviating suffering. After 70 years of independence most social oppression and economic exploitation in India is generated in the caste system. The destruction of caste itself is necessary to eradicate the social and economic evils in Indian society. The caste system itself needs destruction, rather than perpetuation, their needs to be an anihalation of caste itself.

Social boycotting is not a thing of the past, Buddhist have been the victim of social boycotting in Maharashtra at Bawada for setting up their own candidate for the Zilla Parishad elections. Hindu casts issued threats to the Buddhists to withdraw their candidate. As a result 300 men and women lost their bread and many were beaten and intimidated with dire consequences. Bhia vidya an article treated concern with a knife, an untouchable India (*Volume.1 No.4*) The pernicious doctrine of discrimination rooted in the desire of the Savarnas to dominate the schedule caste by preventing them exercising their rights for improving their lot by breaking ancient shackles of slavery.

DISCRIMINATION

Discrimination is another menace to be guarded against if fundamental rights are to be a reality, available only if it is recognized, implemented and protected the world over. Discrimination from bigotry in India against citizens by government officers in public administration on grounds of caste or creed or 'social statute should be treated as an offence, welfare of the schedule caste tribes under article 338 of the constitution of India. The untouchable fences Act is a central Act - and the special responsibility of The Commissioner for schedule caste and schedule tribes under article 338.

The literacy rates of females belonging to schedule castes are very low and their educational level is at rock bottom level with the rate of increase in the level of education is slow. This is because schedule caste population is socially backward and oppressed within them the position of females is the worst as a result of a patriarchal mindset. Most women are forced to into scavenging by the societal attitude. There are more than seven million scavengers who develop diseases resulting in 23,000 deaths annually, is this the modern India today.

INTERDEPENDENT AND INDIVISIBLE

All human beings are indivisible, whether they are civil and political rights, such as the right to life, equality before the law and freedom of expression; economic, social and cultural rights, such as the rights to work, social security and education, or collective rights, such as he rights to development and self determination, are indivisible, interrelated and interdependent. The facilitates advancement of others. Likewise, the deprivation of one right adversely affects the others.

EQUAL AND NON-DISCRIMINATORY

None discrimination is a cross cutting principle in .international human rights law. The principle is present in all the major human rights conventions such as the International Convention on the Elimination of all forms of racial discrimination and the Convention on the elimination of all forms of Discrimination against Women.

The principle applies to everyone in relation to all human rights and freedoms and it prohibits discrimination on the basis of a list of non-exhaustive categories such as sex, race, colour, and so on. The principle of non-discrimination is complemented by the principle of equality, as stated in Article 1 of the Universal Declaration of Human Rights: "All human beings are born free and equal in dignity and rights."

BOTH RIGHTS AND OBLIGATIONS

Human rights entail both rights and obligations. States assume obligations and duties under international law to respect, to fulfill human rights. The obligation to respect means that states must refrain from interfering with or curtailing the enjoyment of human rights. The Obligation to protect requires States to protect individuals and groups against human rights abuses. The obligation to fulfill means that States must take positive action to facilitate the enjoyment of basic human rights At the individual level, while we are entitled to our human rights, we should also respect the human rights of others.

QUEER BRITAIN

A campaign for a national museum called Queer Britain was formally opened in Kings Cross London. At a reception in London's Cafe Royal which celebrates the richness and diversity of the nation's LGBTQ inheritance and own its place in gay history, commenced in London 28 Feb 2018, A potential site has been identified in Southwark, south London, for the museum. It is hoped the building could be open in 2021 serving as a visitor attraction and social centre. It is time our stories were told in literature, in sport, in art, in engineering, in science, there is no aspect of life in Britain in which LGBTQ people have not had an influence. It is time their stories were told and celebrated. 'Although many museums and institutions, including the National Trust, British Museum and British Library marked the anniversary of the law change. Last year Joe Galliano said there was a danger people would think the job was done. It's time we took up the challenge and told the story ourselves.' 'It is a necessary and long overdue', said Joe Galliano former editor of Gay Times and leader of the campaign. 'We don't underestimate the challenge, but artefacts and peoples stories are being lost every day and we need to save them Already many of the people who directly experienced the discrimination and partial decriminalisation of homosexuality in 1967 are no longer with us. At 86 Paul Clarkson is still with us.

We see it as a place for instance, where a young man or woman who has just come out to her parents could visit with them, and understand that this is a much deeper richer history than most people realise.' It is acknowledged the cost would be' many millions' both to establish and run the museum centre.

ENSLAVEMENT

When we look at history, we discover the genius of James Madison, chief writer of the US Constitution, The federalist and the bill of rites. We learn Maddison 'owned', 100 slaves, that George Washington 'owned' 600 slaves. James Munroe 75 enslaved. people. All but ten Presidents owned enslaved people. The tour guide round Maddison's office in the basement showed small hand prints of enslaved children who made the bricks of the building a metaphor of American history, the bodies, hands arms and legs the very souls of the marginalised and huddled mass yearned to breath free. Enslaved people involved in the construction of Capitol in 1793. In 2012 Congress finally gave the of the Artisans of the Capitol building a

President Trump makes no secret trans-people are a target he promised to atack in his opening executive orders 2025. The judiciary are trying to block Trump's move against trans-people and made clear that he might simply ignore the judges. It's all about courting the public in bigger game to see marginalized population that needs eradicating.

When the Nazis started marginalizing groups the LGBT+ community trans people were high on the list. In the 1930s targeted the Institute for sexual research the first clinic to provide modern day gender affirming care the research was burnt. It seems likely Trump will follow this part of the Nazi playbook, and if he wants to target trans-people, we are an extremely vulnerable group.

President Trump signed an order against Law Firm Jenner & Block for challenging his healthcare ban affirming care for transgender youth under 19. The order has already been declared unconstitutional by a Federal Court.

The US Department of Health and Human services has published a proposed ruling removing gender affirming treatment (Dysphoria) from essential healthcare benefits covered by insurance under the affordable care Act. Revocation of medical protections threatens to impact over 200,000 transgender people who rely on ACA to afford transitional healthcare. A study from a Human Rights Campaign finds that almost 3 in 10 adults are living in poverty.